D0445104

U. S.-EUROPEAN MONETARY RELATIONS

A Conference Sponsored by the
American Enterprise Institute for Public Policy Research
and Georgetown University

U. S.-EUROPEAN
MONETARY RELATIONS

Edited by Samuel I. Katz

American Enterprise Institute for Public Policy Research
Washington, D.C.

Library of Congress Cataloging in Publication Data

Main entry under title:

U.S.-European monetary relations.

(AEI symposia ; 79B)
"Proceedings of a conference held March 17-18, 1977
in Washington, D.C." and sponsored by the American
Enterprise Institute and Georgetown University.
    1.   International finance—Congresses.   2.   Monetary
unions—Congresses.   3.   Money—European Economic
Community countries—Congresses.   4.   Foreign exchange
problem—European Economic Community countries—Con-
gresses.   I.   Katz, Samuel Irving, 1916-
II.   American Enterprise Institute for Public Policy
Research.   III.   Georgetown University, Washington, D.C.
IV.   Series: American Enterprise Institute for Public
Policy Research.   AEI symposia ; 79B.
HG3881.U644   332.4′5   79-11718
ISBN 0-8447-2150-6
ISBN 0-8447-2149-2 pbk.
AEI Symposia 79B

PARTICIPANTS

Bela Balassa
Johns Hopkins University
Baltimore, Maryland

Henri Baquiast
Ministry of Finance
Paris

Giorgio Basevi
University of Bologna
Bologna

Edward M. Bernstein
EMB, Ltd.,
Washington, D.C.

F. Boyer de la Giroday
Commission of the European Communities
Brussels

Sir Alec Cairncross
St. Peter's College
Oxford

Jean Deflassieux
Credit Lyonnais
Paris

Tom de Vries
International Monetary Fund
Washington, D.C.

William Fellner
American Enterprise Institute
Washington, D.C.

Charles Frank
Department of State
Washington, D.C.

Armin Gutowski
Goethe University of Frankfurt
Frankfurt

Gottfried Haberler
American Enterprise Institute
Washington, D.C.

Wilhelm Hankel
Goethe University of Frankfurt
Frankfurt

Alexandre Kafka
International Monetary Fund
Washington, D.C.

Samuel I. Katz
Georgetown University
Washington, D.C.

Peter F. Krogh
Georgetown University
Washington, D.C.

Alexandre Lamfalussy
Bank for International Settlements
Basel

Fritz Leutwiler
Swiss National Bank
Zurich

Assar Lindbeck
Institute for International Economic Studies
Stockholm

Bruce K. MacLaury
Brookings Institution
Washington, D.C.

C. W. McMahon
Bank of England
London

Giovanni Magnifico
Bank of Italy
Rome

Stephen N. Marris
Organization for Economic Cooperation and Development
Paris

Thierry de Montbrial
Ministry of Foreign Affairs
Paris

Hubertus Müller-Groeling
Institut für Weltwirtschaft
Kiel

C. J. Oort
Ministry of Finance
The Hague

Jacques J. Polak
International Monetary Fund
Washington, D.C.

Wolfgang Rieke
Deutsche Bundesbank
Frankfurt

Horst Schulmann
Commission of the European Communities
Brussels

Andrew A. Shonfield
Royal Institute of International Affairs
London

Robert Solomon
Brookings Institution
Washington, D.C.

Hideo Suzuki
Nomura Securities Company, Ltd.,
Tokyo

Niels Thygesen
University of Copenhagen
Copenhagen

Pierre Uri
French Economic and Social Council
Paris

Jacques van Ypersele
Ministry of Finance
Brussels

Roland Vaubel
Institut für Weltwirtschaft
Kiel

Jacques Henri Wahl
International Monetary Fund
Washington, D.C.

Jacques Waitzenegger
Bank of France
Paris

Henry C. Wallich
Board of Governors of the Federal Reserve System
Washington, D.C.

Hans-Herbert Weber
Ministry of Finance
Bonn

Thomas D. Willett
U.S. Department of the Treasury
Washington, D.C.

John Williamson
University of Warwick
Coventry, England

CONTENTS

PART FOUR
NEXT STEPS IN EUROPEAN INTEGRATION

PART FIVE
PROBLEMS OF GLOBAL MONETARY INTEGRATION

PART ONE

INTRODUCTION AND OVERVIEW

INTRODUCTION

Samuel I. Katz

A widespread pessimism about the drift in international financial affairs prevailed in early 1977. There were two principal grounds for a growing uneasiness about monetary trends. First, efforts over the previous ten years by U.S. and European officials to agree on ways to introduce highly structured reforms into the international monetary system had ended in failure. Second, in 1976 the leading Western industrial countries were becoming economically polarized into two blocs: a group of "weak" countries with high domestic inflation, large balance-of-payments (BOP) deficits, and depreciating currencies; and a group of "strong" countries with much lower inflation, a tendency toward continuing BOP surpluses, and appreciating currencies.

The earlier efforts at world monetary reform had visualized sweeping changes in both global and European regional monetary arrangements. The negotiators of global reform had in mind a broad-based modernization of the original Bretton Woods system: greater exchange-rate flexibility than before through a regime of "stable but adjustable parities"; more symmetrical adjustment constraints than before both between surplus and deficit and between reserve and nonreserve currency countries; and international control over global liquidity through the creation by the International Monetary Fund (IMF) of special drawing rights (SDRs). Perhaps it was inevitable that major differences would arise between U.S. and European officials on key elements of proposals in each of these areas. In any case, there was a deadlock in the negotiations that was broken only when major disturbances in the world economy—especially the 1972–1974 global inflation and the abrupt rise in oil prices in late 1973—swept away the par-value exchange regime and forced reluctant national authorities to accept widespread floating among the major industrial currencies.

The goal of negotiations among European officials had been even more carefully formulated than the global monetary goals: to proceed step by step toward European monetary union on the basis of an agreed timetable, extending to 1980, which had been accepted in 1970 as part

3

of the Werner plan. Despite the strong desire of European officials to achieve this goal and the general agreement among them on strategy, however, the forces of economic separatism seemed too powerful to be resisted. These difficulties were intensified when, with the floating of currencies after 1973, the fragmentation of European trading partners into blocs of countries with "weak" and "strong" external positions was accelerated. The divergent rates of domestic inflation among them seemed to doom any hopes for progress toward the goal of regional integration. The position became even more worrying by 1976, in fact, when several deficit countries either turned to—or were known to be seriously considering—the introduction of selective restrictions on intra-European trade, a step that threatened the continuance of the substantial benefits the countries of the European Economic Community (EEC, or Common Market) had achieved from the common trading arrangements and from some significant advances in sectoral economic integration among them.

In addition, new issues had arisen in international monetary affairs by early 1977 that had not been widely considered in the debates on international financial reform in the preceding decade. There was no longer an overriding interest in establishing a formal exchange-rate regime based on national intervention commitments, extensive financing and settlement arrangements, and procedures for prior review of national decisions about exchange rates—a dominant theme of the earlier debate. Instead, attention had turned to the effective management of the national economy as the dependable basis for a stable world monetary order. The right of members of the IMF to have exchange-rate arrangements of their own choice, which had been agreed on at a meeting in Jamaica in January 1976, meant that hopes for stable exchange rates had come to depend not on commitments for market intervention but on management of the domestic economy. Regional unification on the basis of target dates had ceased to be discussed. In its place was a revitalized debate about more limited ways in which European officials could seek to reduce regional BOP surpluses and deficits and to diminish the widening differentials in price and wage increases among European countries.

A third element made a review of international financial policies particularly timely in early 1977: a growing uneasiness about the way the system of floating currencies was working out in practice. The continuing BOP deficits of Italy and Great Britain in 1976 and the surpluses of West Germany and Switzerland were bound to raise doubts about the effectiveness of floating arrangements in promoting international adjustment. By early 1977 the efficacy of exchange-rate policy under modern conditions was being debated in terms of a vicious-circle/virtuous-circle hypothesis. The VC hypothesis was advanced in several forms. A rather naive version seemed to argue that the downward floating of the exchange rate of a deficit country could be expected to set off a self-sustaining cycle of domestic inflation and of further exchange-rate decline, which could become an explosive sequence of first internal and then external disequilibrium. Advocates of this version sometimes seemed to be maintaining that the decline in the exchange rate could itself be considered an independent source of domestic inflation. A parallel sequence of uncorrected BOP disturbance was envisioned for surplus countries in this version. That is, a country with a strong BOP position would seem to get stronger in an unbroken circle of appreciation and then of relatively slower rates of price advance. Steady rises in the value of the national currency would not seem to reduce the external surplus.

Proponents of a less naive version of the VC hypothesis could agree with critics of the theory that exchange-rate depreciation could not be the cause, but was only the result, of accelerating inflation in a deficit country. But these proponents of the VC hypothesis still questioned the efficacy of exchange-rate policy in promoting international adjustment under contemporary conditions. Some of them focused on extraeconomic factors as major sources of continuing disturbance. Many also pointed to the phenomenon of "overshooting" in the foreign exchange market, when the short-term decline in the market rate would be pushed significantly below the medium-term equilibrium rate, usually as a result of short-term capital movements. When overshooting brought the exchange rate below the equilibrium value, domestic prices would be pushed higher than they would otherwise be. That is, a further advance in domestic prices and costs would be set into motion by the lower exchange rate, which eventually could validate the lower value of the currency.

The VC hypothesis was being widely challenged in early 1977 by economists who could not accept the view that the downward or upward floating of currencies had worsened the problems of domestic stability in surplus or deficit countries. In their view changes in currency values could not have worsened inflation in a deficit country when the decline in the market rate was itself the result of internal inflation. They maintained that overshooting could produce additional domestic inflation only if the national authorities adopted accommodative financial and incomes policies. For example, they maintained that a central bank that did not expand the domestic money supply could by itself frustrate the drift toward a higher national price level.

5

It was against this background of growing uneasiness about the process of economic fragmentation, both global and regional, and of a sharpened controversy about the contribution floating currencies were making to the processes of international adjustment that the Conference on U.S.-European Monetary Relations was convened in Washington, D.C., on March 17 and 18, 1977. The meeting was cosponsored by the American Enterprise Institute for Public Policy Research and Georgetown University and was supported by the German Marshall Fund of the United States, the Volkswagenwerk Foundation, and the French-American Foundation.

The purpose of the conference was to consider the practical next steps that might be taken to halt and to reverse these unfavorable global and regional monetary trends. Participants drawn from diverse national and international agencies and from banking and academic institutions were asked to review past experience and to evaluate alternative ways to renew efforts at multilateral and regional integration. Because national financial strategies were known to be under review in the United States, West Germany, and several other countries in the aftermath of federal elections held during 1976, the conference was intended to contribute to this review process. It was to focus on key policy options the thinking of experienced economists of more varied backgrounds and points of view than would normally participate in an evaluation of national policy. To this end the papers prepared for discussion at the conference and the written commentaries on them by invited discussants were widely distributed. After the meeting a transcript of the conference discussion was made available to participants who requested them for further study and for circulation among colleagues and associates at home.

The four conference sessions dealt with: (1) an overview of problems of global and regional monetary integration; (2) the main problem areas and policy options for European regional integration; (3) the specific next steps to be taken toward European integration; and, more broadly (4), the key strategies to promote global integration —the coordination of national policies and the control of the evolving exchange-rate mechanism. Most sessions were opened with a broadly based survey of the range of views on a topic, drawn from the current professional literature; the paper was not to be limited to the author's particular viewpoint. Each main paper was then reviewed by discussants selected for the diversity of their national origin, experience, occupation, and personal views.

These main papers and the written assessments of the discussants for each session compose the remaining four parts of this conference volume. The reproduced papers and commentaries represent considered personal statements of the views of their authors and are to be regarded as the formal record of the proceedings. The overview of the conference proceedings which follows in this chapter introduces the main papers and discussant responses and gives the general reader a summary—however personal in its choice and emphasis—of the proceedings and of the themes of primary interest to participants. The overview and the assessment that concludes Part One are intended to suggest the flow of the main themes of the discussion and are not to be regarded as a record of the proceedings.

OVERVIEW OF CONFERENCE PROCEEDINGS

Samuel I. Katz

Monetary Integration: Global or Regional?

The opening paper by Lamfalussy was intended to provide a common background for participants through a general introduction to the problems of global and regional integration. Could these two objectives be reconciled? Or were European attempts at regional union necessarily in conflict with efforts at global monetary arrangements? Did European leaders have to choose whether to give priority to policy strategies aimed at global or at regional objectives?

The Lamfalussy Paper. Alexandre Lamfalussy (economic adviser, Bank for International Settlements) attributed the recent failure of regional integration to the European response to the series of external shocks in the world economy after 1973. Differences in policy response based on differences in economic structure and in policy preferences, not the external shocks themselves, were responsible for destroying hopes for regional integration.

Despite this experience, Lamfalussy thought that a reopening of the discussion about European integration was justified at this time, primarily because the adjustment process under floating rates had not worked well in Europe. He found a disenchantment there with floating on the grounds that it had discouraged private investment and had encouraged a process of vicious and virtuous circles that was encouraging disparate rates of inflation and of changes in currency values among the European trading partners. The discussion of the vicious and virtuous circle argument (or, as we shall call it, the VC hypothesis) was to prove perhaps the topic of primary interest to conference participants.

Lamfalussy presented an analysis of the VC hypothesis applicable to small European countries that (1) are price takers, (2) have substantial tradable goods in domestic output, (3) transmit higher prices for tradable goods to home goods through expenditure switching and adjustments of wages to the retail price index, and (4) experience occasional "overshooting" downward of exchange rates because of expectations. In his view the basic argument ought to focus not on the mechanics of the VC hypothesis but on concrete policy issues: where and how to break the sequence of inflation and depreciation.

Lamfalussy recognized that the VC spiral could be broken by proper domestic policies, but the political costs might be too high for such policies to be regarded as feasible. In such a situation, an incomes policy was necessary. In Great Britain, for example, the second stage of the incomes policy agreed upon in August 1976 had assumed a deceleration of price rises; but the downward drift of the pound later in 1976 had speeded up the inflation and raised doubts that the unions would be willing to renew the wage-restraint package in mid-1977. By contrast, unions in West Germany and Switzerland could be satisfied with modest wage increases because currency appreciation had helped slow down domestic inflation and raised real income more than the unions had expected.

However, there were arguments against reopening the discussion about monetary union in Europe. First, the VC hypothesis might justify exchange market intervention, but it did not demonstrate that fixed exchange rates would provide a better framework for BOP adjustment than present arrangements. Second, the West German authorities preferred to encourage BOP adjustment not by reflating the domestic economy but by allowing the deutsche mark to appreciate. Monetary unification in Europe would make further deutsche mark appreciation very difficult.

Furthermore, world economic trends would not encourage regional unification anywhere. A new attempt in Europe would be facilitated only by a lower average world inflation rate, reduced BOP deficits, especially in the smaller countries of the Organization for Economic Cooperation and Development (OECD), and less uncertainty about the outlook for the dollar.

In Lamfalussy's view some technical proposals offered at this conference were interesting. In addition, attempts within Europe to coordinate monetary policy should be continued. But he did not think that such proposals were fully reopening the monetary integration issue.

Commentaries

Alexandre Kafka (executive director, International Monetary Fund) approached the Lamfalussy paper from the point of view of the less developed countries (LDCs). He accepted Lamfalussy's loose definition of monetary integration—greater exchange-rate stability and freedom for current and capital transactions—and thought that the LDCs had the same difficulties in progress toward integration as the developed countries: a deterioration in effective policy coordination compared with that of the earlier periods of the gold standard. Policy attitudes were changing; exchange-rate fluctuations were now more acceptable, but the progress toward trade liberalization, so evident before the 1970s, had apparently ceased. Redistributing the oil deficits required trade liberalization as much as exchange movements.

Outsiders sometimes found it difficult to understand the pronounced preference among LDCs for avoiding floating rates. But an LDC often faced difficult political or economic choices in a floating world whether to peg to a major currency or to a basket, or whether to attempt to formulate an explicit exchange policy on its own.

Finally, Kafka added, monetary integration among the LDCs was limited to a rudimentary form of reserve saving (that is, interim finance) and some limited reserve pooling. Substantial reserve pooling is resisted in the Third World, as it is in Europe, where monetary and fiscal policies are not adequately coordinated or spontaneously in step.

Pierre Uri (French Economic and Social Council) took up four main points.

1. Devaluation might be ineffective in restoring a country's BOP equilibrium when its competitors did not enjoy full employment. At present, the world was condemning itself to competitive deflation, placing the BOP deficits, which were the counterpart of the oil surpluses, on the weakest countries.

2. A worldwide policy might be undertaken in the context of the North-South dialogue: the holders of oil surpluses might be induced to make long-term investments in LDCs on the basis of a guarantee by the industrial countries. Those countries would then return to full employment through their delivery of capital equipment, and they could agree, in turn, to accept imports from the LDCs in a new division of labor that would be the core of a new international economic order.

3. Stabilization of primary product prices might be facilitated by the issue of SDRs linked to commodity prices and distributed as compensatory finance to LDCs with export shortfalls. With these resources the LDCs could produce for storage and still maintain their demand for industrial products.

4. As to the European picture, he noted that, even before the oil price increased, the four major partners of the EEC had completely different BOP structures. There was little hope of progress toward European integration unless there were funds within the community to

assist changes in BOP structure. An essential feature of monetary union was a large common budget, partly financed by a common system of progressive direct taxation; the political character of such budget and tax arrangements would help pave the way toward political union.

Armin Gutowski (professor of economics and member, West German Council of Economic Experts) emphasized the need for predictability of government policy. He defined "stability of exchange rates" in terms of the predictability of their movement. Stability in this sense did not require identical, or even common, policies among countries. It could be achieved through the predictability of national policies, a view derived from past experience that each country in a group would behave in a specific way. There could be greater exchange-rate stability among countries with different, but predictable, policies than among countries with pegged rates but unpredictable domestic policies.

The 1973 shocks to the world economy had brought to light underlying differences in social and political attitudes that had defeated European attempts at monetary union. In Gutowski's view readiness to invest depended on the degree of stability not of exchange rates but of medium-term expectations.

As to the VC hypothesis, an initial inflation could produce an inflation-depreciation spiral only when monetary policy was accommodating. In his view acceptance of inflation by the surplus countries would not help the deficit countries. In particular, reflation was not the right policy prescription for West Germany. In 1975, for example, additional fiscal expansion had had a negative feedback on private investors and consumers. In West Germany the unions had come to realize what a strict monetary policy meant for employment if wage policy was too aggressive.

Gutowski recognized the point Lamfalussy had emphasized: that restrictive policies needed to break the VC cycle might lead to an unacceptable amount of unemployment. But "something real has to give" to break such a cycle. Incomes policy, as a complement to restrictive demand management, could be helpful only if it ensured that real wage increases lagged behind the rise in productivity. In addition, official exchange intervention could be necessary where the price effects of further depreciation would put too great a burden of adjustment on wages; but it would be helpful only if a restrictive monetary policy continued to be applied.

The European countries could move toward monetary integration if each of them would accept jointly agreed upon, though different, monetary policy targets. The West German Council of Economic Experts had recommended the monetary base as the common policy target.

11

Each country could set an initial level appropriate to its situation; but, over time, each central bank would be obliged to move closer to the group target, which would be based on the monetary policies of the most stable economies of the group.

Gutowski therefore was prepared to argue in favor of a renewed attempt at monetary integration in Western Europe, but in a way to avoid the old mistakes. The monetary program he recommended would ease the three sources of global disturbances identified by Lamfalussy in that it would (1) reduce inflation rates between countries, (2) ensure a more equitable distribution of OPEC surplus funds, and (3) promote stability among European currencies to minimize any disturbance to exchange markets from renewed distrust of the dollar.

Andrew A. Shonfield (director, Royal Institute of International Affairs) directed his comments primarily to the longer term effects of the extended oil deficit of the OECD countries on the national policies of countries with weak BOP positions. Exchange rates tend to be more unstable among deficit countries than among countries with balanced BOP positions because, in the latter, the exchange market does not react negatively to a temporary BOP deficit. He concluded that the exchange market badly needed guidance from a credible authority about the "tolerable" ranges of fluctuations around some acceptable BOP deficit.

In Shonfield's view, Oort's program of target zones would be far more difficult to operate when a few industrial countries have surpluses with their OECD partners greater than their oil deficits. Contrary to proposals for sharing the aggregate oil deficit, West Germany had remained consistently and substantially in surplus. A continued West German surplus would threaten the free-trade arrangements within the Common Market because it dangerously aggravated the difficulties of partners with BOP deficits, particularly by putting them under pressure to accept a significantly higher rate of unemployment than existed in West Germany. Given the customs union, West German domestic policy determined the level of unemployment in other partner countries.

Because it seemed too difficult to persuade countries to adapt their policies to the needs of their trading partners on a worldwide basis, Shonfield proposed an attempt to reach agreement among a limited group of countries. The European group was the obvious candidate. The trade gains already secured by the EEC were relatively large, and they had more at risk if the union were menaced by persistent payments imbalances between members. In addition, the Europeans had mechanisms for mutual aid to cushion BOP adjustment costs, such as the modest EEC Regional Fund and devices like the Common Unemployment Fund proposed by the Marjolin group in 1975.

On the other hand, Shonfield did not agree with Lamfalussy that regional coordination should be pursued independently of any effort to secure greater European monetary integration. Mutual aid could be made conditional on meeting certain monetary performance criteria.

Indeed, the two aspects of policy were by their nature mutually dependent. Shonfield stressed the difficulties of structural adaptation of certain important European countries. It was not an accident that the most acute inflation emerged in the mid-1970s in two major countries that faced long-term structural difficulties and were inadequately equipped with the political means of carrying through the required policies systematically.

C. W. McMahon (executive director, Bank of England) shared Lamfalussy's doubts about the effectiveness of floating rates in promoting BOP adjustment. To him the core of the problem was an empirical matter: the fact that the real (that is, the relative price-adjusted) changes in exchange rates had been small under floating. He thought the VC problem, as Lamfalussy had put it, was a realistic model for some countries. There was a secular rise in the difficulty of securing adjustment within deficit countries that was paralleled by a secular rise in the share of labor and a fall in the share of profits over several business cycles. McMahon cited a number of specific factors: increased unionization and greater pressure by unions to maintain real wages, the social climate, a growing use of indexation, and a weakening of government authority. One aspect of these changes was the regime of floating exchange rates.

In the late stages of the Bretton Woods system, it was thought that liberating the exchange rate would make it easier for countries that were adjusting very slowly to adjust more quickly. Paradoxically, the experience had been the opposite: it was harder under floating for governments to use the exchange rate as a positive policy tool. In practice, if a government needed to improve its BOP structure, how could it achieve the appropriate change by exchange depreciation—that is, how could it get other countries to accept the depreciation and not have the gain vitiated by union pressure for higher money wages?

Accordingly, McMahon favored a greater degree of exchange stability, as Lamfalussy had defined it, not because he wanted the rate to be maintained at any particular level but because he believed such a regime makes it more possible to use the exchange rate as one tool of BOP adjustment.

McMahon understood why the West German authorities become a little irritated at continued outside pressure for them to expand demand at home. In theory, however, the combined policy of a strong general stimulus and a strong appreciation should be able to reduce the West German current-account surplus without adding to domestic inflation; but it would obviously be very difficult to achieve the result in practice in a purely floating system.

On the other hand, McMahon would agree, it was hard to see how the existing degree of stability could be expanded, even on a regional basis. It would be better if countries had some kind of exchange policy that they could discuss and agree on among themselves. While some OECD countries had BOP surpluses, it was difficult operationally for countries—with the best will in the world and with an acceptance of the need for international cooperation—to accept policies that worked to the norm of a current-account deficit. Deliberately to accept a deficit policy extending over time posed severe problems of national economic management and created political problems of sustaining a government in office.

European Monetary Integration: Problems and Options

The conference turned from the interrelation of global and regional problems to a general review of the European experience in efforts at regional unification. Balassa was asked to identify what had proved to be the principal problem areas and then to consider the range of policy options before European officials in response to them. Discussants with different national origins and professional experience were then asked to interpret Balassa's analysis in the light of their particular experience and vantage point. The objective was to try to find common ground on the European integration experience among participants from widely diverse backgrounds.

The Balassa Paper. Bela Balassa (professor of economics, Johns Hopkins University) identified three main problem areas for discussion: exchange-rate management, policy coordination, and European financial markets. His paper considered various actions that might usefully be taken regarding European monetary arrangements under present conditions. To avoid excessive fluctuations in exchange rates, it has been suggested that "target zones" be established to provide a frame of reference for national policy actions and for consultations on the Common Market level.

While such consultations would be of an ex post character, the interdependence of the national economies of the member countries and the objective of avoiding the emergence of balance-of-payments disequilibria would call for ex ante consultations on domestic policies, eventually leading to policy coordination. Balassa argued in the paper that consultations, and eventually coordination, would have to extend to monetary as well as fiscal policies.

The paper further examined arguments made for coordination of national control measures on capital movements and, in particular, on Eurocurrency flows. It concluded that controls on the Common Market level would not be useful. In turn, the integration of capital markets would be beneficial for the EEC.

While implementing the recommendations made in the paper would limit the sovereignty of the Common Market countries in economic policy making, it was suggested that the freedom of action of those countries was presently more circumscribed than commonly assumed. That was because the increased interdependence of their national economies through trade had reduced the effectiveness of policy measures taken by the individual countries, including the larger ones.

In his comments on the paper, Balassa touched on several analytical issues prominent in the conference. In his view the VC argument in an extreme form meant that exchange-rate changes would never affect the BOP—would never restore BOP equilibrium. This was an extreme conclusion. He suggested three qualifications to the hypothesis: (1) that price and wage adjustments were not immediate; (2) that some contracts were designated in nominal, not real, terms; and (3) that there were lags in the adjustment process and, therefore, that an initial random change in the exchange rate would usually produce a change in the real exchange rate.

Balassa questioned the view that the difficulties of European monetary integration would be solved only if intercountry differences in inflationary trends were reduced. There would still be speculation-induced fluctuations in real exchange rates. In addition, it was not realistic to expect that inflation differentials could be reduced in the foreseeable future. What can then be done? He proposed in his paper a target zone approach that was "crawling," not "stationary," moving gradually in step with inflation differentials.

On the question of policy coordination, Balassa invited participants to discuss the experience of their own country in terms of four questions: (1) the choice of monetary target; (2) the policy objectives of monetary policy—that is, domestic versus BOP; (3) the possibilities of monetary stabilization; and (4) the effectiveness of national monetary policies, given capital flows, institutional differences, and the role of fiscal policy in the European countries. Viewing the policy coordination issues in general terms, he concluded that there was a role for both monetary and fiscal policies if countries were to reach national price and BOP targets. Hence policy coordination should consider targets that are monetary, are fiscal, and relate to the financing of public sector deficits.

Finally, Balassa thought that some of the issues concerning European financial markets were reasonably well resolved. The Euro-system was not itself a major inflationary force, because the multiplier appeared to be small. It did not seem to be a mechanism for transmitting U.S. inflation to Europe since the U.S. inflation rate was then below the European average; nor was it one that allowed U.S. actions to reduce the effectiveness of European policies since the exchange rate could change. On a cost-benefit analysis, he concluded, it was not desirable to move toward some kind of joint control of this market.

Commentaries

Sir Alec Cairncross (master, St. Peter's College, Oxford) discussed mainly two issues: exchange-rate management and the implications of Great Britain's experience as a country faced with the need for BOP adjustment. On the exchange-rate side, he preferred not to establish a target zone among European countries but to seek more stability among the three major currencies—the deutsche mark, the dollar, and the yen. He also concluded that countries should not try to coordinate monetary and fiscal policy merely to stabilize exchange rates; either such coordination was desirable for its own sake, or it should not be attempted.

In general, Cairncross was skeptical about the capacity of governments to carry out national policies, whether intended or indicated. In his experience they were much more helpless than they pretended. Progress toward regional integration required something approaching a common view about objectives and about the use of the instruments of stabilization policy. It was a mistake to speak as though officials had only two or three policy instruments to employ to control the domestic economy. Because of the numerous policy options, each country should maintain continuous contact with trading partners so that each would understand the full complexity of the situation in the other's country and try to work out, more or less ad hoc, agreed measures appropriate to the situation.

In the British experience, the volatility of spot rates under floating did not make Cairncross optimistic about the practicality of securing

16

exchange stability through the target zone approach. Within Europe countries seemed to remain obstinately either in surplus or in deficit. Some economists had become profoundly pessimistic about a country's ability to improve the trade balance through exchange-rate changes.

Behind the differential rates of inflation were major sources of disturbance that could not easily be corrected. In the British experience, two factors needed to be stressed: the external shocks that created BOP deficits and the rise to political power of wage earners, which made it difficult to ensure that real or even money wages could be made to respond predictably.

In general, stable exchange rates are possible only if the structure of world trade and payments is consistent with such stability. It was unrealistic in a period of severe world disequilibrium to expect to approach stability by multiplying either policy targets or mechanisms for international cooperation. Any constellation of exchange rates would be inherently unstable, given the large oil-induced collective BOP deficit, and short-term capital movements were likely to worsen the instability. Hence agreement on target zones through BOP forecasting was not promising. Action on the part of surplus countries was needed either to run BOP deficits or to invest their surpluses in weaker countries.

In Cairncross's view more attention might be paid to two devices developed in the 1930s: the Exchange Equalisation Account and the Tripartite Agreement. A target zone would seem appropriate among countries in BOP surplus. Would it not do the world more good if there were some kind of stable relation among the deutsche mark, the dollar, and the yen rather than among the deutsche mark, the pound, and the franc? If the EEC wanted to pursue integration, he added, it should set up lender-of-last-resort facilities, with means at its disposal comparable to those of the IMF. In his view there was not much point at this time in pursuing target zones for most of the European countries.

Giovanni Magnifico (economic counsellor, Bank of Italy) concentrated primarily on direct action on intra-European exchange rates. The target zone proposals were really a three-pronged approach that included exchange-rate zones, effective mechanisms for policy coordination, and enlarged EEC facilities for financing. There was no conflict, as he saw it, between the target zone and European snake approaches.[1] In his view there could be no European integration if member countries were unwilling to approach a common exchange-rate policy, especially vis-à-vis the dollar. The snake was no longer a communitywide arrange-

---

[1] See Oort, esp. pp. 193 ff. for a review of the European snake arrangement.

ment. Three of the four major currencies had been withdrawn, leaving the snake a one-way relationship between a number of smaller countries and the deutsche mark. One merit of the Oort proposal was to put an end to this state of affairs and to try to introduce the first elements of a truly communitywide exchange-rate system of which the snake would become merely a special case.

In the Italian experience, wage developments had been critical. There had been large labor migrations among the EEC countries, but they had not created a communitywide market for manpower. On the contrary, manpower is organized in unions, national in scope and pursuing different wage strategies. What can be done to foster a truly unified European labor market?

In Magnifico's experience communitywide policy coordination had floundered on two obstacles: national objectives could differ from community objectives, and members could differ on priorities and on the sharing of the burden of BOP adjustment. As it worked in practice, he thought, the adjustment burdens under the Bretton Woods mechanisms were shifted mainly to the countries with BOP surpluses. In contrast, the burdens under floating had fallen largely on the deficit countries— that is, mistakes in demand management were felt mainly in domestic prices and the exchange rate, less in the BOP. In Italy progress had been made in reabsorbing the current-account deficit; but, because changes in nominal wage rates had not led to real wage adjustments, Italy suffered from domestic inflation. Restrictive policies in Italy had reduced resource utilization and tended to be counterproductive—to push up costs.

The suggestion that the EEC adopt and announce a stringent monetary target would have an effect only if expectations were altered. But the costs of such a policy could be high, with a strong adverse impact on employment and output. Magnifico thought there was a role for income policy, at least during the transition period. In Italy it had been very difficult to stick to monetary targets when the public sector deficit was not also curbed. The "crowding out" effect of the fiscal deficit on private investment in Italy had been high—closer to 100 percent than to zero.

Jacques van Ypersele (adviser, Ministry of Finance, Belgium) concentrated on problems of exchange-rate management, particularly against the background of the Belgian experience.

He began by pointing out that the concept of target zones had different meanings in the several conference papers. It was his understanding that both Oort and Balassa conceived of target zones as a mechanism primarily to trigger consultation. Oort had emphasized that it was essential to his proposal that countries were not in any way obliged to maintain their effective exchange rate within the target zone by intervention. On the other hand, Willett and Cairncross seemed to regard the target zone as a mechanism to require, or at least to encourage, a country to intervene to dampen exchange-rate fluctuations away from the target zone.

There was general agreement that the exchange ratios should reflect underlying economic conditions. But "underlying conditions" and "erratic fluctuations" were being defined differently. In the United States a broad and extensive interpretation was given to "underlying conditions" and a narrow one to "erratic fluctuations." In Europe the reverse was occurring: a substantial proportion of capital movements was included in the "erratic fluctuations" that were to be neutralized.

Van Ypersele stressed the benefits of the snake, especially for small open economies with strong wage indexation to be pegged to the deutsche mark through the snake. In such countries the VC argument was valid; an active exchange-rate policy to avoid depreciation, together with an incomes policy, had an effective role in restoring economic stability.

Belgian experience during the past three years contained useful lessons for the global problem of exchange-rate management. Between December 1973 and 1975, the rise in the consumer price index (CPI) in Belgium had been more than double the rise in West Germany. Van Ypersele was convinced that allowing the Belgian franc to depreciate would have been harmful precisely because of the VC spiral. The authorities had fought back and held the exchange rate with market intervention, a tight monetary policy, and the two-tier exchange market, which helped them to resist capital pressures.

Later the policy of pegging the franc to the deutsche mark also meant an appreciation of the Belgian franc during 1976. This, together with an incomes policy to slow down wage rises, enabled Belgium to reduce its inflation rate to 7.5 percent. He concluded from this experience that the Belgian economic situation would be much worse today, and its inflation rate much higher, if the authorities had allowed the exchange rate to depreciate in 1975 or 1976.

Van Ypersele disagreed with Balassa's recommendation that there was need for more frequent changes in exchange rates among snake countries. Contrary to the Bretton Woods experience, the snake countries had demonstrated that they were able to adjust at the appropriate moment. He also had doubts about applying the target zone concept to the snake countries as a group. The snake mechanism had, on the whole, functioned well. He thought the concept of a target zone would

19

best apply to the currencies of European deficit countries that had been floating downward.

Van Ypersele also welcomed the contribution of the target zone proposal to creating a framework for triggering consultation so as to encourage meaningful policy discussions among EEC members. In practice, no real measures had been taken to ensure greater convergence among EEC members; but important measures had been taken in the broader IMF framework, where there was less psychological and political reluctance to discuss corrective actions and where large credits could be more easily gathered to support the stabilization effort.

Finally, he pointed out that floating had not relieved the authorities of the need to take measures to counteract unwarranted market fluctuations. However, it was a question not necessarily of more extensive exchange-market intervention but rather of making more active use of other instruments of stabilization, especially of interest-rate policies and, in some situations, of control of capital movements.

Hubertus Müller-Groeling (Institut für Weltwirtschaft, Kiel) was opposed to the attempt to introduce target zones for exchange rates not because a reduction in rate fluctuations was undesirable but because this strategy put the cart before the horse; it proposed to define exchange-rate targets and then to try to force the necessary policy harmonization on European governments. The suggestion of a target zone could also be a very sophisticated attempt at reintroducing an adjustable peg or similar fixed rate.

He favored the exactly opposite procedure: first to harmonize economic policy as much as governments would accept. This gain in itself would eliminate some important causes of rate variations. There were at least four reasons why fiscal policy was singularly unsuitable as a target for harmonization efforts: (1) there was doubt whether fiscal harmonization was feasible, as the recent West German difficulties in trying to form an appropriate anticyclical fiscal policy illustrated; (2) fiscal policy usually lagged behind overall economic developments, and the effects of fiscal policy changes were often delayed; (3) fiscal policy already had several objectives in each country: income redistribution, financing economic development, and anticyclical goals; and (4) fiscal policy was the central core of sovereignty of the nation-state, and it would be a mistake to overestimate the willingness of governments to make concessions in this area.

Müller-Groeling thought monetary policy could serve as an instrument for international harmonization: it is under the control of national authorities; it usually leads changes in business trends; and it could be the subject of international negotiations. He proposed that nations negotiate preannounced, but different, monetary targets. Such agreement should lower inflation rates in Europe and narrow existing differentials.

He was cautious about proposals for target zones and instead regarded the introduction of a European parallel currency of stable purchasing power as a serious proposal. It had the advantage, as pointed out in the Vaubel paper, of attempting to bring about currency union without passing through the stage of exchange-rate unification. The lesson to be learned from recent European experience was that there is no substitute for a willingness of European governments to give up sovereign rights in favor of a European union.

F. Boyer de la Giroday (director, Monetary Matters, Commission of the European Communities) first informed the conference that the Council of Ministers of the European Communities had very recently taken a decision on the proposals of the Dutch minister of finance. Rather than focusing specifically on an exchange-rate scheme of the target-rate kind, the council decided that a new exercise in policy coordination was needed, one more precisely defined than those previously undertaken, and that it should cover the various short-term policies affecting exchange rates. He then explained why the implementation of a target-rate scheme would be premature. This whole concept belonged to the family of "fixed rates." While there would be no commitment to intervene at a given point, something like this would indeed be expected from the participants. It could impose unbearable constraints on member countries at times of widely divergent inflation rates because, among other reasons, countries would inevitably find themselves creating money to finance excessive wage claims by trade unions. Economic integration could not be achieved, it was said, unless one could 'integrate the trade unions." That might come some day, but the goal was still distant.

Boyer de la Giroday thought the review of policy options in the Balassa paper was helpful. He expressed some disagreement with the use of comparative unit labor costs as a reference for moving exchange rates, criticizing it on practical grounds such as the unreliability of statistics and delays in their preparation.

He hoped that the limited suggestion for exchange-rate consultations proposed in the Oort paper might produce more in practical terms than had been achieved by the grand designs agreed upon in the past. He could not hope for a big leap forward into a single currency for Europe, as discussed in the Vaubel paper. He anticipated further attempts within the machinery of the Commission of the European

21

Communities to advance toward that goal on the basis of specific cases as they arose.

He thought that in the third section of the Balassa paper, "European Financial Markets," the concern with communitywide organization and control of the Eurodollar market was premature in view of the conditions of today and the possibilities for tomorrow. Freedom of capital movements and unification of relations with Euromarkets would indeed be indispensable in approaching monetary union. At this time, however, the whole argument could well have been dispensed with and replaced by a discussion of the Europa as an international instrument that might be of use in breaking the present deadlock in the debate on international monetary matters. The three contributors to the conference who had dealt with the Europa had done so entirely from a European point of view, thereby deserving fully the criticism quoted in Thygesen's paper about the inward-looking character of the debate. It was surprising to have to agree with this criticism in a conference convened under the title "U.S.-European Monetary Relations."

Boyer de la Giroday questioned Cairncross's remarks that the European Monetary Cooperation Fund (EMCF) was useless because it had no money to spend. This comment showed ignorance of the way the EMCF worked, and in any case the importance of an institution did not depend on the amount of money it had.

Boyer de la Giroday noted that the conference lacked any discussion of the famous asymmetry in the role of the dollar. Fred Bergsten had concluded in his new book that the economic bases for the dollar had diminished and would no longer support the dollar's role as the sole world currency. R. I. McKinnon had proposed a tripartite agreement between the deutsche mark, the dollar, and the yen.[2] Lamfalussy had reminded this conference of the role played by the dollar in wrecking the hopes of European monetary union and he would stress that confidence in the dollar rate was essential for greater stability of intra-European rates.

Next Steps in European Integration

This session concentrated on two proposals that were actively under discussion in early 1977 as realistic immediate steps to be taken in a renewed move toward regional integration in Europe. The proposal by Vaubel envisioned the introduction of a Europe-wide parallel currency

---

[2] Ronald I. McKinnon, "A New Tripartite Monetary Agreement or a Limping Dollar Standard?" Princeton Essays in International Finance, no. 106 (October 1974).

to circulate alongside existing national currencies. The second proposal, by Oort, was an attempt to devise arrangements in the field of exchange-rate management that would enable the non-snake countries in Europe to move into loose association with the much constricted group of snake currencies. Oort's paper was an in-depth exploration of a proposal made by Finance Minister Willem H. Duisenberg of the Netherlands to the European Council of Ministers to create a loose framework of rules for floating to apply to all EEC members during a period in which the snake arrangement would continue to function among the more limited number of snake countries. It was, in addition, an evaluation of the experience within the European snake by an official of a participating country since he was at the time a senior official at the Netherlands Finance Ministry.

As background to this discussion, Niels Thygesen, a member of the Optica group of independent experts (which had been set up by the Commission of the European Communities in 1975 to evaluate European monetary trends, in particular the role of exchange rates in regional experience), reported on the work of the group in the two areas. In its reports for 1975 and for 1976 the group had discussed the attempt to further regional integration by the creation of a parallel currency and by agreement on common rules of exchange-rate management. Neither of the Optica reports had been evaluated or acted on formally by the European commission. The Conference on U.S.-European Monetary Relations, in fact, provided the occasion for a broadly based discussion of several of the recommendations of the Optica group at a time when its reports were being actively considered by European commission personnel.

Creation of a Parallel Currency in Europe? The conference papers reproduced in this volume demonstrate that the debates over European monetary unification had entered a new phase by early 1977. Earlier efforts had aimed at a full monetary union based on fixed exchange rates and geared to a specific timetable. The Werner report of October 1970 had laid down a step-by-step program for a European Monetary Union (EMU) by 1980 that called for: (1) the progressive narrowing of exchange-rate margins among European currencies; (2) the pooling of foreign exchange reserves; (3) the eventual establishment of a common currency as the end product of the process of eliminating exchange margins; and (4) the creation of a European central bank as the key organ of an economic and monetary union. There was no serious reference to the Werner approach as a feasible concept at the conference. The remaining vestige of the earlier efforts—the European

23

snake—had been diminished by 1977 by the withdrawals of other large European countries into a de facto deutsche mark area made up of smaller countries with substantial trade with West Germany that were prepared to keep their monetary and aggregate-demand policies roughly in step with those of West Germany.

The looser concept of regional integration advanced in the Optica reports had focused on proposals for common exchange-rate management, supplemented by mechanisms to promote closer policy coordination. The group had also recommended the gradual introduction of a parallel currency; but they regarded it, as Thygesen explained, only as a major instrument of European integration and not, as Vaubel had suggested, as a substitute for other measures. Vaubel's proposal had two wide-ranging goals: regional monetary unification and monetary reform. In his view an indexed parallel currency had a crucial advantage over the earlier attempt to move toward regional unification through fixed exchange rates. Its introduction would enable European countries to proceed toward a monetary union without having to pass through the graduated stages of exchange-rate consolidation. He regarded his approach as a substitute for, not as complementary to, the Werner approach.

Vaubel spelled out in his paper the reasons why he regarded the earlier approach as unpromising. As he saw it, the deutsche mark might be the key currency in Europe, but it was unsuitable as a pivot for exchange-rate union. After all, it had appreciated steadily in real terms, and its adoption as a pivot rate would require other members of a European union to accept substantial domestic deflation.

The parallel currency would be indexed, but it would not have the status of legal tender, as a true common currency would. Thus it would be an additional foreign-currency asset available to private parties in Europe on demand. But this status raised the problem of coexistence because an indexed parallel currency might be resisted by national governments as a threat to their local currencies.

Three distinct models for a parallel currency in Europe could be distinguished: (1) the already existing European unit of account, which was spreading only slowly and had not proved very attractive to private markets; (2) a fully indexed parallel currency, as proposed by Vaubel, which private markets might find quite attractive; and (3) the Optica compromise, as developed by Thygesen, which would create a currency as attractive and at least as strong as the least inflationary European national currency. There was a further difference: where Vaubel would intend the parallel currency to be attractive to residents in all countries, the Optica approach emphasized the need to

24

make it attractive primarily or only to residents in countries that had been inflating the most.

European Exchange-Rate Management

Giorgio Basevi (professor, University of Bologna) emphasized that the main purpose of the Optica recommendations in the exchange-rate field was to halt the process of economic disintegration among EEC members. In particular, their proposals were intended first to avoid any further divergence in domestic inflation rates and then to reduce existing differentials. The group took a pessimistic view about current trends within Europe toward national fragmentation. He added that the recommendations about exchange-rate management were not to stand alone but were only one part of a whole package of policy instruments and guidelines. The package included coordination of budgetary, fiscal, and monetary policies, incomes policy, exchange-rate policy, and a parallel currency.

In Basevi's view exchange-rate policy ought to be subordinated because some European countries seemed to be relying on it to reconcile disagreements among social partners by allowing the exchange rate to float. It was unfortunate to carry out an incomes policy in this way; he thought that agreement on exchange-rate coordination might bring to a halt the present arrangement under which some social partners were being cheated as a result of exchange-market fluctuations.

The Optica group had concluded from their research that the purchasing power parity (PPP) formula for determining long-term equilibrium relationships appeared to be a good objective indicator for adjusting exchange rates. The Optica rules were neither mandatory— there was no automatic rule to force actual exchange rates to crawl on the basis of a PPP determination—nor symmetrical; intervention was to be required only when the market rate of a depreciating currency was *below*, not when it was *above*, the PPP value. The aim of the intervention rules was to avoid a further drifting of non-snake away from snake currencies; hence both the snake and the minisnake could hope to survive.

The theory behind the rate management rules rested in part on the "overshooting" element in the VC hypothesis. In Basevi's view the fact that assets moved faster than goods markets was all that was needed to explain the phenomenon of overshooting. Even if the central bank kept to an agreed money-supply rule, it would not reduce the inflation associated in the short run with overshooting but would merely either alter the distribution of income for a given level of employment or reduce the level of employment. It would be hoped that the market would form stabilizing expectations when it knew what the central bank intended to do.

The Optica group had debated for more than a year the question of choosing price indexes and determining the meaning of the real exchange rate. There are at least two meanings of the latter concept. In a two-commodity model with import and export goods, the real exchange rate could be defined as the ratio between them—that is, the terms of trade. In that case, there would have to be an adjustment in the terms of trade, and it would be undesirable to link the exchange rate to the ratio of export to import prices. This definition was not what the Optica group had in mind.

A second definition was based on the domestic terms of trade: the ratio of tradable to nontradable goods prices. The group had initially thought to use unit labor costs as the key indicator, as Balassa had suggested. Because unit labor costs are not a reliable indicator for many countries, however, they had compromised by choosing wholesale prices for manufactures as the best available statistical measure among the European countries.

Finally, Basevi wanted to clarify the asymmetry in the scheme. The rule was symmetrical in that it applied to both depreciating and appreciating currencies; it did not allow falling currencies to depreciate below PPP but also did not allow rising currencies to appreciate above the PPP level.

C. J. Oort (Ministry of Finance, the Netherlands) agreed with Basevi that we must think seriously about how to stop the disintegration of the EEC. Two strategies were being offered to this meeting: to devise a great leap forward or, alternatively, to make whatever small steps were realistic at this time. In his view small steps were more likely to be helpful than attempts at great forward leaps.

The Oort paper explained a proposal that was being discussed in the EEC to set up a system of "rules for floating." Two approaches had been advanced: (1) to adapt the present snake arrangement to enable countries with floating currencies to join or (2) to agree upon a looser framework of rules for floating to apply to all community members while maintaining the snake as it then was. The paper focused on the second approach.

The proposals outlined in the paper had already been studied at Brussels. The first official initiative along these lines had been taken by Duisenberg, the Dutch minister of finance, in a letter to his European colleagues July 6, 1976. The proposals had been examined by the Monetary Committee and Committee of Central Bank Governors, who had submitted their reports on how and when the scheme could be applied in practice. The council had had a first round of discussion on them on February 14, a month before the present meeting.

Oort offered these propositions in introducing his paper:

- that the economic and monetary union envisaged in the Werner report was for all intents and purposes an entirely dead issue
- that certain rules of the game for active exchange-rate management in the community were needed to maintain its basic achievements
- that the present European minisnake was a stable and workable arrangement, essentially because the smaller partners tried to align their policies with West German economic and monetary policy and not the reverse
- that the minisnake arrangement was not a suitable model for an exchange-rate system for the community as a whole because economic tensions between the major near-equal partners had led to the breakup of a communitywide arrangement in the past and were likely to do so in the future
- that the European countries could choose between a weakening of the current snake arrangements and the creation of a looser set of rules of behavior for an interim period until each member could rejoin a snake-type arrangement in the future.

According to Oort, there was a strong political bias against prompt and adequate changes either in parities or in central or target rates. Adjustment actions were usually too limited and too late. Arrangements were needed to offset the bias in the political system; however, the guidelines should not be automatic rules but presumptive triggers for consultation and action.

Dutch officials were unhappy that they had formulated their proposals in terms of a "target zone" because the words commonly implied a much more formal structure than was being contemplated. The Dutch concept was not meant to imply either (1) an objective currency value intended as a country's policy target or (2) a commitment to any kind of obligation for market intervention or policy action; it was to be, in the first phase, merely a very loose framework for consultation. Hence the proposal was not really for an exchange-rate but for a consultation system. The effective exchange rate was to be a signal of disturbance and of the need for consultation. It was to trigger consultation and, later, coordination of economic and monetary policies. It would permit members with floating currencies to retain that freedom and not be obliged to peg their rate or even to intervene in the exchange market.

Oort stressed two advantages in the proposal. First, the triggering arrangement was concrete and clearly defined. Second, the focus on effective exchange rates and the need to discuss the exchange-rate implications of economic developments and policy actions would make community discussions more useful than they had been when such implications of policy measures were not discussed.

In addition, the proposals were both flexible and dynamic. Flexibility was desirable because it would be counterproductive to attempt, in a great leap forward, to impose common arrangements on a community that was disorganized and was attempting to absorb new members with different economic, social, and structural backgrounds. The proposals also had a dynamic quality in that they could have as much policy content as was realistic at any time.

Finally, Oort thought it essential that the deutsche mark zone, however defined, participate in the scheme. It was necessary to stop further disintegration within Europe by taking small pragmatic steps forward when possible, rather than to waste efforts on grandiose approaches that had not the slightest chance of being realized in the foreseeable future.

Selected Topics from Conference Discussion. Haberler pointed out that we were in a "second" round of discussion on monetary integration in Europe. The first round was started by the Werner report of 1970 and had culminated in the excellent volume, *European Monetary Unification and Its Meaning for the United States*, based on a Brookings conference in 1973.[3] There had been perhaps even more criticism of the European monetary unification then than there was today. He thought that there were two pillars of the new approach to European monetary integration: the reference rate idea and the VC hypothesis. In his view the difference between the reference rates and par values had been exaggerated, and the reference rate approach had been greatly oversold. He doubted that the reference rate proposal would be much less prone to stimulate destabilizing speculation than the par-value system had. It has been suggested by Robert Mundell and reiterated by John Williamson[4] that the floating Canadian dollar has great stability because it is called a dollar. It is thus identified with the U.S. dollar and serves as a sort of "reference rate" and focus for stabilizing speculation. Haberler thought it was the history of political stability and prudent

---

[3] Lawrence B. Krause and Walter S. Salant (eds.), *European Monetary Unification and Its Meaning for the United States* (Washington, D.C.: Brookings Institution, 1977).

[4] John Williamson, "The Future of the Exchange Rate Regime," *Banca Nazionale del Lavoro Quarterly Review*, Rome, June 1975, pp. 135–36.

policies in Canada that were at the root of the stable Canadian dollar. The Mundell-Williamson argument suggests that Mexico could promote the stability of the peso by renaming it the Mexican dollar or that Italy could induce stabilizing speculation by renaming the lira the Italian mark. The French franc was not saved by the fact that for many years (1865–1914) it was linked (along with the lira) in a one-to-one relationship with the Swiss franc in the Latin Monetary Union.

The virtuous and vicious circle experience of different countries is due to different internal policies in different countries and is not the consequence of floating exchange rates. A mental experiment will make this clear. Suppose there exist two groups of countries with little or no trade between them. One group pursues inflationary policies, the other has no inflation. The first group will experience a vicious circle, because inflation always tends to develop vicious circle properties. The other group will flourish. The exchange-rate regime has nothing to do with the different development in the two groups of countries, for trade is assumed to be insignficant.

It is true, however, that under floating every country has to swallow the inflation that it generates. Under fixed rates, on the other hand, a country with a sufficient reserve or credit line can alleviate its inflation by "exporting" part of its inflation to other countries by developing an import surplus of goods and services.

Overshooting of the exchange rate is possible, but it can start or intensify a vicious circle only if supported by an accommodating monetary expansion.

Balassa based his criticisms of the Optica proposals on theoretical considerations, not on questions of political expediency nor on the lack of reliable price indexes for PPP comparisons. He explained that, if a price index is to be used, it should relate to nontraded goods, since the prices of traded goods adjust immediately with an exchange-rate change. In his view evidence from a number of indicators would provide a better measure for policy purposes than one price index.

De Vries suggested that economists should not attempt to devise complicated schemes on the assumption that, if arrangements are made complicated enough, governments can be tricked into doing what they do not want to do. It would be better to tell governments that, if they wanted monetary integration, they would have to transfer powers to a federal authority.

Magnifico thought that governments might still have a tendency to view the exchange rate as an endogenous variable to be adjusted in response to movements in domestic costs that they might not be able to control in a particular situation. In Italy all available indexes had been reviewed before a position was taken on exchange rates, and then a judgment was formed by weighting the various indications. Finally, he had doubts about having an indexed parallel currency— the strongest currency by definition—because of the difficulties of managing the dual system.

Oort doubted that private parties would be interested in an indexed parallel currency. He noted that they could have indexed contracts now but used instead either national currencies or the dollar. Further, how could a forward cover be organized in an indexed currency?

Gutowski reported that the West German Council of Economic Experts had proposed that ex ante arrangements on rates of monetary expansion and the monetary base would constitute a tremendous advance in the light of earlier failures to achieve agreement within Europe. If such arrangements were adopted, it was thought, the European countries could live with the effects of differentials in monetary growth on the exchange rate. When a monetarist point of view is followed, fiscal policy is distinguished from monetary policy. A country with a large fiscal deficit that stuck to its monetary target would experience domestic repercussions but would not have so great a problem of harmonization.

Williamson regarded the reference rate proposals as a species of floating and not a par-value system at all. All the safeguards against destabilizing speculation available under any other floating system would be available under reference rates.

Lindbeck was skeptical about the quest for some mechanical formula for altering exchange rates. Economists point out how complex the economic system is and then they advance a formula that assumes that the system is simple. He thought Balassa's point important: the tying of the exchange rate to exports or other tradable goods was a very curious idea. Such a measure does not tell us anything about competitiveness.

In response Thygesen thought that the Optica approach differed from the Werner plan in that exchange-rate changes were envisioned over a long period of time. The Optica economists were in substantial agreement with Vaubel in the analysis of the costs and benefits of a parallel currency. In Thygesen's view the issue of differences in the degree of openness of the European economies had been exaggerated; detailed studies of Great Britain and Italy had suggested that they were extremely open economies, not qualitatively different from the smaller economies. In response to de Vries, he noted that the complexities of the Optica scheme were not meant to conceal that a substantial measure of coordination was required. Under the scheme the exchange-rate mechanism would be confined to a second role among active adjustment policies.

Vaubel hoped that the complexities of the parallel currency approach would not mislead governments into actions they did not want to take. Since governments were not willing to envisage monetary unification, such a goal could only be a long-term objective, maybe so long-term as to be utopian. He mentioned several technical options for stipulating the value of the parallel currency. He thought that, at present, European nationals were not free to choose indexed options; the restrictions by governments and the disincentives were substantial today.

There was a general discussion of the Oort proposal. Some pointed out that there was uneasiness in Europe about floating, in part because BOP surpluses and deficits had remained. But this result meant not that the textbooks or exchange policies were wrong but that the national stabilization policies accompanying the floating rates were inadequate.

There was a consensus against a return to too much intervention. Intervention might produce short-term stabilization, but only national policies of medium-term effectiveness could stabilize exchange rates over a longer period.

Some Europeans noted that Oort's proposal was clear and practical but did not go beyond what European countries were already prepared to do—to consult. The existing commission machinery provided mechanisms for consultation and cooperation and even definite rules for each member, but political leaders had not made much use of these possibilities. On the other hand, a new element was Oort's proposal that there be consultation about exchange-rate policies. Yet this focus was different only in its emphasis, for consultations would still be concerned with monetary targets and fiscal policy.

Advocates of European unification found at least two arguments in favor of action at this time: (1) the need within Europe for monetary integration in purely economic terms and (2) the contribution European union would make not as a substitute for, but as a complement to, worldwide monetary integration. It would make the world system function more smoothly. In addition, they found advantages for participants in the snake in that they could avoid the depreciation-speculation sequence that had produced for some countries overshooting and VC difficulties.

Williamson thought that work by Rudiger Dornbusch and John Helliwell had provided evidence of more undershooting than overshooting of exchange rates. He wondered if, as a general theorem, one might not have undershooting with current-account impacts and overshooting with capital-account impacts.

Lindbeck concurred, emphasizing that overshooting was the consequence of disturbances in markets for financial assets. There were two mechanisms for overshooting: an interest-arbitrage mechanism and the gap between the speedy adjustment in financial markets and the delayed improvement in current transactions.

He noted that Belgium and Denmark had been able to remain in the snake but at a high cost in unemployment. The discipline of the snake had also had a high cost in social relations in Sweden.

Marris thought that the discussion had treated Optica 1976 rather harshly. The report was being criticized because it appeared to put forward a complete system to be adopted as a package, a doubtful expectation at best; in addition, any proposed system was bound to be open to technical and theoretical criticisms. The great value of the report was its focus on what, in practice, was the immediate difficulty: the danger of overshooting. There was now a general agreement among participants at the conference on the analytical framework in which overshooting could emerge, a useful advance in the conference discussions.

Problems of Global Monetary Integration

This session turned from regional to global monetary problems. The first topic—the international coordination of national economic policies —was not introduced by a general paper. Instead there were personal observations by the five discussants whose contributions are reproduced in this volume. The meeting then turned to the question of the exchange-rate mechanism and its control, with an opening paper by Willett and comments by three discussants.

International Coordination of National Economic Policies

Assar Lindbeck (professor of International Economics, Institute for International Economic Studies, Stockholm) distinguished between three purposes of international coordination: (1) to influence the business cycle, (2) to influence long-term price trends, and (3) to avoid policy inconsistencies among trading partners. He considered each of these objectives.

Strategies for cyclical coordination would vary, depending on the disturbance being experienced. The policy choices might be clear-cut in a period of international recession or global inflationary boom, but

32

the purpose of policy coordination in the more normal conditions from the early 1950s to the mid-1960s might not be to harmonize national policies but to desynchronize them to avoid simultaneous boom or recession.

The second purpose—to influence long-term price trends—had to focus on the short-term stabilization policies of each country. But the long-term trend in international liquidity was of some importance in establishing boundaries on the policy behavior of all countries. Private and public markets and national and international markets for credit are now so integrated that it is difficult to differentiate between international liquidity in a broad sense and international reserves in a more narrow sense. The present international system resembles the U.S. banking system before the creation of the Federal Reserve: the lender of last resort and the supply of international liquidity are a collective enterprise of rather uncoordinated national policies. Therefore the only way to influence international liquidity would be by some coordination of central bank policies.

A third objective of a coordination effort could be the attempt to avoid inconsistencies in national policies. Inconsistencies in price targets and differences in national price paths required not coordination but flexible exchange rates. On the other hand, flexible rates would not resolve output inconsistencies because exchange fluctuations do not have strong short-term effects on trade flows. Accordingly, flexible rates did not eliminate the need for coordination of policies as they affect output variables.

Lindbeck thought the case for coordination was even stronger for the third major type of policy target: the balance of payments or the exchange rate. Even with floating, there remained a common concern about the exchange rates of trading partners and the need for coordination; countries were not indifferent whether BOP adjustment took place on current or capital transactions. In addition, there could be disturbance to trading partners when currency rates were being affected either by direct intervention or by aggressive domestic monetary policy. In practice, monetary policy coordination might be more desired under flexible than under pegged exchange rates because monetary actions could have powerful effects on short-term market quotations and because rate fluctuations might have a more dramatic effect at home than would changes in reserves under fixed rates.

Lindbeck identified three choices: (1) reliance on automatic adjustment mechanisms (floating rates and capital markets) as much as possible to reconcile the international character of the economy with the national character of the political system; (2) adjustment of the economic system to the political by a return to protectionism in a more autarchic economic system; and (3) adjustment of the political to the international economic system to achieve policy coordination.

Haberler expressed some doubts concerning one of Lindbeck's points, namely, that the purpose of policy coordination might have to be "not to harmonize national policies but to desynchronize them to avoid simultaneous boom or recession." A deliberate policy of desynchronization of the business cycle would require some countries to interrupt a cyclical expansion and deliberately bring about a recession. What country would be willing to do that?

Stephen N. Marris (economic adviser to the secretary general, Organization for Economic Cooperation and Development) thought that there was need for rather intensive policy coordination today, in part because of the way the foreign exchange market works. Large income and expenditure flows pass through it, along with the shifts among financial and real assets. The reaction time of the sectors of the market differs widely. It takes hours or days for current financial transactions; months for cost and price effects; and one, two, or more years for flows of goods and services. In his view the case for international coordination under floating depends on the way exchange rates are thought to influence critical real and nominal national economic variables.

Marris thought that the naive model of the VC hypothesis ought to be rejected because, as Willett had shown, a movement of the exchange rate in line with the inflation differential cannot itself be regarded as a source of inflation. But overshooting was more than a theoretical possibility; events during 1976 had demonstrated that it had actually occurred.

It was important to recognize that external discipline under floating can be tougher than it was under the par-value regime. But it was worrying that the disequilibrium among the major industrial countries had gone on so long that it had been built into the industrial structures, and even the attitudes and behavior, of each country. The main industrial countries were having increasing difficulty in coexisting.

William Fellner (American Enterprise Institute) distinguished between two meanings of international coordination: (1) the exchange of information and the adjustment of national policies to what others are doing and (2) the subordination of short-term national objectives to the interests of the world community. The second concept of coordination ought not apply, in his view, when a country with a good demand-management record was called on to become more expansionary to enable its trading partners to expand export sales. Such a recommendation would not be an advantage for its trading partners if it led the country actually to destabilize its domestic economy.

This approach began to acquire political and policy significance as a result of the global oil deficit. It has been argued that, because the oil-importing countries will run a large current-account deficit for many years, the deficit should be shared somehow among those countries. If it is to be shared properly, the argument runs, certain countries with current-account surpluses should generate more domestic expansion to direct output away from export markets.

This reasoning, Fellner suggested, was based on unconvincing propositions. One was the assertion that a country with a current-account surplus was somehow violating the rules of international good behavior. However, such a judgment depended on whether a case could be made for artificial interferences which subsidized exports and restrained imports. To determine that a country had adopted objectionable measures required a complicated procedure, and he thought that some oil-importing countries might well run surpluses even if there were no interference with competitive processes. Furthermore, if objectionable practices were found, this would lead not to a recommendation of domestic expansion but to insistence that the undesirable trade measures be withdrawn.

If a surplus country had adopted undesirable measures, it would be advised to shift resources from exports to home consumption, but this assumption would not justify additional domestic expansionary action in terms of effective demands. Once a country had agreed on a noninflationary output target, the amount of effective demand should be equivalent to domestic output, and to no more, regardless of whether the current account was or was not in surplus. In either event, domestic inputs would be paid for in domestic currency.

Jacques J. Polak (economic counsellor, International Monetary Fund) suggested that the title of the session might be rephrased as "coordination or adjustment of national economic policies." Coordination could be defined as the adoption of policy measures that differed from those preferred on purely national grounds; in contrast, adjustment involved the adoption of national policies designed to correct an external disequilibrium. Can one specify which of these two approaches is the most suitable? He proposed to consider three cases.

The first case, an easy and slightly facetious one, dealt with the recent reduction in world coffee supply. Coordinated government action would tend to encourage an allocation among importing countries to reduce total hardship. Instead demand was being adjusted to supply

35

through the price mechanism. If there were a similar situation for wheat or for oil, the coordination approach for allocating available supplies would almost certainly be invoked.

The second case concerned wide fluctuations in the exchange rate between two currencies as a result of a lack of coordination of national monetary policies. Polak used as an example the deutsche mark–dollar exchange rate between the United States and West Germany. Even though it might be difficult to effect monetary coordination between the two countries, it still seemed unlikely that in such a situation the optimum solution would be no coordination of monetary policy and total reliance on adjustment through exchange-rate fluctuation.

The third case involved the effects on the world economy of the $40 billion or so current-account surplus of the members of the Organization of Petroleum Exporting Countries (OPEC). Should the offsetting deficit be allocated (or distributed by some mechanism of policy coordination), or should one rely on adjustment actions by individual countries to produce a satisfactory structure of current-account surpluses and deficits?

The assumption that this is a problem for multilateral coordination almost inevitably leads to the simplistic conclusion that each country has to accept a fair share of the total: that is, that each country must have a current-account deficit. This new morality seems to be replacing the morality of only five or ten years ago which decreed that none of the industrial countries should have a current-account deficit. Polak suggested that the data (found in the table on p. 240) demonstrated that this problem cannot be solved by appealing to coordination. That approach was neither logical nor practical; it overlooked very important facts. For the data revealed that the OPEC surplus (in real terms and adjusted for growth) was of the same order of magnitude as the pre-1973 traditional surplus of the industrial countries. In addition, the $30 billion deficit of the LDCs was no larger than their deficit before 1973.

In practical terms there has been a change in the source of funds to the LDCs. They are now coming from the savings of OPEC and not, as in the past, from the domestic savings of the industrial countries. In addition, the funds are flowing to a large extent by intermediation through the banking system of the industrial countries.

But the question was: Can the present problem be resolved by the adjustment approach? The answer seemed to hinge on two further questions: the level of aggregate demand and the financing arrangements. Uncertainty must remain whether there could be a reasonably high level of aggregate demand in the world economy with an autonomous savings of $40 billion by OPEC countries. The data in the table could support an affirmative answer, not an oversavings or underconsumptionist theory. On the financing question, it was evident that the recycling process had thus far performed rather well.

Charles Frank (senior economist, U.S. Department of State) attributed differences in macroeconomic policy between the United States on the one hand and West Germany and Japan on the other not only to differences in values but to differences in the perception of the effects of policies. There were those in the U.S. government who felt that an expansionary policy would have only limited inflationary dangers.

He thought that, even if there were an aggregate U.S., West German, and Japanese deficit of $5 billion, a substantial amount of financial intermediation would be required. More official financing was needed to supplement the role of the commercial banks.

Important issues of trade policy also required international coordination. Within the U.S. government, a number of significant trade matters were pending as policy issues. The industrial countries had to find ways to meet the problem of increased import penetration in ways consistent with international obligations. Frank also thought it important that these countries coordinate their policies in two other fields: energy and commodity prices.

The Evolving Exchange-Rate Mechanism and Its Control

Thomas D. Willett (formerly with the U.S. Treasury Department and now professor of economics, Claremont Graduate School) identified two main issues in his paper: (1) international surveillance of the adjustment process and (2) the need for official intervention and international stabilization loans to break the alleged vicious circle between exchange-rate depreciation and inflation.

Willett proposed two main conclusions. In his view many versions of the VC hypothesis greatly exaggerated the case for international intervention and for stabilization loans. Further, it could not be assumed that an exchange-rate depreciation was always the cause of additional domestic inflationary pressures when in fact the depreciation might itself have been merely a reflection of underlying inflationary trends. On the question of international surveillance, he did not recommend the adoption of an internationally agreed upon set of reference rates or target zones but favored a case-by-case judgment of individual situations.

In his discussion of the VC hypothesis and exchange-rate policy,

37

Willett emphasized the need to analyze the cause or causes of exchange-rate movements. He showed that, where an exchange-rate depreciation was a reflection of underlying inflationary pressures, the depreciation could not meaningfully be termed a source of additional inflationary pressures. In such cases, he noted, the country would be exporting inflationary pressures to others.

At the same time, he recognized that, because of destabilizing speculation of particular types of capital flows, it would be possible for the market exchange rate to depreciate below its equilibrium value. Such a development could worsen the country's trade-off between short-run inflation and unemployment and could create incentives for expansionary domestic macroeconomic policies to validate the stepped-up rate of price increases.

Willett cautioned that the possibilities of such private market failures should not be viewed alone; they had to be compared with a realistic assessment of the likely results of government action—how accurately officials could identify such episodes and whether they would tend to have biases toward excessive intervention. For example, he pointed out that the professional literature had established that one could not automatically assume that an exchange-rate decline greater than the differences in relative inflation rates was an indication of "excessive" depreciation. There were not enough simple statistical ways of identifying when an exchange rate had overshot the equilibrium value. In his personal judgment, while there were episodes in which international stabilization loans were called for to complement domestic anti-inflation programs, such loans needed to be granted and used with considerable caution. The extent to which flexible exchange rates had worsened domestic inflationary problems could, in his experience, easily be exaggerated.

Turning to the international surveillance of the adjustment process, Willett noted that proposals for internationally agreed sets of reference rates or target zones were based on the assumption that government officials could forecast equilibrium exchange rates with a fairly high degree of accuracy. He doubted the accuracy of such an assumption and cited, as one piece of evidence, the large errors made in official current-account forecasts. He also questioned whether, in present circumstances, official targets or norms would help to stabilize the private market, as their advocates had suggested.

Willett then considered the major alternative formal approach to the international control of the BOP adjustment process: the establishment of a system of reserve indicators. This approach rested on the assumption that private speculation was usually stabilizing; hence it followed that cumulative official intervention—one way or the other—became evidence that the market rate was being held away from the "equilibrium" rate. However, countries could indirectly bring about the same effects on market rates in numerous ways without showing changes in their reserve levels. Thus a reserve indicator system alone would not be a reliable basis for international surveillance.

In addition, Willett suggested that, as a practical matter, many countries might be willing to modify "inappropriate" exchange-rate practices in a favorable response to quiet pressures even though they might not be prepared to accept a meaningfully tight set of international regulations, whether defined in terms of target zones or of reserve indicators. Many countries desired to preserve as much formal national sovereignty as possible. On the basis of all these considerations, Willett concluded that formal agreement to avoid exchange-rate manipulation should be sought not in terms of specific economic variables but on the basis of a fairly general statement of principles on which a body of case-history precedents could gradually be built up.

John Williamson (professor of economics, University of Warwick, England) favored a system of reference rates. He noted several points on which he agreed with Willett. He agreed that managed floating had performed better than one would have expected the adjustable peg to do. Advocates of target zones were not pushing for a return to the par-value system.

His main concern was the operation of the surveillance process and, in particular, the maldistribution of the oil deficit. Polak's table did suggest that the burden being carried by the LDCs was not as severe as had been assumed, but Williamson still found grounds for disquiet about the distribution of the deficit among the industrial countries. The excessively deflationary policies adopted by some countries in quest of financial stabilization had a severely damaging effect. Under floating, he recalled, financial stabilization in one country leads to exchange-rate appreciation and to a cost-push inflationary effect in countries whose currencies depreciated.

He interpreted Fellner's criteria to mean that each country should pursue its domestic goals without concern for the interests of trading partners. This view was not an appropriate policy approach in an interdependent world. A West German acceptance of monetary or fiscal expansions could have helped other countries without intensifying West German inflation if, for example, the authorities had offset the rise in aggregate demand by selling reserves in the foreign exchange market.

In Williamson's view one could approach international consultation directly in terms of discussions about the coordination of demand managements if there were not the political obstacles Lindbeck and others had discussed. An alternative approach, which he favored, was to instigate talk about policy instruments with a relatively large effect on the country's external sector. By focusing on surveillance over exchange rates, one could hope to achieve within the multilateral surveillance process an international discussion of significant aspects of national policy. It was on these grounds that he favored more formal arrangements than Willett was prepared to accept. Williamson continued to favor the reference rate proposal as the basis for an orderly and effective exchange-rate surveillance exercise.

Henry C. Wallich (Board of Governors of the Federal Reserve System) suggested that the United States had been comfortable with managed floating because the convertibility obligation had been lifted and the dollar exchange rate was no longer being determined by our trading partners. Under floating, since neither the United States nor other countries have much control over the dollar rate, the dollar cannot be as overvalued as it was in 1971. In addition, West Germany and Switzerland were grateful that under floating they were not forced to buy incoming foreign exchange and hence to inflate the money supply.

On the VC argument, Wallich saw a virtuous circle for countries like West Germany or Switzerland: higher exchange rate, lower import prices, less inflation, still higher exchange rate, still lower import prices —a continuing upward circle. There was a parallel case on the part of the deficit country: if the exchange rate depreciated in line with purchasing power parity—the naive case—the country suffered worse inflation than if it had maintained a fixed rate. Since the fixed rate could not be maintained in that case indefinitely, the country merely postponed the depreciation that would occur promptly under floating. Finally, in the case of overshooting—where the rate of depreciation exceeds the level appropriate to maintain purchasing power parity— everyone agrees that this can be considered a vicious circle situation.

Willett's remedy was to advise the country to bite the bullet and follow appropriate policies. But countries in that situation had been unable to follow that prescription. The result had been a polarization: the weak countries grew weaker, the strong grew stronger. The latter had made substantial financing available to the deficit countries to overcome this polarization. One should recognize that this BOP financing was a form of official exchange-rate intervention and that the amount of it had been massive under floating.

Wallich drew two conclusions from the experience with floating:

(1) the countries that had benefited from floating had been prepared to help their trading partners through lending; and (2) countries that had found their freedom of national policy making disappointingly limited under floating had found it much more attractive to adhere to an optimum currency area.

On the surveillance issue, the United States had a strong interest in a clean float. Only then is the dollar rate determined by the market and not by the intervention of other countries. A system of target zones or target rates would deprive the United States of the benefits of floating in that a control would be reestablished over the dollar rate and perhaps even a convertibility obligation.

Surveillance also had to do with the allocation of current-account deficits. The solution of international BOP surpluses and deficits was not found exclusively in domestic expansion by surplus countries or exclusively in an exchange-rate change. The stronger countries could encourage the weaker countries to borrow and maintain their exchange rate or, alternatively, to reduce their borrowing and allow the rate to depreciate. In the latter case, the exchange rates of the surplus countries would appreciate; it would then be appropriate for them to act to restore the degree of domestic expansion lost by the upward exchange-rate trend. Thus, under floating, we seemed to be back to the old argument about the distribution of the burden of adjustment between deficit and surplus countries .

Gottfried Haberler (American Enterprise Institute) found himself in substantial agreement with Willett and in some disagreement with Williamson.

He emphasized that any long-drawn-out inflation acquires vicious-circle properties that are the consequence of inflationary policies and are independent of the exchange-rate regime. If there is overshooting of the exchange rate, the obvious remedy is intervention in the exchange market. But the exchange market interventions of Great Britain and Italy financed by large borrowing abroad had not broken their vicious circle of inflation.

Haberler next considered Williamson's view that the recession could be attributed to the priority given to price stability at the cost of real output. He felt that the choice was no longer so simple. In the post–World War II period, there had been no case of deflation in the traditional sense of declining price levels or contraction of either the money supply (M) or money GNP (MV). In his view a clear-cut trade-off between employment and inflation no longer existed. And for economists and policy makers the choice between lower unemployment and lower rates of inflation was no longer available. With the Phillips curve approximating the shape of a vertical straight line, we must expect inflation to accelerate quickly and output and employment to gain only a little when expansionary monetary-fiscal measures are applied.

Haberler questioned whether the burden of the oil *deficit* (as distinguished from the higher oil price) had to be shared equitably so long as the deficit could be financed by petrodollars. Similarly, if West Germany and Japan had an export surplus, it did not necessarily mean that they were exporting deflation and unemployment. The surplus could be financed by direct investments or portfolio investment abroad, thus "transferring real resources" to the deficit countries. Even if the surplus countries added to their international reserves, under floating the deficit countries were not compelled to deflate and accept more unemployment. No country in the modern (post-Keynesian) world has been willing to accept a real deflation.

ASSESSMENT OF CONFERENCE DISCUSSION

Samuel I. Katz

Participants at the conference seemed to be primarily interested in three major policy issues in the field of U.S.-European monetary relations:

- To what extent could they regard the VC hypothesis as valid?
- Were the West German authorities justified in their unwillingness to reflate their sluggish domestic economy?
- Should European officials approach regional monetary integration through the creation of a parallel currency or through the adoption of general rules for the management of exchange rates?

Only the first two topics attracted the attention of all participants. On the question of the next steps in European integration, there was a reluctance on the part of American participants to offer advice or to take strong positions for policy action. The immediate approach to regional integration was primarily a concern of the European participants, and the main points raised in the debate among them can be found in the papers in this volume by Balassa, Vaubel, Oort, Thygesen, and Basevi and in the commentaries of several participants.

In contrast, all the participants seemed to have views about the validity of the VC hypothesis and the need to reflate the West German economy. Participants raised their main points both in the various conference papers and in the discussion. They are scattered throughout the conference record and cannot be found in any of the specific papers. In this section, therefore, I will try to draw together the main themes of the discussion on these two topics.

Validity of the VC Hypothesis

The validity of the VC hypothesis was perhaps the major topic debated by the participants. The formulation of the hypothesis in the Lamfalussy paper served as the basic analytical framework around which each of the participants expressed his own views. In general, although there were individual exceptions, most European participants considered that the European experience had confirmed the relevance of this hypothesis, at least in the cases of individual countries. The strong opposition to the analytical validity and practical relevance of the theory came primarily from U.S. participants.

The narrowing of these differences between critics and advocates of the VC hypothesis was perhaps the major by-product of the conference. By the end of the two days of debate, it had become clear that proponents and opponents of the theory had found substantial common ground. Proponents had backed away from naive versions of the hypothesis. They accepted the fact that an inflation-depreciation spiral could not develop without an accommodating monetary expansion and that depreciation could not appropriately be regarded as an independent source of inflationary pressure in situations where the exchange-rate decline merely reflected domestic inflation. They also recognized that the use of official reserves to support an overvalued currency might temporarily help a country hold down inflation, but only at the cost of exporting more inflation to trading partners.

On their side, the critics of the VC hypothesis came to acknowledge the possibility of exchange market "overshooting"—the decline in the market rate below the equilibrium value—as a threat on some occasions to domestic stabilization in a regime of floating rates.

But the convergence among participants was mainly in the realm of analytical agreement. At the end of the conference substantial differences remained, both on the mechanics of the processes of the VC spiral and on the policy implications for corrective action. Critics of the theory could not regard an occasional overshooting as a mechanism that by itself could set off a cumulative sequence of depreciation and inflation; on the contrary, such a continuing spiral was credible only when there were accommodating domestic financial policies in effect. To them, therefore, the appropriate policy response even to episodes of overshooting was firmer monetary control, rather than dependence on official exchange market intervention. The critics were sensitive to, and continuously resistant to, the VC theory to the extent that it could be interpreted as a serious criticism of the regime of managed floating. Thus there was an element of the perennial debate among economists about fixed or floating rates in the background of the discussion of the inflation-depreciation spiral hypothesis.

As it turned out, therefore, the conference debate focused not on theoretical models of a self-sustaining sequence from depreciation to inflation but on policy issues: where and how could the VC spiral be broken? Thus the debate became a broadly based reappraisal of the role of exchange-rate policy in BOP adjustment under contemporary conditions.

Many European participants voiced a general disenchantment with the way floating rates had worked in their countries. They were impressed with the fact that, despite widespread changes in European currency values, the large BOP surpluses and deficits did not seem to be diminishing. Equally disturbing was a general economic fragmentation in the area: the emergence of two blocs of countries, one with "weak" BOP positions, high inflation, and depreciating currencies and one with "strong" BOP positions, low inflation, and appreciating currencies. Furthermore, some of them attributed the sluggishness of the European recovery, especially the lag in private investment, to the uncertainties created by floating currencies. They saw a process of regional economic fragmentation under way—a much wider divergence of inflation rates within the region under floating rates than had ever taken place under pegged rates.

Those participants who interpreted the European experience in terms of the VC hypothesis thought that the primary factor that had limited the effectiveness of exchange-rate policy was the rapid communication of the inflationary effects of a depreciating currency to domestic markets for goods and labor. According to traditional theory, the use of exchange-rate policy to eliminate a BOP deficit will necessarily be inflationary. That is, the decline in the exchange rate will lower the foreign-currency prices of local goods (thereby promoting export sales) and will raise the local-currency prices of foreign goods (thereby stimulating price advances in import and in import-competing goods). These changes in relative prices in the depreciating country will speed an improvement in the trade balance on the external side and speed price rises and an expansion in aggregate spending on home goods on the domestic side. Even in the standard theory, the acceleration in domestic inflation gradually erodes the temporary competitive advantage local entrepreneurs can hope to obtain from a depreciated or devalued currency.

The common theme among advocates of the VC hypothesis was the rapidity with which the inflation associated with the fall in the exchange rate was being transmitted to prices for home goods and to wages in the European experience. This process had been speeded up by (1) the adjustment of wages and other incomes to the rise in retail prices, especially with indexing under law or under contract; (2) the existence of social policies and income transfers that reduced the effects of rising unemployment on wage trends; and (3) the demands of

45

organized labor to preserve the level of real wages or of existing skill differentials in the face of advancing prices.

In 1977 wage-sector behavior had been central to the recent European experience. The feedbacks from a depreciating currency to wages were particularly troublesome in situations where the country was relying on incomes policy as a crucial element in its anti-inflation effort. The national authorities sought to avoid a situation in which an unstable or a widely fluctuating exchange rate would make wage negotiations with the unions more difficult by its effects on domestic price trends or on expectations. In some cases they had therefore undertaken substantial exchange market intervention.

In addition, advocates of the VC hypothesis stressed the significance of the phenomenon of overshooting in the exchange market. There was general recognition that there had been episodes of overshooting among both "weak" currencies (the lira and the pound) and "strong" ones (the deutsche mark and the Swiss franc). The phenomenon was commonly interpreted as a form of short-term capital flow. A change in expectations (about prices or the exchange rate) could lead asset holders temporarily to alter the proportion of foreign- and domestic-currency assets in their portfolios, even without any change in interest rates or in expected underlying yields. An additional factor was the precautionary shifts out of weak currencies (including leads and lags in payments and in physical trade) by multinational corporations and private firms engaged in foreign trade. Such shifts by private parties had, on occasion and in the absence of support from the central bank, led to episodes in which spot rates registered wide temporary swings out of all proportion to the recorded changes in trade flows or to the perceived changes in comparative costs of export goods. These were the grounds on which some participants concluded that the VC hypothesis justified official intervention.

The West German Economy: The Need to Reflate?

The basic VC model applicable to "weak" countries with depreciating currencies could also be applied to the cycle of continuing appreciation experienced by countries with strong BOP positions. The transmission mechanism was identical in sequence and opposite in direction. An appreciating deutsche mark had acted as a brake on domestic inflation through the same channels through which the depreciating lira and pound had acted as a stimulant to inflation in Italy and Great Britain. Thanks to the rising value of the deutsche mark, union members could accept what appeared to outsiders to be modest increases in money wages and still have a significant realized rise in real wages.[1] In these circumstances it was easier for the authorities and the employers to get the unions to accept moderate wage agreements, which in turn helped to make West German goods competitive in inflationary foreign markets despite the higher value of the deutsche mark.

The appreciating deutsche mark did not seem to be effective in reducing West Germany's BOP surplus. There seemed to be in West Germany a VC spiral in the form of a virtuous circle of appreciation and comparatively low levels of price and wage inflation. When the West German economy fell off during 1976 and the growth in real GNP turned out to be substantially below the levels originally forecast by the authorities, there developed a growing criticism of the West German failure to act more vigorously to stimulate business recovery.

This criticism was introduced into the conference in the form of a recommendation endorsed by several participants that officials of West Germany take expansionary monetary and fiscal measures to speed up its growth rate. These participants urged that West German policy was offending an appropriate international code of good behavior in that the continuing BOP surplus—in a period when the industrial countries as a group were faced with a large and enduring oil deficit—pushed onto its trading partners an additional payment deficit that ought to be borne by Germany in a "fair sharing" of the OPEC surplus. Given its external surplus, therefore, these participants regarded the refusal of West German officials to promote recovery as wholly without justification.

The conference discussion of the theoretical bases of these recommendations was prolonged. The external considerations advanced by critics of West German policy—the need for a fair sharing of the OPEC surplus and the acceptance by West Germany of its responsibility to speed world economic recovery—are defended and questioned in several of the commentaries in this volume.

West German participants without exception resisted this advice. They argued that (1) reflation attempted in West Germany in 1975 had been frustrated by the reaction of private investors, who cut back their projects, and of consumers, who raised their level of savings;

---

[1] This process is contrary to the Mundell-Laffer ratchet theory, which holds that prices rise in the depreciating country but do not fall in the appreciating country; hence there would be an acceleration in world inflation even when the currencies of surplus countries are allowed to rise (Morris Goldstein, "Downward Price Inflexibility, Ratchet Effects, and the Inflationary Impact of Import Price Changes: Some Empirical Tests," *IMF Staff Papers*, November 1977, pp. 571 ff.). However, the West German and Swiss experience led proponents of the virtuous circle hypothesis to stress that prices of imported commodities decrease in terms of local currency and can slow down the rise in wage rates.

(2) inflation by a surplus country would not help the deficit country but would merely create a rise in the latter's import price level that would spread throughout the domestic economy; and (3) West German domestic policy depended on predictability of government action, which precluded attempts at fine tuning.

Concluding Observations

Conference participants were really exploring the relation between exchange-rate and demand-management policies under modern conditions as they debated the validity of the VC hypothesis or the appropriateness of West German macroeconomic policy. The central fact that they confronted was the stubbornness of the BOP surpluses and deficits of several major European countries, especially the association between exchange-rate change and inflation in Great Britain and Italy during the 1975–1976 inflationary surge.

This experience could serve as the basis for doubts about the effectiveness of currency changes in promoting international adjustment. But the same facts could equally be interpreted as evidence that exchange-rate policy could be expected to promote international adjustment only when supported by appropriate domestic policies.

For example, surplus countries that allowed their exchange rates to appreciate could expect the higher currency value to slow the pace of domestic expansion. A steady appreciation of the currency made urgent the introduction of additional expansionary measures to offset this slowdown. In brief, it was realistic to expect a prompt adjustment in the external surplus only when the rise in the exchange rate was complemented by offsetting internal fiscal and monetary measures. If the sluggishness in the domestic economy were allowed to persist, the effects of the domestic business slowdown on domestic costs could make local exports increasingly competitive and set the stage for a further round of currency appreciation.

Similarly, the deficit country with inflation that allowed its exchange rate to decline could expect an acceleration of inflationary pressures and could hope for a lasting improvement in its external position only if it introduced domestic measures to contain the impact of the lower currency value on domestic incomes, on prices and wages, and on expectations. Conference participants agreed that the need for such complementary measures had become much stronger since 1973 in most European countries. In cases where the national authorities did not, or *could* not, introduce appropriate policies of domestic restraint, it had been a common experience for the deficit country to find that the lower exchange rate would induce offsetting rises in prices and wages and would create internal cost conditions that made a further fall in the exchange rate unavoidable.

Accordingly, the recent experience had demonstrated that changes in exchange rates could not by themselves ensure the elimination of external surpluses and deficits, especially under contemporary social and political conditions. On the contrary, it was as necessary for BOP adjustment under floating as it had been under the par-value system for domestic aggregate-demand policies to be integrated with exchange-rate policy. The recent European experience clearly demonstrated that a country's willingness to allow its exchange rate to move upward or downward in response to exchange market developments could not by itself restore external balance. Nor could it create the sustainable balance in domestic goods and financial markets required to bring to a definite end the upward or downward drift of the exchange rate.

PART TWO

MONETARY INTEGRATION: GLOBAL OR REGIONAL?

AN OVERVIEW
OF THE PROBLEMS

Alexandre Lamfalussy

The purpose of this short introduction to the panel discussion is to raise two questions without really trying to answer them. The first of these, to which I shall devote most of my time, is whether recent experience with the working of the adjustment process (or its failure to work) warrants a reappraisal of current negative attitudes to regional monetary integration—especially in Western Europe. In addition, I shall consider briefly the implications of any such reappraisal for worldwide monetary management and, more specifically, for relations between the dollar and European currencies.

In what follows I propose to use "monetary integration" rather loosely, by insisting on two minimal features of an integrated monetary area: a greater stability of exchange rates within the area than between its members and third countries; and a high degree of freedom within the area for payments on current- and capital-account transactions.

Even on this deliberately loose definition it is clear that little has survived of earlier attempts at promoting monetary integration within the European Economic Community (EEC). A cursory glance at exchange-rate graphs (Figure 1) suggests that the four large Western European economies—France, West Germany, Italy, and the United Kingdom—have been moving away from integration rather than toward it. That is true not only for the diverging trends of exchange rates but also for the great number of restrictions on capital movements introduced by these countries, which apply to intra-EEC payments as well as to payments with third countries. Admittedly the snake has withstood quite a few adversities, but since it has been reduced to little more than a deutsche mark zone, it can hardly be regarded as a "natural" nucleus for a broader revival of European monetary integration. On the whole, it is probably correct to say that today predominant attitudes toward monetary integration within the EEC range from skepticism about its feasibility to doubts about its desirability. This is indeed a far cry not only from the visionary hopes of the 1960s but even from

FIGURE 1
Changes in Effective Exchange Rates and Current-Account Balances of Payments in Selected Industrial Countries, 1970–1976

— Effective exchange rates; 1969 = 100.

 Current-account balance-of-payments surplus or deficit minus net balance of unilateral transfers as a percentage of gross receipts from exports of goods and services.

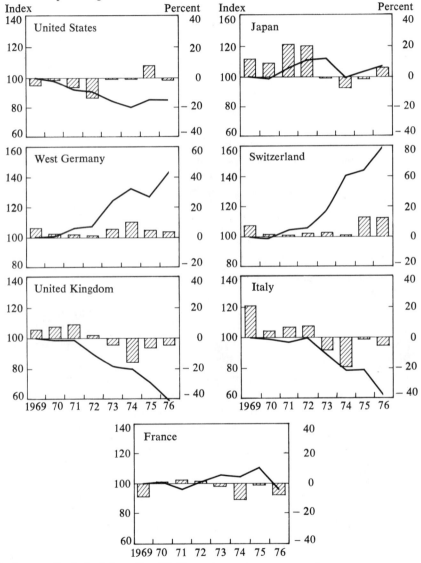

SOURCE: Bank for International Settlements.

the more modest ambitions entertained in the early 1970s of creating an island of exchange-rate stability in a world of floating currencies.

We now know the reasons why the EEC, despite its growing trade integration, has not managed to turn itself into a currency area. A series of external shocks has revealed fundamental differences in the social and political attitudes, as well as in the economic structures, of the larger member countries. These differences had been concealed by the exceptionally favorable conditions for balanced growth prevailing until about 1968–1969, but they came to light under the pressure of three major external forces. First was the flight from the dollar. When this began to happen and the holders of dollar balances had to make up their minds which other currencies they preferred, the choice had already become relatively easy. The underlying economic performance was clearly better in some countries than in others, although the differences were then much smaller than they have subsequently become. But the differential influx of funds into Europe definitely widened the emerging divergences in the BOP pattern and therefore contributed to the instability of intra-EEC exchange rates. The second shock came from the sharp acceleration of world inflation in 1972 and 1973—in considerable measure because of the general rise in commodity prices, but of course most European countries themselves contributed to this rise by their domestic expansion. The third was the sudden rise in the price of oil at the end of 1973.

Not only did these shocks affect countries differently, but the reactions to them varied from country to country: in labor markets and domestic price formation, in export performances, and, most important, in the choice of policy priorities and therefore in effective policy measures to deal with their consequences. The outcome was a substantial aggravation both of differences in inflation rates and of intra-European payments imbalances. In these circumstances, what amount of foreign exchange reserves would have been needed to peg the franc, the lira, or the pound to the deutsche mark? No one can tell. At any rate, the deficit countries' reserves proved insufficient while the surplus countries refused to continue accumulating reserves indefinitely. Exchange rates therefore had to go—in most instances, vis-à-vis the dollar, but in the process also one against the other.

It is tempting to conclude from this experience that the EEC should *not* be regarded as an optimum currency area and hence that there is no reason for reviving attempts at monetary integration among its members. But is that so obvious? Two groups of arguments run counter to this contention. Both reflect some disenchantment with floating.

The first group deplores the disruptive influence on trade of unpredictable and sizable exchange-rate changes within an area where different national economies are increasingly integrated. There seem to be two versions of this very general argument.

According to one version, exchange-rate uncertainties—or, more specifically, sharp declines in exchange rates—are accompanied by, or at least foreshadow, restrictive measures by governments. These can be general monetary or fiscal measures; but they may also comprise direct, often discriminatory, restrictions on trade. Such restrictions hamper trade and could increasingly endanger the customs union. I do not find this argument convincing: restrictive measures are the consequence of payments imbalances, not of exchange-rate changes. One could even reverse the argument and say that, without appropriate exchange-rate adjustments, there would be a higher probability of an external deficit's leading to restrictions on trade. The real culprit is the intra-European payments disequilibrium rather than its reflection in exchange-rate changes.

The second version of this general argument, however, carries more weight and does not seem to be vitiated by a logical flaw. Exchange-rate fluctuations *do* of themselves create a climate of uncertainty, and while trade transactions can in most cases be insured against exchange risks (at a cost), investment cannot. When capital expenditure is undertaken with a view to supplying goods to a variety of foreign markets, the entrepreneur will add a special risk premium to his calculation of the financing cost, and this is likely to have an inhibiting effect on investment—especially in the trade-integrated area of the EEC, where a substantial part of manufacturing investment goes into industries supplying internationally traded goods and using inputs of the same kind. In a world where uncertainties already abound, one does not really need an additional one—hence the feeling shared by many Europeans that exchange-rate uncertainties may have played a role in the stubborn sluggishness of industrial investment.

To some extent, of course, one could reply to this argument too that, since exchange rates respond to external imbalances, the responsibility for the climate of uncertainty should lie with the latter, just as in the previous version of the argument. This sounds convincing when one looks at, say, Italy and West Germany. But what kind of underlying imbalances would justify the marked swings that have occurred in the deutsche mark–Swiss franc rate? Or, to take the example of the French franc, has there been any change in the basic balance of payments of France (on any acceptable definition) that would have warranted first the appreciation, then the depreciation of the franc?

I would attach much greater importance to a second group of arguments, which in essence cast doubt on the effectiveness of exchange-rate changes in promoting balance-of-payments adjustment.

On a somewhat superficial level, this doubt is derived from observation of the facts presented in Figure 1. The dramatic depreciations of the lira and the pound have not so far been accompanied by a return to external balance in Italy and the United Kingdom (although in both the deficits were smaller in 1975 and 1976 than in 1974). At the same time, both West Germany and Switzerland have remained current-account surplus countries despite the appreciation of their currencies (although the West German surplus has declined). The fact that the adjustment in the U.S. current account occurred after the depreciation of the dollar and after a decline in real wages suggests that exchange-rate changes may have different impacts on the current account according to the relative size of the economy, its degree of openness, and the degree of stickiness of its real wages.

To arrive at this conclusion and to give some plausibility to the vicious and virtuous circle argument, one needs of course more than a look at Figure 1. The argument is being actively debated by many academic economists. At the risk of appearing presumptuous, I shall try to sum up a set of propositions that, put together, would tend to explain the self-defeating nature of some currency depreciations.

- "Small" countries are price takers; hence prices of internationally traded goods expressed in the national currency tend to increase, after a relatively short time lag, by the amount of the depreciation of the currency. This applies both to import and export prices.
- When a "small" country is at the same time "open," there will be a high proportion of tradables or effectively traded goods in the domestic output. The price increase therefore directly affects a large proportion of the goods produced and consumed domestically.
- This price increase is transmitted to the nontradables through expenditure switching and the adjustment of wages (and other incomes, such as rents) to the rise in the retail price index, especially where wage indexation is contractual. The effect is amplified whenever the institutional setup forces money wages up by more than the rise in retail prices.
- When a country has been living for some time with an inflation-depreciation spiral, expectations will have a further destabilizing effect by producing periodical downward "overshooting" of exchange rates and by transmitting price increases to the nontradables in anticipation of the rise in the price of inputs.

Many economists would probably agree that some such mechanism might have been at work, although some of them would argue that its practical importance remains to be empirically verified. However, the really fundamental divergence between those who insist on the vicious circle approach and those who reject it lies not so much in the analysis as in policy prescriptions: more precisely in recommending *where* and *how* to break up the sequence of events.

On the one hand, the extreme monetarist would argue that the increase in domestic prices induced by a depreciating exchange rate is an essential part of the adjustment process, which will function properly on condition that monetary authorities prevent the money supply from rising in such a way as to frustrate it. In this case inflation will lead to a decline in real balances, which will bring about the appropriate adjustment in both the current and the capital account of the balance of payments, while at the same time putting a brake on domestic inflation. The decline of the exchange rate will then come to a halt. A somewhat milder version of this view is that, provided the national authorities do not accommodate domestic inflation by letting the money supply expand or by maintaining an expansionary government budget, the vicious circle will stop functioning, since depreciation simply reflects faulty domestic policies. Apply the right kind of domestic policies, and there will be no destabilizing expectations.

On the other hand, proponents of the vicious circle approach do not deny that there is always some degree of restraint in monetary and fiscal policies that would by itself break the circle; nor do they deny that the spiral cannot be interrupted without applying restrictive domestic policies. But what is the cost of applying *only* these policies? And given these costs, would such policies be feasible? In the kind of country described above, the cost will be an unnecessarily high level of unemployment coupled with a shift in income distribution against profits leading to sluggish investment. This is clearly not desirable, nor is it feasible in countries where large-scale unemployment is politically unacceptable. Hence their first conclusion for those countries is that incomes policy in some form or other is an unavoidable complement, though not an alternative, to appropriately restrictive domestic policies in any attempt to bring about a temporary decline in, or at least a stabilization of, real wages. Once this conclusion is accepted, a second follows closely. In a country caught in a depreciation-inflation spiral, the chances of enforcing a successful incomes policy without stabilizing the exchange rate through intervention are very slight indeed. Under the impact of a depreciating exchange rate there is the major risk that accelerating inflation will lead to declines in real wages on a scale that produces a wage explosion. That is the real risk today in the United Kingdom. On the other hand, currency appreciation, leading to lesser inflation, will ex post justify earlier wage restraint accepted by the unions and therefore make it easier to renew wage agreements on moderate terms.

Although I do not want to hide my sympathy for this line of reasoning, I do not suggest that its acceptance should lead one straight back toward arguing in favor of a renewed attempt at monetary integration in Western Europe. For one thing, while the European experience seems convincing enough negatively—in the sense that it raises many questions about the role of floating rates in the adjustment process —it has not so far conclusively demonstrated the opposite thesis, namely that fixed rates provide (for small, open economies with rigid real wages) a better environment for appropriate adjustment policies and therefore for an effective adjustment process. It is a fact that the countries that have remained in the snake have experienced less inflation than those that have left it. But to be able to answer this question one will have to watch very closely future developments in the small snake countries. There can be little doubt, for instance, that the combination of a tight domestic monetary policy and massive intervention in the exchange markets has—through the pegging of the Belgian franc to the deutsche mark—slowed the rate of Belgian price and wage inflation without apparently affecting Belgian exports. And if this experience continues to prove successful, it may provide useful lessons for European countries larger than Belgium but small in relation to the world economy as a whole.

Second, one is justified in having some doubts about the practicability of a new approach to European monetary integration because of likely objections coming from the largest appreciating country, namely West Germany. On the other hand, West Germans have become increasingly aware of how appreciation has assisted their fight against inflation. On the other hand, while they refuse to play the adjustment game by undertaking strongly expansionist demand management, they see no objection to letting the deutsche mark appreciate as their own contribution to reestablishing current-account equilibrium. On both counts they are likely to be reluctant to participate in a process of integration that would make it more difficult for the effective exchange rate of the deutsche mark to appreciate.

The last but not least reason for being cautious in recommending an immediate reopening of the currency area issue is that the external shocks that were responsible for revealing the intra-European differences in social economic structure and policy preferences have not yet been fully absorbed.

First, inflation is still running at intolerably high rates in almost all European countries. It is obvious that a reduction of the absolute differences between individual inflation rates must imply reducing the average European inflation rate. This is a simple matter of probability: relative differences between inflation rates are bound to subsist. The point, then, is that a 14 percent inflation rate is double a 7 percent rate; the difference between the two is significant and will lead to exchange-rate disparities. Equally, 4 percent is double 2 percent, but one can probably live more easily with such a difference without experiencing diverging exchange-rate movements. Therefore an absolute precondition for even a modest stabilization of intra-European exchange rates is a further, significant decline in the *average* European inflation rate. The downward stickiness of inflation rates in all but those countries whose exchange rates have appreciated makes this unlikely in the very near future.

Second, the international oil imbalance is also still very much with us, although its aggregate size is smaller than in 1974. But since the surplus is now concentrated in a handful of low-absorbing countries, its further decline appears improbable in the near future. Moreover, one can have doubts about the continued smooth functioning of the financing flows so far provided by the private banking system. This raises problems analogous to that mentioned in the previous paragraph, since in this context one has to assume, and even wish, that a significant part of the current-account oil deficit will remain in Europe. Otherwise, how could one ensure adequate financing? This would imply that even the complete disappearance of the few surplus positions in Europe would lead not to balanced current accounts in the vast majority of the European countries but simply to smaller deficits. I feel that it is more difficult, both psychologically and operationally, to stabilize exchange rates between deficit countries than between countries in balanced positions. On more general grounds, the current imbalance in world payments, implying the accumulation of huge debts outside as well as inside Europe, simply does not provide an adequate framework for successful regional monetary integration.

Third, Europeans would be well advised not to forget the role played by the dollar crisis in wrecking their hopes of monetary union. It is hard to imagine even an approximate stability of intra-European exchange rates without continued confidence in the dollar or, to put it more pointedly, without a fair degree of stability in the dollar–deutsche mark rate. This would require not only that the success in fighting inflation remain similar in the United States and West Germany but also—on this assumption—that excessive interest-rate fluctuations between the two countries be avoided and that the U.S. authorities adopt a more positive attitude toward exchange market intervention. I am of course not suggesting any formal agreement to peg one currency to the other. Even on the assumption of comparable inflation rates in the two countries, the many uncertainties and the vast sums of liquid assets involved would make any such agreement wildly unrealistic. But there is a long distance from pegging to today's refusal even to consider the problem.

My tentative and not very original conclusion therefore is that our first priority should be the appropriate handling of the three broad problems mentioned before we embark on any new scheme of regional monetary integration in Europe. While the creation of a European area of exchange-rate stability may be highly desirable in a world of uncertainties, its practicability remains doubtful so long as these three potential or actual problems remain unsolved. That is not to say, however, that European policy makers should not regard achieving greater stability of intra-European exchange rates as a major objective. They could work in this direction in two ways. First, by making a serious attempt to coordinate economic policies rather than simply paying lip service to such coordination. Second, by exploring both technically and politically new approaches (of which the target zone proposal is just one) that at a later stage might become a useful starting point for monetary integration in Europe.

COMMENTARIES

Alexandre Kafka

In speaking about Lamfalussy's excellent paper, I shall pay particular attention to those points that concern the LDCs. Since I seem to be the only underdeveloped participant in this meeting, I assume that that is where my comparative advantage lies.

I very much like Lamfalussy's loose definition of monetary integration: increased exchange-rate stability and a high degree of freedom of current and capital transactions. It seems to me that that is a much more useful approach than restricting the concept to absolute fixity of rates and complete and everlasting freedom for capital- and current-account transactions.

One would not deny that the stricter standard, if it could be imposed, would be likely to make things easy in some respects; for instance, by avoiding speculative capital flows. But to proceed even on the softer standard might be worthwhile. After all, the gold standard achieved many of the advantages expected from "integration" without living up to quite so strict a standard. There were tariff changes and rate fluctuations between gold points, and central banks sometimes monkeyed about with the gold points.

If the world was once—at least in its industrial core—enough of an optimum currency area to sustain the gold standard, two questions are raised; (1) Why has it become less so? (It obviously is not an optimum currency area today.) (2) How could it be an optimum currency area in gold standard days without institutionalization of monetary and fiscal integration or harmonization, of which we hear so much these days?

The deterioration in the conditions for an optimum currency area is, obviously, a deterioration not with respect to Robert A. Mundell's criterion (factor mobility) or Ronald I. McKinnon's (openness of the economies) but with respect to Charles P. Kindleberger's criterion (policy coordination).[1] Under the gold standard, of course, policy coordination came about without institutionalization in the monetary field as a result of the importance attributed to maintenance of fixed par values. And it was less of a necessity in the fiscal sphere—if it ever is—because the scope of government was so much smaller.

Professor Lamfalussy claims that all may not be lost with respect to monetary integration in Western Europe, although first it is necessary fully to absorb the three great recent shocks about which he spoke: the new inflation plateau in most industrial countries, the oil crisis, and the dethronement of the dollar as the safest currency—though I would suggest that the latter is simply an aspect of the new inflation plateau.

Nobody could quarrel with Lamfalussy's priorities. Monetary integration can help to induce governments to suffocate shocks that cannot be quickly suffocated and that affect countries differentially.

Although absorbing the oil shock is not a problem of exchange-rate adjustment between oil-exporting countries and oil-importing countries, the distribution of the oil deficit among the latter is, in part, such a problem. In other words, it is necessary not merely to recycle the petrodollars but to recycle the oil deficits among countries so that no country will have to go too much into debt year after year while the world's oil deficit remains.

Unfortunately the problem is not only an exchange-rate problem. There has been a curious change in attitudes toward economic policies. Exchange-rate movements, including appreciation, are now a good deal more acceptable than they used to be. But trade liberalization has apparently ceased to be acceptable although much progress was made until the early 1970s. Yet redistributing the oil deficits requires trade liberalization as much as exchange-rate movements, which, however, may also have been insufficient in some cases.

One feels that many large industrial countries in strong BOP positions would rather do anything—lend to the hilt—than import one dollar's worth more from weaker countries.

Lamfalussy has given an excellent account of two areas where floating rates may not be ideal. He is careful not to claim that stable but adjustable, or even fixed, rates may be better. His concern is simply to temper the initial enthusiasm for floating rates. He has said, first, that floating rates may not be ideal in their effect on investment because one cannot normally hedge for the time period relevant to the invest-

---

[1] For a comprehensive summary of the literature on an optimum currency area, see Yoshihide Ishiyama, "The Theory of Optimum Currency Areas: A Survey," *IMF Staff Papers*, July 1975, pp. 344–83.

ment decision and, second, that floating rates may not be ideal because of the possibility of an exchange-rate–wage-price–exchange-rate spiral.

The investment argument requires qualification. Although currency movements in some developing countries have often involved quite sharp temporary devaluations as well as appreciations in real terms, they have nevertheless not inhibited domestic investment largely addressed to exports or direct investment from abroad, as long as one condition was met: that there was confidence that government would not, in the medium term, attempt to inhibit the adaptation of the exchange rate to cost and price differentials between the country and the rest of the world.

It seems to me that the fluctuations of the currencies of the industrial countries have been considerably shorter than the periods one would assume to be relevant to most investment decisions and that, over time, rate fluctuations have corresponded rather well to relative price movements. That has not, however, invariably meant that exchange-rate relationships—which are also influenced by their starting point—have been most conducive to the most desirable adjustment process, as I have already suggested.

But I would conclude from this that Lamfalussy is probably right, that exchange-rate uncertainty is likely to inhibit short-term international investment as well as portfolio investment. But I do not think that exchange-rate uncertainty—to judge from my experience with the developing countries—will depress investment in export industries, specifically, to any great extent if there is no medium-term exchange maladjustment existing or expected.

Developing countries, like industrial countries, have been influenced in their exchange policies by concern for Lamfalussy's exchange-rate–price-wage–exchange-rate spiral, although they have sometimes, like industrial countries, gone beyond what is reasonable in trying to avoid depreciations. What is probably more difficult to understand is the LDCs' announced preference for the avoidance of floating rates—not among themselves or between themselves and industrial countries, but among industrial countries. Yet there are some reasons for such an attitude, along with some pure prejudice.

A developing country with a geographically well-diversified trade would have to decide in the floating world whether to peg to a major currency. And that decision may involve disagreeable political choices and may create problems for the BOP and internal stabilization because of events unrelated to the economy of the developing country itself. Failure to peg to a major currency, or frequently changing the currency to which one does peg, creates the need to formulate an explicit exchange-rate policy. This can also be quite difficult if a country is not accustomed to doing so. It may also be necessary for a country floating independently, or for one pegging to a basket, to create a forward market that may have high operating costs because of diseconomies of scale.

The floating of industrial countries' currencies can have other consequences for developing countries. For example, monetary as well as trade integration among developing countries will be impossible, or at least more difficult, if the natural propensity of different countries in the integrating group is to peg on different industrial currencies.

I should say a few words about experience with monetary integration among developing countries themselves. There are some movements in this direction, particularly in Latin America. They are limited to the most rudimentary form of monetary integration, which is reserve saving—what used to be called in Europe, "interim finance"—plus some very limited reserve pooling. There are, by present standards, areas of quite impressive monetary stability in the Third World; in Central America, for example, it is politics, rather than economics, that militates against greater monetary integration.

It has been suggested that, even elsewhere, limited monetary integration might help LDCs increase the mutual opening of their economies by allaying fears of payments imbalances. Substantial reserve pooling through regional funds, it has been suggested, could be helpful in this direction even without more far-reaching integration. But the practical problem is that substantial reserve pooling is resisted in the Third World, as it is in Europe, where monetary and fiscal policies are not adequately coordinated or spontaneously in step.

Pierre Uri

I am inclined to share Lamfalussy's doubts about the effectiveness of the adjustment process under floating exchange rates as well as about. the feasibility and even the advisability of an attempt to create a comparatively stable exchange-rate area in the EEC as long as inflation is unequally controlled by its various members and their BOP react differently to external shocks.

Since I am not aware of any consistent position on the part of French authorities either on the international monetary system or on the path to monetary union in Europe, my comments will be more personal. They may reflect more the potential thinking of the opposition than the actual thinking of government circles.

One may try to list the successive creeds or their cycle in the

French official policies, proposals, or statements. General de Gaulle had denounced the exorbitant privilege of the dollar, which can be issued for the payment of external liabilities; he apparently ignored the limitation of the freedom of movement on the part of the U.S. authorities, which is the counterpart of the role of the dollar as an international currency. More than by the force of persuasion of Jacques Rueff, the general was probably impelled by his anti-American stand to extol the impartiality of gold as the only genuine means of international settlements; he was prone to ignore how far its value in the present world was determined by the policies of countries affected by racial conflicts or by a superpower whose main interest is not to prop up the functioning of the capitalist market. When Michel Debré was finance minister, this faith in gold was temporarily revived. His predecessor, who was due also to become one of his successors, Valéry Giscard d'Estaing, had presented a new version of the gold standard in which settlements in bullion would be accompanied by a defined proportion of payments in a newly created "composite reserve unit" based on the currencies of the Group of Ten, which alone appeared to offer a reliable backing. The consequence, with this tag attached to every piece of metal, would have been a de facto revaluation of gold limited to the transactions between the rich countries. The IMF had to fight against this discrimination and insist that any newly created fiduciary instrument of reserve be fully international. Debré was very reluctant to support the SDR scheme and insisted that part of the allocations should be repaid by the recipients. After the short-lived experiment with SDRs, it is hard to know what the French view is about the international means of settlements except that the nominal protest against the use of the dollar could be revived to please the Gaullists despite the acceptance of the Jamaica agreement. French reserves are still largely composed of gold, mainly because it cannot be used and is moreover valued at near the free market price.

Inside the EEC, France supported the idea of getting a monetary union started by narrowing the margins of fluctuation between the European currencies. It joined the snake, then had to leave it, then decided, more for political than for economic reasons, that it should join it again, and then abandoned it apparently for good. Until recently there was no more striking contrast than between the official position in favor of stable exchange rates and the most frequently devalued or downward floating currency of all industrialized countries. The present prime minister and finance minister tries to maintain the external value of the franc, at least in relation to the dollar, if not to the deutsche mark, for reasons of fact even more than of principle. The depreciation of the franc in relation to the deutsche mark that occurred in 1969 had given a spurt to French exports, industrialization, and growth. In a more recent period, the perverse effects of depreciation seem to dominate: imports are immediately more expensive, whereas exports are less dynamic in a half-stagnant world economy, and long-term contracts require a heavy involvement of the government to guarantee the exporting firms against increases in costs. It may seem extraordinary that some of the highest authorities denied the seriousness of the BOP problem. The recession in 1975 had been deep enough to restore a temporary equilibrium through a drop in the volume of imports; and little attention was paid to the warnings of the Planning Commission that, as soon as activity picked up, the long-term character of the imbalance would again be revealed and that a decisive effort at conquering new markets for a broader range of products and wider array of firms would be required over a number of years.

This is only part of a more general story. Western governments have treated cost inflation as if it were caused by a demand pull and not purely by the increased price of imported oil. In so doing they have transferred the burden of the deficits that are the necessary counterpart of OPEC surplus to those parts of the world least able to shoulder and finance them. The world situation can be summarized in a few sentences. Industrialized countries used to complain about their agricultural surpluses in the face of a hungry or starving Third World. They are now suffering from large-scale unemployment in the face of sorely unsatisfied fundamental human needs. The problem of agriculture has been duplicated in industry.

In a sense those who maintained that OPEC surpluses would not stay idle and would finance deficits were right: there is no complete vacuum. But it remains to be seen how the funds are being recycled. For a time part of them went to London, where they were badly needed, but most of them were absorbed in strong-currency countries. By and large, developing countries have to borrow indirectly.

With widely different rates of inflation, there is no alternative to floating rates of exchange. But there is no denying that they in turn contribute to inflation, in the surplus countries through the accumulation of reserves, in the countries with depreciating currencies through the increase of import costs and other mechanisms decribed by Lamfalussy. The countries in deficit have to inspire confidence in other governments, in the banks, or in the Euromarkets. This leads to a process of competitive deflation. There is a remarkable convergence in the attempts to slow down the movement not only of money wages, which is quite appropriate, but also of real wages. As long as unemployment prevails, it is hard to see how this damping down of consumption can revive investment. The only justification is to reduce the demand for imports and release more resources for exports so as to come closer to external balance. It is very doubtful, however, that a restriction of real wages can of itself increase profit margins, which are better restored through the fuller utilization of capacity and of labor productivity reserves that is induced by a real recovery. It is even more doubtful that the reconstituted profit margins will be invested when the medium-term prospects for growth are more limited than in the past, so that increases of capacity can be spread over a longer period.

One of the fundamental changes since World War II that made for the unprecedented rate of growth was that world trade was increasing faster than world output. There has been an absolute decline followed by a limited recovery and now another slowdown. It is an irritating fact that the import absorption of OPEC countries is restricted by their lack of infrastructure and harbor facilities. An application of Western technology to remove that bottleneck would do more for balanced world growth than exchange-rate mechanisms. But beyond those local actions, the future depends on a concerted effort by all the parties concerned to apply the surplus funds more directly to the aims of development. Some courageous efforts, but on a narrow scale, have been attempted in that direction through the oil facilities, the "Third Window" of the World Bank, and direct grants or loans by oil-producing countries; but the key lies in a much broader approach that would give its full significance to the North-South dialogue. The oil producers should provide the capital, industrialized countries the technology and equipment goods, the developing world its manpower. Grants and concessional loans are certainly required on a broader scale. For productive investment, however, the decisive issue is not the rate of interest, but a guarantee against default. Experience shows that, even in the countries of the Third World, default is not a very frequent risk: a guarantee given by industrialized countries would not be very costly. The purpose would be to bring about a new international division of labor, which cannot be divorced from a higher level of employment. The workers in the industrialized world would benefit from a redeployment from low-wage to high-wage industries by accepting the higher imports from the developing world that would accompany the sale of more equipment. It is hard to believe that the private financial markets can achieve this ambitious goal: it requires an unprecedented degree of intergovernmental cooperation and an enormous stepping up of the role of international financial institutions.

As to the monetary system proper, I do not think that the "link" as conceived by the representatives of the Third World—that is, the contribution of a part of international money creation—to long-term lending institutions, would be the most appropriate direction: it would not preserve the flexibility called for by monetary management. My own preferences go very much along Robert Triffin's lines, with a few amendments. I am in favor of a substitution account that would re-absorb the dollar overhang. Otherwise I would want to restrict the discretionary allocation of SDRs to developing countries and make the industrialized ones earn their reserves, as they normally do except when gold is revalued. As to the rate of creation and methods of distri-bution, I would add to Triffin's proposals the following features. I would accept a normal rate of increase of international liquidity based on the anticipated noninflationary growth of trade but would make the formula a binomial one. Considering that industrial raw materials shoot up when industrial production accelerates and fall when industry slows down, let alone recedes in absolute terms, the global price index of such materials should be considered the prime indicator of world economic tendencies. Thus the creation of SDRs should be stepped up or retarded—subject to the exercise of judgment on abnormal factors such as war or droughts—according to the movement of that index. The SDRs would be distributed to the developing countries in relation to the fall of their normal external receipts (calculated on the basis of their share of the markets) for the primary products they export. This compensatory financing would be used for continued production con-ducive to storage, which in turn would avert an explosion of prices when industrial production recovers. The primary producers would receive the means to meet their demand for industrial products, which would contribute to maintaining the prices of primary products and the export proceeds of the developing countries.

As to monetary integration in Europe, my own insistence is on structural factors on the one hand, on fiscal policies on the other.

One should confess that the Rome Treaty relied too optimistically on the prevention of wide price divergences through the very movement of goods and on the convergence of labor union attitudes. The fact is that structural discrepancies have developed between the main mem-ber countries rather than being smoothed out. With a grain of salt, I would argue that West Germany sells the right things on the right markets, France the wrong things but on the right markets, Great Britain the right things but on the wrong markets, and Italy, after years of economic miracle, was prevented by social troubles from keeping up the rate of investment that would have allowed it to reach the level of technology appropriate to its level of wages. The various funds set up by the Rome Treaty or by more recent decisions are not geared to the redressing of such structural deficiencies. Even a steep depreciation of the currencies does not make up for them, since there is a long lead time for investment in new products or markets.

One of the key factors in keeping a country in monetary union with itself is the importance of a public budget that draws most of its resources from the more prosperous areas and spreads its expenditures throughout the territory, thus accomplishing a lot of automatic transfers. The development of a federal budget in the EEC and of a European tax system that would not only rely on customs duties, agricultural levies, or the value-added tax but would comprise an element of direct progressive taxation is an indispensable ingredient of monetary union and regional balance if those objectives are taken seriously. Meanwhile I agree that the use of a unit of account based on a basket of European currencies could provide a good vehicle for the movements of capital and eliminate hot money shifts between European countries. But a large-scale fiscal policy alone would achieve the purpose and moreover, by politicizing the debate at the European level, would pave the way for political union.

Armin Gutowski

To comment on Lamfalussy's paper without merely stressing some points he has made is not easy, for his reasoning is convincing. First I shall try to clarify what could be meant by greater stability of exchange rates; then I shall add a few remarks on the issue of the vicious circle; and finally I want to draw some policy conclusions concerning monetary integration.

I certainly agree that a minimal feature of an integrated monetary area is a greater stability of exchange rates within the area than between it and outside countries. The question is, what is meant by stability of exchange rates? I suggest expressing stability of exchange rates in terms of predictability of their movements. If one feels fairly certain from past policy performance that each country within a group will behave in a specific way—let us say one country will stick to an 8 percent rate of inflation, another will gradually bring down its 9 percent rate to 5 percent within three years, and so on—this could be called a rather great stability of exchange rates in spite of the different policies in each of the countries. The contrasting situation would be where the rates are pegged to each other and the economic policy of each country is not fairly foreseeable, so that it cannot be known when and to what extent devaluations and revaluations will become unavoidable. I should not say that better predictability of exchange-rate movements means monetary integration, but it probably is a necessary condition of forming an integrated monetary area.

Certainly exchange-rate fluctuations can of themselves create a climate of uncertainty and thus impair the propensity to invest, but such a climate arises only if short-run exchange-rate fluctuations reflect quick changes in medium-term expectations about the policy performance of the countries concerned. One can argue, therefore, that there is no close connection between uncertainty and either fixed or flexible exchange rates. To me it seems that the readiness to invest depends rather on the degree of stability of medium-term expectations.

I agree with Lamfalussy that a series of external shocks has revealed fundamental differences in the social and political attitudes of the larger member countries of the EEC. But I want to underline strongly the word "revealed." The shocks themselves were not the reason the EEC has not managed to turn itself into a currency area; they merely brought to light the differences in the underlying factors. These differences would have turned up sooner or later in any case because the member countries were not ready to harmonize their policies, especially their monetary policies. From this it does not necessarily follow that attempts at reviving monetary integration would be in vain.

Lamfalussy discusses in his paper two groups of arguments that run counter to the conclusion that one should give up attempts at reviving monetary integration among EEC members. I shall confine myself to the second group of arguments, especially to the vicious circle argument, which questions the effectiveness of exchange-rate changes in promoting BOP adjustment. The impact of exchange-rate changes on the current account—and here again I agree—may be less, the smaller the relative size of the economy, the greater its openess, and the more sticky its real wages. But the last condition, the stickiness of real wages, makes the statement an almost empty shell.

I do not deny that the vicious circle can be observed. If, for a while, depreciation of a currency has led to price increases in the tradable goods sector, and these have led to factor price increases, which have in turn pushed up the general price level, and if an expansionary monetary policy has accommodated the inflationary process, the result will be an inflation-depreciation spiral. If policy measures are taken to stop this process but everybody still expects it to go on, it may come to downward overshooting of exchange rates.

One can argue that under a regime of fixed exchange rates a similar outcome is not unlikely. If a country encounters a cost-push inflation exceeding the rate of inflation of its trading partners, it will run into employment problems. If, as assumed in the vicious circle argument, real wages are not flexible and if the government resorts to further monetary and fiscal expansion, inflation will accelerate, and the current-account deficit will grow. As is well known, this cannot go on forever; the system of fixed exchange rates is bound to break down unless the surplus countries finally accept a higher and accelerating inflation for themselves. Acceptance of inflation by the surplus countries, however, would not help the deficit country, because the inflationary impact of rising import prices again would be spread over the whole economy. For exactly the same reasons, reflation in more stable economies would not help countries experiencing a vicious circle under a regime of flexible exchange rates.

Let me insert a footnote on this widely discussed issue of reflation. I do not deny that reflation could be helpful if lack of demand were the only cause of slackening investment and growth. By fiscal and monetary expansion a basically strong economy could improve growth of its own GNP without stepping up the pace of inflation, and by subsequently importing more from abroad it would help other countries to overcome their problems. But I do not believe that reflation would be the right policy prescription in, for example, West Germany, which is under pressure to reflate from groups inside and outside the country. More fiscal expansion over and above the programs already in motion and over and above the general budget deficits central and state governments already run would probably, as we learned from experience in 1975, give rise to skepticism in private investors and even consumers about the consequences of continually high government borrowing for mainly consumptive purposes. The negative feedback on private investment and consumption might almost or even fully offset the positive fiscal effect on demand. More monetary expansion would immediately attract the unions' attention. They have learned the hard way what a strict monetary policy can do to employment if wage policy is too aggressive. But they would, since money illusion is gone, be the first to demand higher wages if room opened up for prices to rise.

No monetary trick applied by the more stable countries can solve the problems of countries that absorb more resources than are compatible with their long-run growth potential. Something "real" has to give in the countries experiencing a vicious circle. What, then, could be done to interrupt it?

Again I agree with Lamfalussy that an answer like "apply the right kind of domestic policies, and there will be no destabilizing expectations" is too simple. The degree of domestic restraint in monetary and fiscal policies that would by itself break the vicious circle might lead to unemployment of a politically unacceptable magnitude. I also agree, therefore, that adequate incomes policies could become a necessary complement of restrictive demand management. Otherwise unions would probably push wages up too much, not taking into account the change in domestic policies, with all the detrimental effects on employment. But incomes policies will be helpful only if they make sure that real wage increases lag behind the rise in productivity and that the consumer price index used in the calculation of the real wage increment is corrected for the price effects of changes in value-added and sales taxes, subsidies to producers, and the terms of trade.

Finally, I agree with Lamfalussy in principle but not without restriction that intervention in the foreign exchange market will be necessary because the price effects of further depreciation would put too great a burden of adjustment on wages. Such intervention would imply the extension of credits to the countries in question. On the one hand, such additional credits could facilitate the adjustment process launched by adopting more restrictive policies. On the other hand, the credits would temporarily remove part of the pressure that made the adoption of such policies necessary; if those restrictive policies were subsequently relaxed, all the efforts undertaken might have been in vain. I feel, therefore, that it has to be made sure by all means that the restrictive policy will continue to be applied.

In trying to describe how this can be achieved, I diverge from Lamfalussy's policy conclusions by bringing in monetary integration again. In its last report the West German Council of Economic Experts, of which I am a member, devoted a chapter to monetary policy in Europe, making some proposals and showing that they can be implemented in spite of differences in the tools used by European central banks.[1]

The council recognizes the limits on member countries' solidarity and willingness to adapt imposed by their individual political and social situations. Taking for granted that all EEC members still intend to arrive finally at an economic and monetary union, the council feels that one possible new basic principle would be to make multilateral assistance from other member states conditional on all member states' forsaking some of their independence in national monetary policy and adhering to jointly agreed upon monetary policy targets. As the most

---

[1] Sachverständigenrat zur Begutachtung der Gesamtwirtschaftlichen Entwicklung (Council of Economic Experts) *Jahresgutachten 1976/77* (Stuttgart, Mainz, 1977), paras. 467 ff.

adequate monetary aggregate, the council chooses the monetary base. Its expansion should move in line with the growth of productive capacity and with the rate of price increases deemed unavoidable.[2] For each member a monetary policy objective has to be set at a level that varies according to the initial situation in the country. Over a period of time, the rates of central bank money supply would have to move gradually closer to the target of the group of the most stable economies, which form a floating bloc (for this group stricter rules have to apply). If member countries agree on such rules for their monetary policy, a complementary commitment has to be made that joint assistance will be provided for intervention in the foreign exchange market as soon as exchange rates leave the path corresponding to the monetary targets —that is, the target zone.

For example, if it is agreed that for a particular year the expansion in the monetary base should be 6 percent for countries in the hard-core floating bloc and 11 percent for an outside country, the maximum rate of depreciation of the outside country's currency vis-à-vis the currencies in the bloc should not be less than 5 percent during the year. If the 5 percent limit is exceeded, any intervention by the central bank of the country concerned should trigger the support of the others, provided that the expansion in the monetary base in the country concerned has been in line with the preset agreement. More precisely, the intervention point should be determined by the change in the weighted exchange rate of the currency of the country concerned with respect to the countries of the joint float.[3] Such a scheme takes care of the problem of downward overshooting of exchange rates, which causes great apprehension today. The necessary means of intervention would be jointly provided by the EEC countries as soon as the exchange rate of

---

[2] Allowance also has to be made for the trend in the effectiveness of the monetary system. On several occasions the council has discussed which monetary aggregate would be most suitable as the control variable for managing monetary policy, for example *Jahresgutachten 1974*, paras. 374 ff. There is also a brief discussion in the chapter on monetary policy in Europe, *Jahresgutachten 1976/77*, paras. 476 ff. In para. 478 the council concludes, "Control of monetary base eliminates most of the serious drawbacks of the money supply concepts, as high powered money can be created only by the central bank. It is this money which clearly provides the framework for monetary expansion, at least in the medium term. It is also the prerequisite for an allocation of responsibilities within the stabilization policy process. . . . Households and firms can resist the pressure to adjust . . . in the short term only by economizing on their cash holdings through the use of forms of financing which will save central bank money. This elasticity of the monetary system is limited, however, as long as only central bank money or claims on central bank money are used as a generally accepted means of payment."

[3] Since it is difficult to determine the "correct" intervention point, it might be more advisable to have target zones.

the country troubled by a vicious circle hits the bottom of its exchange-rate target zone while it is trying to break that circle by restricting its monetary expansion to the preset rate.

I do argue, therefore, in favor of a renewed attempt at monetary integration in Western Europe, but in a way that avoids the old mistakes. I strongly believe that the best thing Europe can do and the first thing Europe should do is to launch such an attempt. Although I agree with Lamfalussy that the three external shocks he lists have not yet been fully absorbed, I do not share his caution in recommending monetary integration. To my mind, a scheme such as I have described would make it easier to solve the three worldwide problems revealed by these shocks:

1. Setting rules for monetary expansion would pave the way for reducing not only the differences between individual inflation rates but also the average European inflation rate.
2. Sticking to the rules for monetary expansion and for corresponding interventions in the foreign exchange market made possible by joint credit extension would help to ensure and even to improve the distribution of financial means from the oil-exporting surplus countries among EEC members.
3. Although it is highly desirable to have a fair degree of stability (in terms of better predictability) of the exchange rates between the U.S. dollar and the currencies of a hard-core floating bloc, this is probably not a necessary condition for the functioning of the process of monetary integration in Western Europe.

Andrew A. Shonfield

My comment is addressed chiefly to the latter part of Lamfalussy's paper, specifically to the longer term effects of the oil deficit on the national policies of industrial countries with relatively weak BOP.

The evidence both from recent developments in OPEC and from the projections of available oil resources in the 1980s suggests that the international transactions of the "low import-absorbing" countries of the Middle East (mainly Saudi Arabia and the United Arab Emirates) will give rise to a large collective OECD BOP deficit on current account for a number of years to come. As Lamfalussy points out, exchange-rate relationships between individual deficit countries tend to be more unstable than between countries whose BOP is normally in equilibrium. It is worth asking why. Presumably the main reason is that the foreign exchange market is in these circumstances bereft of conventional criteria by which to judge the significance of any given deterioration in an already negative payments account. It badly needs guidance from some credible official authority on what are to be regarded as tolerable ranges of fluctuation around some accepted deficit position.

Here is a further argument for the establishment of target zones for exchange rates, as suggested by Oort elsewhere in this volume. There are two points to be made about the institution of a system of current-account deficit norms applicable to individual countries in the particular conditions we have been experiencing in the late 1970s. First, such a system is likely to be far more difficult to operate if a small number of advanced industrial countries, while incurring substantial deficits with OPEC, achieve a persistent current-account surplus with other OECD countries that more than offsets their oil deficits. Nothing that has happened subsequently has weakened the force of Robert Solomon's warning about the danger of "mutually frustrating and destructive" policies that could follow from a failure to reach international agreement on some principle for sharing out the worldwide deficit on oil account.[1] His own suggested formula for doing so—a formula that had the attraction of simplicity combined with a readily recognizable equity— would have moved West Germany's target balance of current account some billions of dollars into the red from 1974 onward. Instead the West Germans have stayed consistently and substantially in surplus.

Whatever the criteria adopted for sharing out the global deficit, economic policies pursued by any individual nation that result in its chronic accumulation of reserves earned from other OECD countries, which are in any case involved in a process of steadily increasing indebtedness on oil account, are highly likely in the long run to prompt retaliatory action. In my view, the continuance of a large West German current-account surplus over any extended period will threaten even the well-established free trade arrangements of the EEC. It will do so because the surplus will be viewed as dangerously aggravating the difficulties of other members of the EEC, whose economic and political capacities—including the capacity to take long-range rational decisions on public policy—have been weakened during the slump of the mid-1970s and the halting recovery from it. In particular, the adjustments required of them by the free trade system in the changed situation put them under pressure to accept a significantly higher rate of unemployment than that of the surplus country in their midst. Given the customs union, West German domestic economic policy determines the level of unemployment in the other countries of the EEC.[2]

---

[1] Robert Solomon, "The Allocation of Oil Deficits," in *Brookings Papers on Economic Activity* (Washington, D.C.: Brookings Institution, 1975).

[2] The assumption is that public authorities in the weaker countries are unable, except for short periods, to control the level of real wages. An effective and *sustained* incomes policy in these countries would open up different options.

This leads to the second point about the institutional character of an international authority with the capacity to persuade individual countries to adapt domestic monetary and fiscal policies to the manifest needs of their neighbors. It seems highly unlikely that such a capacity can be established worldwide in the foreseeable future. That is one cogent reason for attempting to reach the necessary agreement initially among a more limited group of countries that are members of a regional grouping with recognized common aims and that have become habituated to mutual intervention in the details of one another's domestic affairs. The EEC is the most obvious candidate. There is of course no guarantee of success when such a group applies itself to intervention in matters of domestic macroeconomic policy, but at least the EEC offers a more promising field for international experimentation than any other in sight.

It is promising partly because the trade gains already secured through membership in the EEC are relatively large, and the members therefore have more at risk if the union is menaced by persistent payments imbalances between them that, in the context of the oil deficit, cannot be offset by large trade surpluses earned outside the Common Market. Furthermore, it is clear that the stability of the EEC requires a systematic effort to *desynchronize* the next business cycle—and probably other cycles following it. The countries that run to structural surpluses must be encouraged to expand faster during the upturn, while the others must deliberately lag. Lagging in this sense implies the systematic maintenance of a higher level of unemployment than that of their neighbors. Once again such a requirement is likely to be acceptable only when made within a group of countries that have adopted the principle of mutual aid for collective purposes and have at least the minimum of common institutional instruments serving that end. The EEC Regional Fund, although excessively modest in scale, and such devices as the Common Unemployment Fund (proposed by the Marjolin group)[3] are examples of what is required.

Such devices would help to mitigate the forces making for the destabilization of exchange rates noted by Lamfalussy. It seems to me, however, that it would be an error to argue, as he appears to do in his final paragraph, that this objective, together with the others that he mentions, should be pursued independently of ("before we embark upon") any effort to secure increased monetary integration in the EEC. Monetary integration is predicated on the assumption of mutual aid on a wider front. There is no reason the provision of such aid should

---

[3] Marjolin Study Group, *Economic and Monetary Union 1980* (Brussels: EEC, 1975).

not in turn be made conditional, in part or as a whole, on meeting certain criteria of monetary performance.

Indeed the two aspects of policy are of their nature mutually dependent. That point is underscored in present circumstances by the manifest requirement for the structural adaptation of major industries in certain important Western countries, which will have to be undertaken in conditions of economic strain and relatively high levels of unemployment. On the one hand, there is the pressing need, urged by Lamfalussy as a condition for more exchange stability, for an early reduction in the *average* rate of inflation in the Western world. On the other hand, it is evident that a number of countries will fare especially badly if the prospective rapidity of the desired monetary effect becomes the overriding consideration in the choice of common policies. Great Britain and Italy will serve as topical illustrations of the problem. It is, in my view, not an accident that the most acute form of inflation emerged in the mid-1970s in two major Western European countries that are (1) faced with the problems of long-term structural adaptation of their economies and (2) inadequately equipped with the political means of carrying through the required policies systematically. In both countries there are marked inelasticities of supply of some tradable goods, combined with a high income elasticity of demand for imports, which results in a propensity to run into BOP deficits at levels of activity well short of full employment.

The problem is worsened in times of relatively low growth of international trade, especially when this coincides, as it has done in the middle and late 1970s, with a marked increase in the competitive power of the leading industrial economies in certain internationally traded goods. To put the point in somewhat oversimplified shorthand, Italy is not able, through a rapid enlargement of its tourism industry, to match the West German or Japanese capacity to capture a larger share of the exports of manufactured goods to third country markets. Nor does Italy have the political capacity to force down real wages sufficiently to offset the adverse effect on its BOP, either by cheapening its exports or by reducing the volume of imports.

Without an effective incomes policy, countries of this type—typically those with a relatively low output per capita that also have a relatively low proportion of gross domestic product (GDP) derived from manufacturing—are compelled to adopt deflationary policies involving high unemployment, if they are to maintain their competitive position in international markets. Popular pressures to have recourse to import controls during a period of structural industrial change are likely to be strong. If there were in fact an incomes policy that promised to contain the secondary inflationary effects of restraining imports, the temptation to arrive at a higher level of employment by means of import controls—indeed to use these as a bargaining counter in persuading organized labor to moderate its wage claims—might in certain countries, especially those with weak governments, come to be well nigh irresistible.

All this amounts to an argument for not pressing the pace for the desired reduction of inflation too hard. The worrying aspect of the present international situation is not simply the unevenness of the economic performance of different nations. It is the sheer size of the gap that appears to have opened up between leaders and laggards inside the small group of countries that make up the hard core of the Western alliance. So much that has gone right in the international economy since the war has depended on the cohesion of this core group.

It now looks as if bigger demands are going to be imposed on it, at a time when the underlying forces, if left to themselves, are likely to make for a greater divergence in the perception of national interests. Some of the additional demands arise because there are more problem industries, such as shipbuilding, which will require collaborative international action over a long period, even if the world economy returns to a steady rate of expansion in line with long-term historical trends. Major structural changes seem likely to be required in the countries of the Western world in the late 1970s and early 1980s in a variety of established industries whose employees and managers together deploy considerable social and political power. The conflicts they are likely to engender will in any case complicate the business of social management on which the effective control of short-term movements in our economies, and above all the containment of the constant threat of cost inflation, ultimately depend. We should not overestimate our capacity for flexible social response in these circumstances.

C. W. McMahon

It is difficult for me to comment on Lamfalussy's paper because I agree with virtually everything in it. He put his arguments well, and they are arguments that convinced me. I share broadly his preferences and his objectives, and I see the same difficulties in the way of achieving those objectives. In my commentary, therefore, I propose to expand a little on one problem that he raises and take the argument perhaps a bit further than he might be willing to go.

I particularly want to take up his doubts about the effectiveness of floating exchange rates in producing BOP adjustment. The figure in his paper supports these doubts by comparing very big movements of rates with fluctuations of BOP surpluses and deficits in what initially seems to be a perverse way.

Many people would say that he has looked only at the nominal exchange-rate changes and not at the real ones, or that he has not presented the real ones. If the real exchange-rate changes were plotted they would be shown to be much smaller. This is true but, in my view, it does not touch the heart of the problem. My own doubts about the effectiveness of the floating-exchange-rate system that we have to produce adjustment do not rest on elasticity pessimism. I am not well enough acquainted with the literature to give an authoritative view on how high the elasticities are. But I am not interested in resting the case on this. There may be quite high elasticities—in fact, I think it likely. In my view, however, the smallness of the real exchange-rate changes constitutes the problem. The real question is how to get, through nominal exchange-rate movements, the real exchange-rate movement that is wanted.

I agree with the vicious circle problem in the way that Lamfalussy put it. There is a naive version of the vicious circle theory that is easy to attack. Of course, one can set up a model—hypothesize that a country and a set of policy makers in that country will follow policies that will produce the domestic adjustment necessary for the exchange rate to produce the effect wanted. There would then be no vicious circle. But that is uninteresting.

The really interesting question is how realistic this model is for the actual countries. This is perhaps the kind of point that Andrew Shonfield was making, at least implicitly. In looking at the world and its problems, one should avoid the temptation to take, as it were, a view about how things *should* be. One could take that view about one's own country when trying to improve things; but for the world at large, one has to take policy makers, political systems, and so on as given data, just like the production functions and other elements in those economies.

There is a good deal of evidence of a secular rise in the difficulty of securing adjustment within countries, particularly deficit countries. Most countries show a secular rise, taken through the cycles, in the share of labor and a fall in the share of profits. I think it is one of the most fundamentally worrying features of the last decade or so. It is still unequally spread, which means that there are differential advantages for some countries over others, but in broad terms all major countries have seen a secular decline in profits and a rise in the share of wages.

There may be many reasons for this. I believe that a very important one is the increased degree of unionization, the greater pressure exerted by unions, and the increased tendency for society as a whole to accept the view that profits are somehow bad and labor incomes good. To make sure that wages are maintained, there has been a growing degree of indexation in most countries around the world, an increased explicit understanding by unions that it is real incomes they are after, and a strong belief in their ability to determine the real income of the employed labor force. (This is, of course, a different question from whether they are actually able to influence it in the long run.)

With all this, coincidentally or not, I seem to see a weakening of governments. In more and more countries governments represent only a small majority of the total population, or there is an increased polarization in the number of parties in legislatures. Compared with the period of the gold standard, and even compared with the period after World War II at the height of the Bretton Woods system, there has been a major change in the relationship of government and policy makers to the mass of the economy. I believe there also has been a major change in the extent to which policy makers, by virtue of particular abstract constraints or views, can impose their policies on the electorate and on the economy.

The gold standard is the classic case of the earlier position. Because people believed in the gold standard it had enormous power to produce adjustment and was not questioned. In the early years of the Bretton Woods system, the fixed rate of exchange was used by policy makers— often badly, of course—to bring about adjustments that would be accepted within the community. It is quite clear that this has changed. One example of the change is the regime of floating exchange rates.

In the late stages of the Bretton Woods system, it was thought that, because a number of countries had been very slow to adjust, the liberating of the exchange rate would make everything easier. Floating exchange rates were expected to bring about adjustment more quickly and more appropriately. Paradoxically, the reverse has been true. Under floating exchange rates, it has in fact become much harder for governments to use the exchange rate as a positive policy tool. There has been a great deal of talk about uncertainty, about predictability, about not fighting the market, and so on. We have lost sight of that crucial element in the Bretton Woods system, the concept of fundamental disequilibrium, and of the need to do something about it where it appears.

In practice, since floating and the almost coincidental quintupling of oil prices, we have experienced much more massive degrees of disequilibrium than we had before. They are proving very stubborn, and very difficult for a government to improve its structural balance of payments partly by an exchange-rate depreciation. How is it to engineer the degree of depreciation that will be appropriate, that will be accepted by other countries as appropriate, and that will not be vitiated by the pressure of the unions inside the country to recapture what they have lost?

In any form of fixity of exchange rates, either regional or more general, there is at least *some* chance of achieving such a depreciation. I am pessimistic, in general, because I think the underlying factors make it difficult in most economies. But at least in a multilaterally agreed upon system of fixed parities, there is scope in principle—and I think there is scope in practice—for a decision to be made and perhaps even shared before being made with the rest of the partners about the appropriate degrees of exchange-rate change that can be beneficial. Under the Bretton Woods system this happened in a number of instances. Uri mentioned a number of earlier French examples in which spectacularly good use was made of exchange-rate change. Under the operation of the snake, it has already, I think—and this is a hopeful sign—been possible. The most recent multilateral arrangement was quite small; but it was significant, it was multilaterally agreed on, and it was able to be maintained.

One reason I would personally favor, if it were possible, a greater degree of stability—or, in Lamfalussy's words, a "loose" degree of stability—is not that I believe so much in the virtues of any particular level over time but that I believe it gives more possibility for decisions to use the exchange rate as one tool to produce the adjustment that may be necessary.

It can also, of course, work upward. It is quite understandable that the West German authorities get a little irritated at continued pressure from other countries to increase the demand in their economy. The West Germans can point quite easily—as Gutowski has just done— to the size of the public deficit that already exists and the high savings ratios. The danger is that by the time they have done enough, they would find they had done too much, a kind of flip-over problem of expectations. At least in theory—it would obviously be very difficult in practice—a combination of a strong general stimulus and a strong upward valuation should be able to reduce the BOP surplus without increasing the inflationary pressure. But this kind of move is very difficult to engineer in a purely floating system.

Nevertheless, I would agree with Lamfalussy that in the present circumstances it is very hard to see how the existing degree of stability could be expanded even on a regional basis. One reason that he cites is the large oil deficits. But here again it would be useful to have some kind of exchange-rate policy that was agreed on between countries, because only then would it be possible to make progress in reallocating the individual deficits that make up the irreducible overall deficit. At present we can merely identify the fact that some countries in the oil-consuming world continue to be in surplus and others in deficit; but it is very difficult operationally, even with the best will in the world and the best international coordination, to produce a set of policies that will do anything to redress the balance.

There is no question but that it is a very difficult task for policy makers to work to a current-deficit norm. We may all give lip service to it because we see the logic of it; but in practice, granted the difficulties of maintaining investment and employment at home, granted the inherent mercantilism of us all, it is difficult for a large industrial country. For an economy like Canada there is less of a problem. Canada has a long history of a current deficit, and it is a structural capital importer. But for most of the Western industrial countries, running a deficit deliberately and over a prolonged period of time poses severe problems of management and of sustaining a government in office.

Here I should like, as Shonfield did, to pick up Lamfalussy's throwaway remark that, in practice, a tight arrangement like the snake is likely to be a surplus-producing arrangement. It is very difficult to conceive of a tight arrangement of monetary stability and exchange-rate stability that does not directly or indirectly lead to a basic surplus.

I agree very much with the remarks in the first part of Conrad Oort's paper about the nature of the snake and the fact that such an arrangement works most effectively with one country plus satellites. Quite apart from the relative inflationary performance of the United Kingdom, France, or Italy, it would be much more difficult to make it work with two or three big centers. It is hard to imagine the snake's persisting in its present form, however, if West Germany were for some years to be structurally in BOP deficit. Maybe it would, but I find it hard to believe.

PART THREE

EUROPEAN INTEGRATION:
PROBLEMS AND OPTIONS

EUROPEAN MONETARY ARRANGEMENTS: PROBLEM AREAS AND POLICY OPTIONS

Bela Balassa

This paper deals with three interrelated problem areas in the general context of European monetary arrangements. They include exchange-rate management, policy coordination, and European financial markets. In each case, outstanding issues will be identified and possible solutions indicated.

Exchange-Rate Management

In recent months several proposals have been put forward to establish target zones for exchange rates in the European Economic Community (EEC, or Common Market). Such a proposal was first made by C. J. Oort in a talk delivered at the Royal Institute of International Affairs on June 18, 1976. It was followed by the proposal of the Villa Pamphili group, reported in the July 23, 1976, issue of the *London Times* and other leading European newspapers and subsequently published.[1] A similar proposal was submitted by the Netherlands authorities to the Council of Ministers of the EEC (the so-called Duisenberg proposal), and issues related to the establishment of target zones were examined in a report of the Monetary Committee of the EEC to the council on November 4, 1976.

Proposals for establishing target zones for Common Market currencies draw on the guidelines for floating established by the International Monetary Fund (IMF) in June 1974, which have not been implemented. Under the IMF guidelines,[2] a country should intervene on the foreign exchange market to smooth out temporary fluctuations in the value of its currency. But it should not act aggressively to accelerate movements in its exchange rate, except to bring this within, or closer to, a target zone of rates that the fund considers "to be within

---

[1] See Bela Balassa, "Monetary Arrangements in the European Common Market," *Banca Nazionale del Lavoro Quarterly Review*, Rome, December 1976.

[2] "Guidelines for the Management of Floating Exchange Rates," Decision no. 4232 (74/67), June 13, 1974; reproduced in International Monetary Fund, *Annual Report 1974* (Washington, D.C., 1974).

the range of reasonable estimates of the medium-term norm for the exchange rate in question." Finally, "if the exchange rate of a member with a floating rate has moved outside [this range] to an extent the Fund considers likely to be harmful to the interest of members, the Fund will consult with the member, and in the light of such consultation may encourage the member . . . (i) not to act to moderate movements within this range or (ii) to take action to moderate further divergence from the range."

The target zone proposals for Common Market currencies reflect the presumption that, given the common interests of the member countries, there is a greater chance for agreement on exchange-rate management among them than in the IMF framework. In particular, in view of the increasing interdependence of their national economies, the EEC countries have an interest in reducing the uncertainty that results from the lack of rules on interventions in foreign exchange markets and the wide exchange-rate fluctuations between snake and non-snake currencies. The proposals also aim at lessening the cleavage between the countries participating in the snake and those outside it that has widened since the withdrawal of France from the snake, which now consists of West Germany, three small EEC countries, and two small non-EEC countries.[3]

In the following, I will examine the possible effects of exchange-rate fluctuations under alternative assumptions. I first consider the case when random variations bring about an initial change in exchange rates in a situation of BOP equilibrium. It is further assumed that the process of adjustment takes the form of a cost-price spiral in the country with the depreciating exchange rate, which immediately and fully validates the initial change in the exchange rate while commensurate changes in costs and prices do not occur in the country whose currency appreciates.

As a result of the operation of this "ratchet effect," random variations in exchange rates have an inflationary bias, which may be aggravated if the amplitude of exchange-rate fluctuations is increased by speculation. This result assumes an accommodating monetary policy in line with Richard Cooper's statement that "the wage level in the modern economy is indeterminant because in the final analysis the

---

[3] In 1975 the EEC countries carried on 49 percent of their total trade among themselves; trade with the associated countries accounted for 6 percent and with Norway and Sweden, the non-EEC members of the snake, 4 percent. The composition of the trade of the individual member countries varies to a considerable extent and differs from the composition of the SDR, which has been suggested as a benchmark for determining reference rates under the Ethier-Bloomfield proposal in John Williamson, "The Future Exchange Rate Regime," *Banca Nazionale del Lavoro Quarterly Review*, June 1975, p. 137.

monetary authorities must—for political reasons—provide a money supply adequate to satisfy any given level of money wages, no matter how it was reached, in order to avoid excessive unemployment."[4] And while the outcome may vary depending on the country concerned,[5] the situation described by Cooper may be approximated through wage indexing in Italy and wage bargaining in the United Kingdom.

Notwithstanding these inflationary effects, the full and immediate validation of exchange-rate changes through wage and price adjustments would not create distortions in trade flows since real exchange rates (that is, nominal exchange rates adjusted for price changes) would remain unchanged.[6] In reality, however, we do not have full and immediate adjustments in wages and prices in the depreciating country.

To begin with, most domestic and some international contracts are denominated in nominal terms, and they are not adjusted after the depreciation of a currency and the domestic inflationary process it gives rise to. There is often no possibility of recontracting transactions entered into beforehand. Lags in the adjustment process may in turn accentuate the effects of a disturbance on the exchange rate through the operation of the so-called J-curve effect, which results in an initial deterioration in the trade balance. Overadjustments in financial markets through interest arbitrage may also accentuate exchange-rate fluctuations.[7] And, taking further account of the possibility that wages adjust with a lag, the delayed effects of successive exchange-rate changes on wages and prices will overlap, giving rise to disproportionate changes between exchange rates on the one hand and wages and prices on the other.

The resulting variations in real exchange rates, in turn, create uncertainty in international transactions. And while exporters can hedge in the forward market, this becomes increasingly difficult and costly beyond the three months relevant for exports of capital goods and for longer term contracts in general. Moreover, fluctuations in real exchange rates create uncertainty for investment in export- as well as in import-competing industries, which will reduce the volume of investment if investors can be regarded as risk averters.

[4] Richard N. Cooper, "The Eurocurrency Market, Exchange-Rate System, and National Financial Policies," in Carl H. Stern and others (eds.), *Eurocurrencies and the International Monetary System* (Washington, D.C.: American Enterprise Institute, 1976), p. 252.

[5] Morris Goldstein, "Wage Indexation, Inflation, and the Labor Market," *IMF Staff Papers*, November 1975.

[6] A different problem is that in the presence of full wage and price adjustments the balance of payments could not be equilibrated through exchange-rate changes. I will discuss this later.

[7] Rudiger Dornbusch, "Expectations and Exchange Rate Dynamics," *Journal of Political Economy*, December 1976.

The described effects of exchange-rate variations do not depend on the existence of intercountry differences in inflation rates, although they are likely to be aggravated if such differences exist. This is in part because of the distortions generated in the process of lagged adjustment and in part because of the tendency toward increased speculation when inflation rates differ among countries. At the same time, one cannot realistically expect that inflationary trends among European countries will be harmonized in the foreseeable future.

Under these circumstances, the application of the target zone approach in the EEC offers possibilities of avoiding excessive exchange-rate fluctuations. For one thing, in application of the rules proposed by the IMF, the countries in question would undertake essentially negative obligations to forego interventions in foreign exchange markets that would accentuate disequilibrating movements in exchange rates. For another, movements outside the target zone would trigger consultations among the member countries, with a view to taking measures such as policy changes or interventions in exchange markets when that is considered desirable.

The next question concerns the use of decision criteria for determining and modifying target zones for individual currencies. Automatic rules based on reserve changes[8] or on the exchange rate's staying at or near the upper (lower) limit of the zone[9] are open to objections, in part because they may reflect the influence of nonrecurring factors and in part because they may engender self-fulfilling speculations, thus giving a "free ride" to speculators. At the same time, as noted earlier, upward movements in the exchange rate may be validated, wholly or in part, through increases in wages and prices.

Another automatic formula was proposed in the 1976 report of the Optica group. According to this proposal, a country's reference rate would be changed periodically (at least quarterly) in proportion to the change of a moving average of the country's effective purchasing power parity (PPP) index, calculated by dividing the country's wholesale price index by a trade-weighted average of the wholesale price indexes of its trading partners. It is claimed that this recommendation rests on empirical evidence presented in the report on the existence of a positive correlation between effective exchange rates and purchasing

---

[8] Raymond F. Mikesell and Henry N. Goldstein, *Rules for a Floating-Rate Regime*, Princeton Essays in International Finance, no. 109 (April 1975).

[9] For a description of such proposals and critique, see Trevor G. Underwood, "Analysis of Proposals for Using Objective Indicators as a Guide for Exchange Rate Changes," *IMF Staff Papers*, March 1973.

power parities.[10] These results are, however, subject to different interpretations.

The estimates indicate that exchange rates correlate best with the export unit value indexes, less well with the wholesale price index, much less with consumer prices, and not at all with unit labor costs. On the face of it, the last result is surprising since, as the authors note, "by combining information on hourly wage and output per man-hour it would appear that one could obtain more reliable information on PPP as an equilibrium relationship."[11] The explanation is that the prices of traded goods tend to be equalized through commodity arbitrage, giving rise to high correlations with export unit values and to somewhat lower correlations with wholesale price indexes that also include some nontraded goods. In turn, intercountry differences in the prices of nontraded goods and labor may persist, leading to low correlation, or the lack thereof, for the consumer price and labor cost indexes, respectively.[12]

With the tendency toward equalization in the prices of traded goods at existing exchange rates, wholesale price indexes—consisting largely of traded goods—will not appropriately indicate changes in the competitive position of the individual countries and should not be used to trigger changes in target zones for exchange rates. A better indicator of competitiveness appears to be the index of unit labor costs, which the IMF also has used for this purpose.

One cannot, however, establish the required changes in target zones for exchange rates solely on the basis of the past behavior of unit labor costs or of any other variables reflecting changes in competitiveness. Aside from the possibilities of error and the delays involved in the statistical estimation, it would be desirable to make changes in the target zone on the basis of the expected future behavior of the BOP. In preparing such forecasts, one would have to take account of actual and anticipated changes in labor costs, the trade implications of the lack of synchronization of business cycles, the BOP effects of the policies. followed, and expected changes in nontraded items.

Automatic changes in target zones and rules of intervention based on changes in price relationships alone would also preclude the use of exchange rates as an instrument to remedy BOP disequilibria that are due to the operation of real factors. At the same time, the observed

---

[10] Commission of the European Communities, *Optica Report 1976* (Brussels, 1977).

[11] Ibid., p. 7.

[12] This point was made in Bela Balassa, "The Purchasing Power Parity Doctrine: A Reappraisal," *Journal of Political Economy*, December 1964.

nonproportionate changes in the prices of traded and nontraded goods indicate the possibility of using exchange-rate changes for such a purpose.

Moreover, whatever the cause of the BOP disequilibrium, exchange-rate variation is not the only—and will often not be the most appropriate—instrument to restore cost competitiveness and reestablish BOP equilibrium. Thus, in a given situation, changes in domestic policies rather than in exchange rates may be called for. At the same time, one would need to forecast the potential BOP effects of the policies that would be applied during the period under consideration.

In making changes in target zones dependent on BOP forecasts, one may avoid the destabilizing speculation that can be expected to occur if automatic indicators are used for this purpose. Williamson goes a step further in claiming that speculation would be stabilizing since reference rates "would provide the market with information as to what the authorities believed to be a realistic estimate of the appropriate rate, as well as providing a basis for informed public debate about exchange-rate prospects."[13] Gottfried Haberler expresses disagreement with this proposition and suggests: "Reference rates that give the impression of being out of line and are therefore liable to be changed at the next 'prespecified' revision, are very likely to cause heavy speculation, unless the revisions are small and are made at short intervals."[14]

Haberler's statement raises the question of the intervals in which the target zone should be modified. The IMF defines the "medium term" for which target zones would be determined as four years, while the Optica group recommends that modifications be made at least quarterly. The former alternative would resemble the par-value system and could be expected to trigger speculation, as Haberler suggests. Taking decisions on target zones at frequent intervals, however, might limit the usefulness of the exercise.

It is proposed here to establish target zones for a year ahead and make actual changes in small steps, in the form of a "crawling zone." In this way one could accommodate intercountry differences in inflation rates and in other relevant variables. It would further appear desirable to review target zones every six months, thus setting them on the basis of a "moving horizon," one year at a time.

The implementation of this proposal would reduce the danger of destabilizing speculation. The chances that speculation will be stabilizing are further increased because the authorities possess information on the

---

[13] Williamson, "The Future Exchange Rate Regime," p. 136.

[14] Gottfried Haberler, "The International Monetary System after Jamaica and Manila," in William H. Fellner (ed.), *Contemporary Economic Problems 1977* (Washington, D.C.: American Enterprise Institute, 1977).

policies to be followed as well as on the interdependence of the variables included in the forecast. And the risk that may be taken appears to be outweighed by the adverse consequences of continued instability in exchange rates among the Common Market countries. In particular, it may be assumed that it would be less costly to offset the effects of speculation on foreign exchange markets by joint action than to attempt undoing its effects through deflationary policies. For joint action to be credible, however, the resources available to the European Monetary Cooperation Fund would need to be increased.

We have seen that judgmental elements would have to play an important role in establishing and modifying target zones. But the question remains as to what role consultation among the EEC countries would play in the process. There are several possible scenarios; the approach suggested here would entail increasing over time the extent of coordination in the establishment and operation of target zones.

Initially each country would have full freedom in determining the target zone for its currency and would assume obligations to consult with the partner countries only if the exchange rate moved outside the target zone. Each country would refrain from taking aggressive action that would accelerate movements in its exchange rate, except for bringing this within, or closer to, the target zone. As a second step, the Commission of the European Communities may be called on to prepare BOP projections in collaboration with the country concerned and to consult with the country on the establishment of the target zone. In this way, one can make use of information provided by the projections of the other countries, and the danger of conflicting projections may be minimized. In case of disagreement about the appropriate target zone, on the recommendation of the commission, the Council of Ministers of the European Communities may set a range for the purpose of the operation of the enlarged European Monetary Cooperation Fund. Eligibility for loans from the fund and support from the other member countries would be denied if the currency of a deficit country remained outside this range for a predetermined period. In turn, a surplus country might be obliged to lend part of its excess accumulation to the fund. Eventually the establishment and modification of target zones would be made subject to joint decision making by the EEC countries on the basis of qualified majority voting. For example, a three-fourths majority in the Council of Ministers might be required to overrule the target zone proposed by the country itself.

One would further need to consider possible arrangements for the snake currencies in the framework of the target zone scheme. In order to avoid compromising the stability of transactions among the countries participating in the snake, it would seem appropriate that these countries maintain present exchange-rate margins among their currencies. They could then adopt a common target zone, determined on the basis of effective rates calculated for the group as a whole. Nevertheless, small exchange margins and a single effective exchange rate for all snake currencies could not be maintained in the face of differential developments in the participating countries, especially since the relative importance of their mutual trade varies.[15] Hence it would seem desirable to allow for the possibility of more frequent exchange-rate changes among snake countries. Such changes should not, however, exceed the limits provided by the target zone for non-snake countries.

Policy Coordination

We have seen that, in a given situation, changes in domestic policies rather than interventions in exchange markets or exchange-rate changes may be called for when the choice of the measures to be taken would be subject to consultations among the member countries. While such consultations would be ex post, the interdependence of the national economies of the member countries and the objective of avoiding the emergence of disequilibria would call for ex ante consultations on domestic policies, eventually leading to policy coordination.

One approach to policy coordination, put forward in the 1976–1977 report by the West German Council of Economic Experts,[16] is to set targets for the expansion of the monetary base in the individual countries. The council has further proposed that the targets be determined on the basis of the expected growth of productive capacity, the rate of price increases deemed unavoidable, and changes in the effectiveness of the monetary system.

Setting targets for the monetary base has been considered, but found to be subject to various shortcomings, in the United States. To begin with, the money supply appears more closely related to economic

---

[15] Their mutual trade accounts for 36 percent of the total trade of the countries participating in the snake, but this share varies between 39 and 46 percent for the smaller member countries and is only 26 percent for West Germany. In the three years after the snake was established in April 1972, effective rates derived by weighting with total trade appreciated 16.0 percent in West Germany, 11.1 percent in the Netherlands, and 3.8 percent in Belgium (see Rudolf R. Rhomberg, "Indices of Effective Exchange Rates," *IMF Staff Papers*, March 1976). During this period the Belgian franc depreciated by 6.6 percent against the deutsche mark and by 5.8 percent against the Dutch guilder.

[16] Sachverständigenrat zur Begutachtung der Gesamtwirtschaftlichen Entwicklung (Council of Economic Experts) *Jahresgutachten 1976/77* (Stuttgart, Mainz, 1977), para. 476.

activity than the monetary base,[17] and the two monetary variables are not strongly correlated. It is generally agreed that central banks should be able to offset variations in the ratio of the money supply to the monetary base that may be due to random changes, unforeseen events, or shifts in liquidity preferences. Finally, reserve requirements vary among the components of the money supply, defined in a wider sense, while there is a high rate of substitution between these components. Such considerations have led Milton Friedman to propose setting targets for M2 in the United States. And, as is well known, the Federal Reserve Board is using both M1 and M2 as targets.

In the Common Market, a variety of monetary targets are used, reflecting largely differences in institutional arrangements, the substitutability of financial assets, and the openness of the economy. Among the EEC countries, West Germany alone has a monetary base target. The principal monetary targets are M1 in Ireland and M2 in France and the Netherlands, with differences shown in the definitions applied. Bank credit is the principal target in Denmark, global credit in Italy, and global credit and level of interest rates in Belgium, while an eclectic approach is followed in the United Kingdom. There is also considerable variation in the degree to which the targets are regarded as indicative or compulsory, as well as in the choice of secondary targets.

Correspondingly, the decision by the Council of Ministers of the European Communities in December 1972 on setting monetary targets in terms of M2 for all member countries was not opportune. The existing diversity among the Common Market countries was recognized in the *Economic Report* of the Commission of the European Communities for 1977, which states that "quantitative guidelines . . . should be defined in relation to the various instruments of monetary policy that are available in the various Member States (central bank money, M2 or M3 or total credit)." In fact, it would appear desirable to establish targets for more than one of these aggregates for the individual countries. This alternative has the additional advantage of reducing the chances of evasion by manipulating a particular aggregate.

In evaluating the merits of monetary targets, consideration should be given to the fact that the effectiveness of monetary policy varies to a considerable extent among the Common Market countries. To begin with, there are substantial differences among them as regards the availability and use of the classical tools of monetary policy—open-market operations, reserve requirements, and discount rate. The United

---

[17] It should be remembered that monetary targets or targets for any other policy variable are intermediate targets used to pursue certain policy objectives, such as increases in output and employment and the avoidance of inflation.

Kingdom alone carries out extensive open-market operations, and several countries rely largely on quantitative credit controls.

The effectiveness of monetary policy is also influenced by institutional factors that may limit the ability of the central bank to implement its policy. Among the original member countries of the Common Market, institutions other than the central bank, such as the Securities Stabilization Fund and the Rediscount and Guarantee Institute, affect the availability and the cost of credit in Belgium; recourse by banks to privileged rediscount categories has reduced the extent of control the central bank has over money supply in France; and the ability of the commercial banks to use Treasury bills and certain long-term bonds as reserves has had similar effects in Italy. By contrast, the central banks of West Germany and the Netherlands have considerable authority over domestic lending.

The intentions of the central bank may also be frustrated by fiscal policy. According to one observer, "central banks usually are not in a position to do more than deplore and protest inflationary deficits by central governments."[18] And it may be unrealistic to assume that setting monetary targets would increase the freedom of the central banks, as suggested in the 1976–1977 report of the West German Council of Economic Experts. According to the report, central banks "might find it very helpful to have to say: There is no more money. Not because we do not want to provide it but because we are not allowed to."[19] Furthermore, doubts may be expressed about the political realism of the recommendations made in the report that "energies must be directed at strengthening the autonomy enjoyed by the central bank."[20]

Leaving apart the question whether monetary policy can act independently of fiscal policy, one needs to consider the effectiveness of monetary and fiscal policy taken independently. In the following, the effects of monetary and fiscal policies on domestic variables and on the BOP will be successively examined.

There is considerable agreement in the United States that over a period of two to three years real GNP as well as the price level is affected by both monetary and fiscal policy. Recent evidence in support of this proposition has been provided by simulating the effects of fiscal policy without accommodating monetary policy, and of monetary policy in the

---

[18] Donald R. Hodgman, *National Monetary Policies and International Monetary Cooperation* (Boston: Little, Brown, 1974), p. 202.

[19] Council of Economic Experts, *Jahresgutachten 1976/77*, para. 473.

[20] Ibid., para. 494.

absence of fiscal actions, in econometric models of the United States.[21] In the simulations, sustained changes in government expenditures (taxes) and a once-and-for-all change in the money supply have been compared.

These results pertain to the business cycle, which is the relevant time frame for target setting. In fact, in pursuing countercyclical objectives, it would be desirable to employ policy tools whose effects do not extend beyond two or three years. The often obtained result that the fiscal multiplier approaches zero in long-term equilibrium would then provide an argument for the use of fiscal policy for countercyclical purposes.[22] The conclusion is strengthened if we consider the long run as a series of short runs when periodical shocks do not ever permit reaching long-run equilibrium and necessitate corrective actions.

In turn, increases in the money supply beyond the needs of increased real incomes will affect the price level over time, pointing to the need for making monetary targets compatible with long-term price objectives. More generally, in line with Tinbergen's principle, the combined use of monetary and fiscal policy is warranted in pursuing more than the domestic economic objective. At the same time, the effects of monetary and fiscal policy on economic activity and prices will vary with the degree of capacity utilization and unemployment. To the extent that Common Market countries find themselves at different stages of the business cycle, these effects will differ even if there are no differences in their economic and institutional structure.

As to the effects of monetary and fiscal policies on the BOP two extreme views may be distinguished. According to the fiscal approach, represented by the New Cambridge School, the size of the current-account deficit is determined largely by the deficit in the government budget. This view is based on the assumption that private savings and investment decisions are made independently of fiscal policy and are stable over time.

Testing this proposition in the framework of an econometric macro model for the United Kingdom, a positive correlation between the public sector deficit and the current-account deficit has been obtained.[23]

---

[21] See Carl Christ, "Judging the Performance of Economic Models of the U.S. Economy," *International Economic Review*, February 1975; and Franco Modigliani and Albert Ando, "Impacts of Fiscal Action on Aggregate Income: The Monetarist Controversy—The Theory and Evidence," in Jerome Stein (ed.), *Monetarism* (Amsterdam: North-Holland, 1976).

[22] This raises the more general issue of lags in policy response, which will not be pursued here.

[23] R. J. Ball, T. Burns, and J. S. E. Laury, "The Role of Exchange-Rate Changes in Balance-of-Payments Adjustment: The United Kingdom Case," *Economic Journal*, March 1977.

While confirming this result for the United Kingdom, a regression analysis of seventeen countries casts doubts on the general validity of the fiscalist hypothesis. Thus "a change in the budget deficit for most developed countries does not seem to affect their balance of trade significantly. In the German case, in fact, results opposite to those predicted by the theory were obtained."[24]

The monetarist approach, represented by the West German Council of Economic Experts and the Optica group, sees the causation running from monetary aggregates to prices and to exchange rates. Under *ceteris paribus* assumptions, changes in the money supply would indeed lead to proportionate changes in domestic prices and the exchange rate in the long run. But the *ceteris paribus* assumptions may not be fulfilled in practice, and changes over time in nonmonetary variables, such as supply conditions and tastes, will also affect the exchange rate.

Furthermore, the described relationship may not hold in the short and medium runs that are relevant for policy making. As Otmar Emminger expressed it, "it is *impossible to forecast*, with any degree of precision, *from an announced monetary goal, or an observed rate of money growth, the resultant future exchange rate movement.* Thus, it is also impossible, to *guarantee* by commonly agreed 'monetary norms' stable exchange rate relationships among the participating countries with any degree of probability" [emphasis in the original]. Nevertheless, Emminger added that " 'monetary norms' that are likely to contribute to better domestic stability are also likely to lead to less instability in exchange rates."[25]

The conclusion emerges that the long-term trend of prices and exchange rates is to a large extent determined by rates of growth of monetary aggregates. Thus the long-term stability of exchange rates among the Common Market countries would require agreement on monetary targets. However, through their effects on economic activity and on prices, monetary as well as fiscal policies will affect the BOP over the business cycle. Correspondingly, in pursuing BOP objectives, sole reliance cannot be placed on monetary targets even if monetary policy could be made entirely independent of fiscal policy. Nor can fiscal policy alone do the job.

---

[24] Elisabeth Milne, "The Fiscal Approach to the Balance of Payments" *Economic Notes*, Monte dei Paschi di Siena, vol. 6, no. 1 (1977). In private conversation, Alan Walters indicated to me that recent results for the United Kingdom also conflict with the fiscalist hypothesis.

[25] Otmar Emminger, "Monetary Policy Coordination and Exchange Rate Stability," paper delivered at the J. Marcus Memorial Conference (Washington, D.C.: International Monetary Fund, November 1976).

It appears then that it would be desirable to combine monetary targets with fiscal targets in the Common Market. This would involve agreeing on the size of the budgetary deficit (surplus) as a proportion of the gross national product just as the monetary targets would be set in relation to GNP. One would also need to ensure consistency between monetary and fiscal targets. This requires determining the method of financing the budgetary deficit through money creation and domestic and foreign borrowing and deciding on the ways of accommodating a surplus.

As a first step toward policy coordination in the Common Market, it would be desirable for the individual member countries to establish monetary as well as fiscal targets. Monetary targets are already in use in several member countries, while fiscal targets are set in conjunction with the annual budgetary process. The coordination of these targets on the national level is, however, generally lacking.

Parallel with the establishment of monetary and fiscal targets in the individual countries, it would be desirable to analyze policy interactions among them since, with increased economic interdependence, the policies applied by any one country influence the others.[26] This may set the stage for consultations between the commission and the member country governments on coordinating monetary and fiscal targets, with account taken of the implications of these targets for economic activity and the BOP in all the EEC countries.

In view of the existing differences in the economic situation and the BOP of the individual countries, as well as their differences in the process of wage and price determination, the coordination of monetary and fiscal policies could not imply setting identical policy targets for each country. However, coordination would aim at lessening the divergence of the policies applied over time.

It would further be desirable to make establishing and subsequently coordinating policy targets a precondition for lending by the European Monetary Cooperation Fund and for support by the other member countries. At the same time, to remedy any adverse effects policy coordination may have on the economic structure of the member countries, there appears to be a need to increase the relative importance of long-term credits in community lending. In this way, the coordination of fiscal and monetary policy and structural transformation could proceed in parallel.

---

[26] Note the various model-building efforts sponsored by the Commission of the European Communities and undertaken in Europe, as well as the results of Stephen A. Resnick, "A Macro Model for Western Europe," in Bela Balassa (ed.), *European Economic Integration* (Amsterdam: North-Holland, 1975).

European Financial Markets

In recent years proposals have been made for coordinating national control measures on capital movements in general, and on flows between national credit markets and Eurocurrency markets in particular, on the Common Market level. The need for joint control measures has been argued on the grounds that Eurocurrency markets represent an inflationary force, impair the effectiveness of domestic monetary policies, and may give rise to large speculative movements.

The fears concerning the inflationary effects of Eurocurrency markets rest on the assumption that Eurocurrencies are created in a multiplier process similar to that of domestic money creation. This argument has been put forward with respect to the transfer of dollar claims from the United States to Europe, which serve as a base for the creation of Eurodollars, representing three-fourths of all Eurocurrencies.

In assigning appropriate values to the relevant parameters (the ratio of the deposits Eurobanks hold with U.S. banks to their own deposit liabilities and the ratio of Eurodollar deposits held by nonbanks to their liquid dollar assets), Niehans and Hewson estimated the value of the Eurodollar multiplier to be 1.1.[27] As the authors note, however, in the absence of fixed reserve requirements for Eurodollar deposits, the multiplier process does not provide an adequate description of the workings of the Eurodollar market. Rather, as Crockett suggests, the market functions as a financial intermediary, and its size is determined by the supply of and the demand for lendable funds.[28]

As a financial intermediary, the Eurodollar (or, more generally, the Eurocurrency) market will increase liquidity to the extent that there is positive maturity transformation, that is, Eurobanks borrow short and lend long. Niehans and Hewson have found that in 1973 the extent of maturity transformation was small.[29] And while these estimates may understate the maturity transformation of Eurobanks whose "rolled-over" longer term commitments are partly shown as short-term loans, the degree of maturity transformation in Eurocurrency markets appears to have been limited until the oil crisis. The increased maturity transformation after the oil crisis, entailing the transformation of deposits of oil exporters into loans to the deficit countries, should be considered a

---

[27] Jurg Niehans and John Hewson, "The Eurodollar Market and Monetary Theory," *Money, Credit and Banking*, February 1976. The value of the multiplier will be even lower if the relation between the money base and the money supply in the United States is taken into account.

[28] Andrew D. Crockett, "The Euro-currency Market: An Attempt to Clarify Some Basic Issues," *IMF Staff Papers*, July 1976.

[29] Niehans and Hewson, "The Eurodollar Market," pp. 12–13.

benefit of the efficient operation of the Eurocurrency markets, since it permitted relief from the stresses caused by the quadrupling of oil prices.

Concern has further been expressed that inflationary pressures in the United States would be transmitted to the EEC through the Euro-dollar market. Since 1970, however, the rate of monetary expansion has been consistently lower in the United States than in the EEC countries, with the exception of West Germany, the Netherlands, and the United Kingdom in 1973.[30] There is no evidence that the establishment of the Eurodollar market would have enhanced the transmission of inflation during the 1960s, when there was rapid monetary expansion in the United States.

It has also been suggested that, given the interconnection of capital markets, variations in U.S. policies over time will reduce the effectiveness of the national monetary policies followed by European countries. This concern appears to be exaggerated, however. A recent study has shown that international interest rate differentials may persist as forward rates adjust in conjunction with covered interest arbitrage.[31] Moreover, variations in U.S. monetary policies can be reflected in exchange-rate changes.

The question remains that capital flows between the national currency markets and Eurocurrency markets may interfere with the conduct of domestic monetary policy. In addition, Eurocurrency markets have been said to be a conduit for currency speculation. Finally, some EEC countries have sought to limit Eurocurrency flows to safeguard the operation of their credit allocation systems or to limit exchange-rate variations for current transactions.

These considerations explain the application of various control measures by the individual member countries. The measures include dual exchange rates for current and for capital transactions, direct controls on capital movements, and market-oriented instruments, such as minimum reserve requirements on the foreign exchange assets and liabilities of banks and cash deposit requirements on nonbank borrowing in Eurocurrency markets.

Among the EEC countries, Belgium has long maintained a system of dual exchange rates, separating transactions in the capital and the current accounts. Such a system has also been tried and abandoned in France and Italy, largely because of the difficulties experienced in main-

---

[30] H. Robert Heller, "International Reserves and World-wide Inflation," *IMF Staff Papers*, March 1976, p. 65.

[31] Malcolm Knight, "Eurodollars, Capital Mobility, and the Forward Exchange Market," *Economica*, February 1977.

taining the separation of the two markets.[32] In fact, it appears that relatively small differences in rates on current and capital account transactions provide inducement for evasion. For similar reasons, in countries such as West Germany and the United Kingdom, it is not considered practical to introduce dual exchange rates. (However, the United Kingdom has a segmented market for the outflow of resident sterling.)

In turn, direct controls and market-oriented instruments of various kinds have been employed on a more or less regular basis in most of the member countries. The principal exception is West Germany, which does not make use of direct controls on capital movements and has used market-oriented instruments mainly in times when the mark was subject to upward pressure.

The effectiveness of these measures varies. According to an EEC study (1973), market-oriented instruments are effective when the purpose is to prevent or to mitigate capital movements induced by interest-rate differentials, but their effectiveness decreases to a considerable extent in the event of speculation provoked by expectations of exchange-rate changes. More recently another EEC report (1976) concluded that national measures aimed at restricting outflows have generally been more effective than measures intended to limit inflows of capital.

The difficulties involved in controlling speculative flows have prompted suggestions to introduce monetary controls on the Common Market level as regards the overall volume of credit generated by, or channeled through, Eurocurrency markets. Regulating the overall volume of Eurocurrency credits may not substantially reduce the extent of speculative capital flows, however, in part because speculation may occur in "conventional" foreign exchange markets and in part because Eurocurrency operations may be diverted elsewhere. Thus, with U.S. regulations more favorable to such operations than in the past, the role of New York may increase at the expense of London.

At the same time, greater exchange-rate flexibility within the snake would tend to reduce speculative pressures on the currencies of the participating countries. This conclusion applies especially to the deutsche mark, which has repeatedly been under upward pressure, culminating in successive revaluations.

---

[32] These problems assume particular importance if the tendency is toward depreciation, as has been the case in France and Italy but not in Belgium, which has continued with its dual exchange market. See Anthony Lanyi, "Separate Exchange Markets for Capital and Current Transactions." *IMF Staff Papers*, November 1975.

The suggested establishment of target zones may reduce speculation in non-snake currencies. And providing greater resources to the European Monetary Cooperation Fund and ensuring mutual support operations among the EEC countries would strengthen the possibilities of individual countries' resisting destabilizing speculation.

The coordination of control measures on Eurocurrency markets has also been recommended to increase the effectiveness of national monetary policies. Yet as long as national policy differences persist, it would seem appropriate that measures aimed at safeguarding the effectiveness of these policies continue to be taken by the national authorities. For one thing, there is no evidence that differences in national regulations would substantially have affected the impact of the measures applied by the individual countries. For another thing, instituting control measures on the Common Market level may reinforce the independence of national economic policies, thereby reducing the chances for policy coordination.

Considering further the advantages of Eurocurrency markets in providing financial intermediation at a low cost, one may question the desirability of attempting to control transactions in Eurocurrencies at the Common Market level. In this connection, it should be recalled that the Eurocurrency markets play an important role in financing trade transactions. This permits cushioning temporary changes in the balance of payments of the individual countries through the operation of leads and lags as well as trade credit.

Eurocurrency markets are also a unifying element in a situation characterized by considerable segmentation of national financial markets, and their operation would make it easier to introduce a parallel European currency, which has repeatedly been suggested. Holdings of Europa-denominated obligations, in turn, would fulfill the role of "generally marketable claims" that can further the integration of capital markets and the financing of temporary imbalances in the EEC.[33]

As Corden notes, exchange-rate arrangements in a common market can be implemented without the integration of capital markets. Nevertheless, the integration of these markets would bring additional benefits.[34] At the same time, for these benefits to be fully enjoyed, it would be desirable to proceed with the coordination of monetary and fiscal policies.

---

[33] J. C. Ingram, *The Case for European Monetary Integration*, Princeton Essays in International Finance, no. 98 (April 1973).

[34] W. M. Corden, *Monetary Integration*, Princeton Essays in International Finance, no. 93 (April 1972).

Concluding Remarks

We have considered in this paper various actions that may usefully be taken in the Common Market in regard to target zones for exchange rates and the coordination of monetary and fiscal policies. Implementing the recommendations made in the paper would, however, involve limiting the sovereignty of the EEC countries in economic policy making.

At the same time, it should be recognized that the freedom of action these countries enjoy at present is more circumscribed than is commonly assumed. This is because the increased interdependence of their national economies through trade reduces the effectiveness of policy measures taken by the individual countries. And while the larger countries are less exposed to foreign trade and hence experience a smaller spillover in the form of higher imports and lower exports, the use of formal and informal wage indexing limits the effectiveness of exchange-rate changes. As a result, a depreciation in the exchange rate occasioned by speculative flows may be validated, at least partially, through higher wages and prices. These consequences can be avoided if mutual support is provided to avoid excessive fluctuations in exchange rates.

Excessive fluctuations in exchange rates also increase uncertainty in international transactions and, in particular, in planning new investments, with adverse effects for the operation of the Common Market. This conclusion is strengthened if we consider the cleavage between snake and non-snake countries that has become increasingly apparent.

Avoiding excessive fluctuations in exchange rates through the application of the target zone approach would thus bring benefits to the member countries. At the same time, for the reasons discussed in the paper, the target zone approach would need to be complemented by the coordination of monetary and fiscal policies on the Common Market level.

COMMENTARIES

Sir Alec Cairncross

When an audience already has the whole text of the play before it and has seen act 1, it is not likely to welcome a critic determined to limit himself to act 2. I propose therefore to extend my comments beyond Balassa's paper and address myself more broadly to the theme of the conference. I shall approach that theme in terms of British experience and problems.

To start with exchange-rate management, on which Balassa, like most other contributors, concentrates, it would be impossible for anyone looking back over the past year at the experience of sterling to award high marks for exchange-rate management. The rate swooped down twice at an alarming rate in the spring and autumn and then recovered from the low point by a full 10 percent. On October 25 it fell against the dollar by nearly 5 percent in a single hour and moved over the year as a whole within a range of 14 percent on either side of the midpoint. These were not changes foreseen and approved by the authorities. The changes over the year were much greater than was expected at the beginning of the year by those responsible for managing the rate.

The market was also unprepared for the changes that occurred. The changes were not large but the day-to-day fluctuations were extraordinary, and there was an overshoot of a full 10 percent before recovery of the rate. Between October 1976 and March 1977 the situation changed from one in which everybody seemed to be convinced that the pound would go to 1.50 to the dollar (and couldn't understand why it did not) to one in which the EEC is said to be exerting pressure for a higher rate of exchange. This volatility in a major currency does not point to great stability in target zones.

These very large changes—on a scale unprecedented in peacetime—seem not to have had correspondingly large effects on trade balances. The surplus countries remain in surplus, and the deficit countries remain in deficit. Only the United States, where such a thing used to be unthinkable, swings to and fro between surplus and deficit. In the five years since the Smithsonian agreement, the share of the leading industrial countries in world trade in manufactures has remained remarkably immune to the most violent fluctuations in exchange rates ever seen in peacetime. The countries that have depreciated most have actually lost ground to their competitors.

What is one to conclude from all this? We have to ask ourselves *why* these fluctuations in exchange rates have occurred and *why* they have failed to remove payments imbalances. It is not sufficient to put it all down to inflation or even to differential rates of inflation. We have to look at the causes of the inflation and why it had differential effects in different countries. A monetarist may find it unnecessary to look beyond the money supply. But if one is not a monetarist one seeks to explain what has been going on by the succession of external shocks that Lamfalussy described earlier and by the constraints on domestic economic policy imposed by the political power of wage earners, which varies from country to country. If the external shocks produce major imbalances, if there is literally no way in which these can be removed, and if the steps necessary to pass them on like Old Maid in the card game are strenuously resisted, then inflation and falling exchange rates are bound to result. Both are likely to reflect also the resistance of wage earners to cuts in real wages or to attempts to make international goods dearer in relation to domestic ones.

So long as the present imbalance in international payments continues, it is hard to see any immediate gain from publicly announced target zones. If we want stable exchange rates, we must aim at a structure of trade and payments consistent with stability. If the structure we have is generating disequilibrium, we will not get very far by multiplying targets. For stability we need a world like that of the 1950s and 1960s in which the countries whose financial strength is beyond challenge are willing to run deficits or to use their surplus for investment in countries weaker than themselves. I see little sign that West Germany and Japan (to say nothing of Saudi Arabia) will pursue policies likely to leave them with a persistent deficit and every indication that there may be a shortage of borrowers of the necessary standing.

Balassa proposes BOP forecasts as a means of reaching agreement on target zones. But this is open to the same objection. BOP forecasts can be translated into appropriate exchange rates only if there is some agreement on what balances are sustainable and consistent with one another. If there is no such agreement or if no set of external balances satisfies the requirement that they should be sustainable in the face of a collective deficit in trade with the oil producers, any constellation of rates will be inherently unstable, and this instability will be compounded and aggravated by movements of short-term capital.

What kind of target zone would be appropriate to the United Kingdom in 1977? Would it be like the target zone recommended by an advisory committee of economists a week or so after Great Britain left the gold standard in 1931? They wanted the Bank of England to "endeavour to keep sterling within certain limits, by buying sterling at the lower limit and buying foreign currencies at the higher."[1] That seems too restrictive, particularly if the limits are far apart. And given the history of 1976, they would have to be far apart. Oort suggests a spread of 3 percent on either side of a central rate. Would anybody attach any importance to an announcement by the Bank of England that it regarded a sterling-dollar rate between 1.65 and 1.75 as a target zone? When a currency can move 5 percent in an hour (and even the Swiss franc has moved 3 percent in a day), what prospect is there of prior consultation within such limits? It would be possible neither to hold the zone constant for long nor to announce a change without making a jumpy market jump to conclusions, as it did in March 1976 when the Bank of England's intervention to sell sterling was interpreted as an invitation to the market to do likewise.

The British case is a particularly apposite one. It brings out how difficult it is to tie exchange-rate management to BOP forecasts. Apart from the worthlessness of most such forecasts—a point emphasized by Willett—and the absurd statistical diplomacy required by collaboration in proposing them, there is the simple issue of principle: If the British BOP is improving (for example, because of North Sea oil), should that be allowed to reflect itself in a strengthening of the exchange rate even if there are large external debts to be repaid—$20 billion by 1985— if inflation is still higher than elsewhere, and if British exports of manufactures are losing ground in world markets? Suppose also that the government is under an injunction to keep a tight grip on the money supply when rates of interest are twice as high as in other industrial countries. If the target zone crawls slowly upward as the BOP moves into surplus—and perhaps even if it remains steady—there may be a large and unwelcome inflow of capital. That would indeed be a curious way of getting rid of sterling balances. In the 1930s Great Britain found an answer to some of the problems of a floating pound in the establishment of an Exchange Equalisation Account and later in the Tripartite Agreement of 1936. I observe no reference in any of the papers to either of these. But I suspect that the way forward may yet involve both

---

[1] Susan Howson and Donald Winch, *The Economic Advisory Council 1930–39* (Cambridge: Cambridge University Press, 1977), p. 101.

a communitywide fund and an agreement to set limits to cross-rates for the dollar, the deutsche mark, and the yen: target zones perhaps for these cross-rates.

I see some virtue in the proposal (in the form elaborated by Oort) in the longer run since member countries ought to have some say in one another's exchange rates. But if it were adopted in a more stable world, I should still want to ask some questions.

For example, how free would countries be to choose their own limits? When countries operated with a fixed parity under the Bretton Woods system, they were nominally obliged to consult the IMF in advance of a change in parity. But it was a fact of life that countries felt free to act first even if they accepted that they had to justify their choice to the IMF afterward. Would the same practice not apply to target zones?

Perhaps within the community it might be possible to go further. Balassa accepts the presumption that "there is a greater chance for agreement on exchange-rate management among Common Market currencies than in the IMF framework." There *should* be. But observing the negotiations over the past few months in London and Rome, I should judge that the IMF carries the bigger punch.

I suspect that the main reason for this is that the IMF has more ammunition in the form of credits. Balassa and others refer from time to time to the European Monetary Cooperation Fund. Balassa suggests as a sanction for enforcing EEC views the power of ministers to limit access to the EMCF or to require a country to lend to it. But strictly speaking there is no fund—only a kind of brass plate for future operations. It has no money of its own and, when it intervenes, uses funds put up specifically for the purpose.

I suggest that, if the community intends to take monetary cooperation seriously, it ought to create a lender of last resort with the means at its disposal to command at least the same attention as that given to the IMF. If the deficit countries in the community borrow outside the community and the surplus countries lend outside it, monetary integration is not likely to flourish.

I leave aside the issues raised by the need to coordinate policies within the community since we are to devote a later session to that subject. I share Balassa's doubts about the idea of setting targets for the expansion of the monetary base or the money supply in each country. I am by no means convinced that either the Bank of England or the British Treasury could bind itself to limit monetary growth to some more or less precise figure without risking the need to take highly damaging action of an irreversible kind. So far as the chancellor has in fact bound himself to a monetary target, he has been careful to do so in a way that throws the emphasis on his budgetary target and to announce a budgetary target that leaves him with some latitude. But these targets are significant only insofar as they affect the level of effective demand and the movement of prices and costs. It is obviously very important that, as far as possible, the member countries of the EEC pursue policies calculated to maintain a high level of employment and bring inflation under control. Some people think that both these things can be done by setting monetary and fiscal targets. I am not one of them, but this is not the place to say why. I see little reason to suppose that, except in extremis, pressure on any country by its neighbors will induce it to embrace policies for the control of inflation that it is not already half disposed to adopt. But I see rather more hope of success if pressure is put on a country to expand or contract demand in the interests of maintaining the world economy in balance or at a higher level.

I turn next to the financial background to exchange-rate management and policy coordination. Here I find myself in general agreement with Balassa. It seems to me that the Eurocurrency market has to be treated as part of a much wider market and that there is very little evidence that lending in Eurodollars has been larger, more imprudent, or more inflationary than lending in national currencies. There is a case for exercising prudential control over any banking operations, and such control calls for international collaboration in the case of the Eurodollar market. But such collaboration already exists, and prudential control is already exercised parentally within the banking system to which the parent of a Eurobank is attached. If the issue is whether control should be exercised as a means of reducing speculative capital flows or preventing international credit expansion, the case is not a strong one.

It is true that there is a real risk of powerful destabilizing movements of capital, not necessarily in Eurocurrencies, because of events and policies outside the community. It is reasonable for members of the community to seek to ward off these flows rather than let their exchange rates take the strain and create distortions within their domestic economies. For this purpose they may seek to make use of capital controls, but these are of limited value. The alternative seems to me to be to create a secret sponge to absorb the inflow without disturbance to the domestic economy—that is, to establish a large fund along the lines of the British Exchange Equalisation Account of the 1930s. This is a role that could be played by the European Monetary Cooperation Fund. A proposal to this effect was put forward two years ago in *Economic Policy for Europe*: The purpose of the account was:

to steady exchange rates without fixing them or preventing adjustments called for by changes in competitiveness reflected in the current account. So far as capital movements took place within the Community, and were ostensibly reversible, no insuperable problems would arise. So far as they represented a movement of capital into the Community from outside, affecting member countries unequally, the proposed account would be a means of broadening the impact, just as would happen if the flow were subsequently outwards. But for this purpose it would have to be very much larger than anything hitherto created.

The management of the exchange-equalization account would presumably be in the hands of the central monetary authority, whatever form that took. If intervention were to be effective, however, the authority would presumably have to enjoy considerable discretion, on the understanding that it would act in conformity with agreed rules and, too, that its operations would in due course be made public and submitted to scrutiny by outside experts.[2]

To conclude, there is not much point, at this moment, in pursuing target zones for most of the European currencies. There is, however, something to be said for target zones for the exchange rates between the three major currencies, the yen, the deutsche mark, and the dollar.

It might be better to approach the problem of exchange-rate stability in the community through an exchange equalization account that would help to prevent excessive fluctuations directly and proceed from this to target zones as a logical consequence of the operations of the account. The creation of a *masse de manoeuvre* of this kind might also serve as a preliminary to future monetary integration.

Coordination of monetary and fiscal policies is desirable for its own sake and can hardly be treated simply as a means of improving exchange stability. If countries do not already have a sufficient incentive to master inflation or industrial depression or both, they will not yield readily to international preaching and proselytizing.

We should bear in mind that governments are much more helpless than they pretend and that there really is not a great deal they can do. They are sometimes full of laudable ambitions, but they rarely achieve what they set out to achieve.

Above all, if we are going to make progress, we need to have something approaching a common philosophy, a common outlook, a

---

[2] Sir Alec Cairncross, Herbert Giersch, Alexandre Lamfalussy, Guiseppe Petrilli, and Pierre Uri, *Economic Policy for the European Community* (London: Macmillan for the Institut für Weltwirtschaft of Kiel, 1974).

common view of the way in which different instruments of policy should be used. This is something we do not have.

I was troubled that references were made this morning to monetary and fiscal targets as if there were only one aspect to monetary policy: either the rate of interest, whatever that may be, or the supply of money, whatever that may be. Monetary policy is highly complex and has many different aspects, not all of them pulling in the same direction or exercising the same kind of effect. The same is true of fiscal policy. Within the things we talk about as single instruments are many subinstruments that have complexities of their own. It is a mistake to speak as if there were only two or three tools for the control of the economies of Europe.

Because this is so, because of the complexity of policy, and because we are so ignorant about how policies operate on the economy, I do not believe that we can do much better than to take Willett's advice: Make sure that we maintain continuous contact with one another, preach at one another if we have to, but each try to understand what the other is up to; try to see the full complexity of the situation in the countries we are dealing with, and then work out, more or less ad hoc, the action that we can take. We can be much too ambitious in a world so precariously poised.

Giovanni Magnifico

From the point of view of the prospects for economic and monetary unification in Europe, the problem with the external factors mentioned by Lamfalussy was that two of them hit different countries to different extents. The most obvious example is the oil price rise, since the resulting additional burden was much greater in terms of GNP for Italy than, say, for West Germany. The diverging performances observed within the EEC cannot be explained only in terms of the differing impact of the exogenous factors. There have also been differences in domestic policies, in the management of the economies—in some cases, outright mismanagement.

Lamfalussy mentioned that real wages continued to rise in Italy during a period when they should have fallen. May I qualify that statement by pointing out that we in Italy have attempted to make the adjustment and have to some extent succeeded in doing so. Some progress has been made toward restoring equilibrium between supply and demand, and therefore equilibrium in the current account of the balance of payments, by curbing the growth of personal disposable income through the use of fiscal instruments. In the summer of 1974 and the fall of 1976 we decided to adopt a restrictive fiscal program, the impact of which on both occasions can be measured in terms of GNP as roughly equivalent to 3 percent—a large shift of resources, indeed.

But I am in agreement with the speakers who have underlined the difficulty of making adjustments in real wages. I feel that, in the light of Italian experience, it is not enough to speak merely of vanishing money illusion. There has been more than this in Italy. There has been, really, a reverse or negative money illusion. The unions are no longer passively resisting a reduction in money wage rates; they have for some time adopted an aggressive attitude and consistently demand increases in money wages far in excess of what the system can give in real terms.

Thus, we now have, with an opposite sign, what used to be known as Keynes's nightmare. He argued that one cannot eliminate the system's tendency toward underemployment of resources by curbing money wage rates, not only because it is difficult to achieve such a cut but also because, in the climate of the Great Depression, he felt that prices would also fall in more or less the same proportion. Consequently the relationship of real wages to prices would remain unchanged, and the tendency to underemployment of resources in the system would not be corrected.

In Italy the same phenomenon is present but with opposite signs. In other words, wages adjust very quickly upward or, more often, precede rising prices, so that the strategic relationship of unit costs to prices is unchanged. Whereas "money illusion" was an instrument of adjustment in that it made it possible to cut real wages notwithstanding the trade unions' resistance to cutting money wages, the "negative money illusion" that unions now seem to adopt in some Western countries tends to prevent adjustment.

Let me turn to the VC hypothesis. Surely the analysis has a lot to do with the automatic indexation of wages and salaries, whether formal or informal.

In my view, there is a strong case for intervening on exchange markets, at least in a couple of cases. One may wish to smooth out exchange-rate changes due to seasonal and to cyclical factors, especially with a desynchronized cycle. The current account reacts very quickly to the change in the trade cycle. If the expanding country allows the current-account deficit to have full impact on the exchange rate—that is, to be absorbed by an exchange-rate depreciation—that depreciation will only in part, if at all, be offset by a subsequent appreciation once the economy slows down and competing economies expand. In other words, there is a "ratchet effect" with widespread indexation of incomes. We in Italy have intervened on exchange markets; on some occasions we were right and were proved right; on others, we were wrong and were proved wrong.

There has been criticism of the role of floating rates in promoting BOP adjustment. One important point that has not been mentioned concerns the effects on the international allocation of investment. In my view the fixed-rate system is biased in that it tends to keep the currencies of more stable countries undervalued. Thus, under fixed rates, the adjustment is only made when overdue. This is the philosophy of the fixed-rate system, at least as the system actually functioned. Consequently, during the 1950s and 1960s, the currency of a country such as West Germany tended to be undervalued. Keeping the currency undervalued means, of course, that exports are subsidized. As a result, competitiveness and exports will increase. It will be possible to realize economies of scale; therefore, productivity will increase more rapidly than in other countries, and so will competitiveness and exports; and so on and so forth. This virtuous circle has gone on for a long time in West Germany and made it a magnet for investment of capital and foreign manpower during the past two decades.

I think this has changed in the 1970s. Although changes in real exchange rates have been small, they have been large enough to alter the situation in at least some trading countries, such as Italy. As a result West German investments abroad have gone to countries other than Italy. But that is on the whole an important phenomenon, which makes for more equilibrium and tends to equalize the price of the factors of production throughout the world.

Let me turn to Balassa's paper, which is mainly about target zones. This proposal has received a cold reception from the technical and political bodies of the community. Some of the reasons for this have been given in the course of the discussion, particularly in Cairncross's remarks. What I have heard has rather confirmed the view that, for the time being at least, any kind of proposal aimed at tackling the present problem of European monetary and economic unification through *direct* action on intra-European exchange rates is unlikely to be accepted or to be feasible.

The target zone proposal, at its inception, was a three-pronged proposal, and the target zones, as such, were just one segment of the whole proposal, as I understand it. It was a new attempt to make policy coordination effective, an experiment in what I shall call a semiflexible system of intra-European exchange rates. For various reasons the parts that concerned policy coordination and the monetary facilities to accompany the adoption of the scheme were never seriously considered. All that really remained of the proposal was the target zone element. And this has proved, in the judgment of those concerned, not feasible now.

The scheme was also intended to make adjustment symmetrical for both surplus and deficit countries, and therefore it was to apply also to countries linked by the snake arrangement. Some snake countries felt that conflicts might arise in operating both the target zone and the snake arrangement, however, and those conflicts might concern not only technical points but also matters of policy, especially the so-called community level of the dollar.

A number of community countries feel that no communitywide monetary arrangement is possible if there is no willingness on the part of all member countries to approach exchange rate policy vis-à-vis third countries—and especially vis-à-vis the dollar—in a way that mediates between the different requirements of the various member countries. I shall return to this point, which of course concerns the process of adjustment.

In my view one can hardly regard the snake as the community exchange system. A truly community arrangement of this sort should provide us with a possibility of stabilizing the exchange relationship among the four major community currencies, and that is not the case today. Since three of the four major currencies of the community have left the snake and are floating individually, the only remaining major one, the deutsche mark, is, in fact, also floating independently. The fact that West Germany normally—and I stress the word "normally"—does not negotiate with the smaller partners its exchange-rate policy vis-à-vis third currencies lends justification to an interpretation of the snake as an arrangement in which a number of smaller countries have pegged their currencies in what tends to be a one-way relationship to the deutsche mark, the leading currency. The deutsche mark itself is therefore, from an economic point of view, on a footing not much different from that of the individually floating currencies. This means that there is not much justification for the discrimination between members and nonmembers of the snake or for the different political connotation that has been attached to membership or nonmembership in the snake. In my view one merit of the Dutch proposal was precisely that it aimed at putting an end to this state of affairs by trying to introduce the first elements of a truly communitywide exchange-rate system, of which the snake would have been only a special case.

Once it has become clear that governments are not in a position to intervene on exchange markets, the declaration of target zones—in other words, of intervention points (without, however, an obligation to intervene, which could not be envisaged under present circumstances) —may become an unnecessary and possibly dangerous exercise.

I agree with the point made in Balassa's paper that the index of relative unit labor costs is a better indicator of competitiveness than, say, wholesale price indexes. In my view the concept of an equilibrium exchange rate implies that prices are kept in the right relationship to the exchange rate and also that costs are in the right relationship to prices. Only for a limited period can exporters maintain competitiveness if unit costs are rising faster than in competing countries. Fairly soon the prices in the exchange rate will have to be adjusted to make room for a "normal" margin of profit. This is borne out by Italy's exchange crisis of January 1976.

Throughout 1975 unit costs kept rising in Italy at a much faster pace than in other industrial countries—costs, but not prices. The weakness of demand did not make it possible to adjust prices more or less in step with cost increases, so that Italy remained competitive in prices. Exports increased fast; in 1975 our share of world exports did not decline. In this process, however, Italy had become uncompetitive in costs, and the adjustment has had to be made through the lira's exchange-rate depreciation, which occurred, as I said, in January 1976. One might ask why the adjustment of the exchange rate was not managed more gradually? The answer is partly that our exports were faring well: in 1975 we practically wiped out the current-account deficit.

One cannot curb price movements in a way consistent with stable exchange rates without curbing cost movements. But costs—the prices of inputs—cannot be curbed when the price of the main input—labor —is determined in the national market. Despite the large labor migrations within the community, there is not yet a communitywide market for manpower. Manpower is organized in unions that have national scope, and the aims of national unions are certainly pursued with different strategies. The dynamics of wages and salaries have developed along different lines in different countries, and hardly any efforts have been made to bring them closer to a common pattern.

What can be done to progress toward a truly unified European labor market? In my view, there is a need to bring the unions and the community closer together, to encourage closer contacts among unions in the economy, and also, perhaps, to associate them more effectively with the coordination of national economic policies on a community level. Perhaps representatives of employers and labor associations should join the representatives of economic ministries and central banks at some stage of the process of defining and agreeing on economic, financial, and monetary targets at the community level. The purpose would be to secure a common undertaking by the national and also the social partners to adhere to agreed targets and to help evolve a community wages policy consistent with those targets.

Policy coordination has floundered, I think, on two kinds of rocks. First, governments have at times been unable to achieve objectives consistent with national policies as agreed at community level, for the reasons McMahon discussed. Second, it has been difficult to define and agree on a community policy because of conflicting views concerning the priorities and the sharing of the burden in the process of adjustment. Lately the very high rates of inflation have made agreement on priorities easier.

But the problem of allocating the burden of adjustment between member countries will be with us for some time. In theory, at least, under the gold standard, both deficit and surplus countries were automatically made to participate in the adjustment process. As the dollar exchange standard with fixed exchange rates gradually evolved from the original Bretton Woods concept, the burden of adjustment shifted mainly to the surplus countries.

Over the past three years, however, the workings of the floating rate system imply a significant turnaround: the onus of adjustment falls, or is left, very largely on the deficit countries. Any mistake made by a country in demand management tends to affect mainly prices and the exchange rate of that country and is less fully reflected in its balance of payments. Under present conditions the adjustments must mainly—if not exclusively—lie with the deficit countries.

Jacques van Ypersele

When I was asked to comment on the excellent paper of Balassa, I was told that I was free to extend my remarks to other related topics discussed in the conference. I intend to make an "appropriate use" of this liberal view of a commentator's job.

Let me first make a short remark on terminology, so that we can avoid some misunderstandings and be aware that the term "target zone" has different meanings in different papers. When Oort—and I believe also Balassa—refer to target zone, they emphasize a mechanism "primarily intended to serve as a trigger for consultation and, it is hoped, for coordination of economic policy in general." Oort emphasizes clearly that "it is and remains essential to the target zone proposal that countries are not in any way obliged to maintain their effective exchange rate within the target zone by intervention in the exchange markets."

116

At the most he envisages for later development of the target zone "introducing certain limited, essentially negative obligations in policy areas directly related to the management of exchange rates," such as that "countries should not take measures that tend to push the effective exchange rate outside or further away from the target zone."

On the other hand, Willett says the target zone approach "would require, or at least strongly encourage, in addition that countries intervene to dampen exchange-rate movements away from and reinforce movements toward the target zone." In fact, Oort and the Villa Pamphili group's target zone approach is closer to what Willett calls "the reference rate" approach, where one focuses on when intervention is prohibited. Thus when we talk about target zones, let us be clear whether we mean Oort's type of target zone or Willett's type.

Let me now come to substance. Rather than stress my points of disagreement with Balassa, I shall put forward my own credo and derive from it the points of difference with his paper.

First, I do strongly believe, as I expect all of us here do, that *exchange rates should reflect basic underlying conditions of the respective economies*. This is the basic philosophy of article 4 of the new IMF articles. Difficulties start to develop, however, when one tries to define what basic underlying conditions are and what is erratic. It can in general be said, I believe, that on this side of the ocean one tends to give a very broad and extensive definition to underlying conditions and a narrow one to erratic fluctuations. In Europe we tend to do the reverse and often include among erratic fluctuations a substantial portion of capital movements.

To come to specifics, the domestic pet I cherish most is the snake, which is probably less admired in this room. I believe that countries in the snake fulfill the basic conditions necessary to maintain fixed but adjustable rates between themselves. This is really to say that the six smaller countries (four EEC plus Sweden and Norway) can and should continue to peg their rates to the deutsche mark. The advantages to the countries in pegging their rates to the West German one come from the fact that the countries are small, open economies, most of them with strong wage indexation clauses. They also come, of course, from the fact that the West German economy has achieved a great deal of stability. In such small, open, wage-indexed economies, exchange-rate depreciation, as Lamfalussy has correctly stressed, leads to little or no BOP adjustment. On the contrary, an active exchange-rate policy designed to avoid rate depreciation, together with an incomes policy, can play an effective role in getting back to stability. In addition this policy mix is probably less costly socially and politically than the

117

strong domestic demand measures that would be necessary to achieve the same return to stable conditions.

Rather than develop again the reasoning implied in this assessment, which is related to the vicious circle (VC) hypothesis, I would like to summarize briefly the experience in Belgium during the last three years, which contains useful lessons. Before 1974, our inflation rate had been broadly similar to the West German one. From December 1973 to December 1974, partly because of the oil price shock and our full wage indexation system, our consumer price index rose by 15.7 percent while the corresponding percentage was only 5.8 in West Germany. Between December 1974 and December 1975, our index rose further by 11 percent while West Germany's rose only 5.4 percent.

Most of the pure believers in market forces in this room and absolute opponents of the VC theory would have advised us to allow a strong depreciation of our currency in 1976 while either remaining in the snake or leaving it. This is in fact also what the market believed, and we had three heavy waves of speculation against the Belgian franc.

But we were convinced that, even if for a short period our price developments had been somewhat out of line with the West German ones, our BOP situation remained basically strong and the so-called basic underlying factors did not warrant a depreciation of the Belgian franc vis-à-vis other snake currencies. This is of course an example of what I mentioned earlier, the divergences of interpretation that can exist on the two sides of the Atlantic about what basic underlying conditions were.

We were convinced not only about the basic position but also that accepting a depreciation of the franc vis-à-vis the deutsche mark, which was also a depreciation vis-à-vis the rest of the world, would have harmed us precisely because of the familiar vicious circle argument. Since our imports are equal to about 50 percent of GNP and our wages are fully indexed, it is understandable that the vicious circle argument, coupled with the conviction of the basic strength of our BOP, led us to resist depreciation of the franc vis-à-vis the deutsche mark.

We fought back speculation by intervening in the foreign exchange market to keep the Belgian franc within the snake and by applying a very tight monetary policy to fight "leads and lags." The existence of a two-tier exchange market, one for commercial transactions that stayed in the snake and one free market that was allowed to float freely, also helped us by providing a kind of safety valve. Strong intervention in the markets, tight monetary policy, and the two-tier exchange rate helped us resist the pressures. When calm came back on the foreign exchange markets, we allowed for a small depreciation of the franc vis-à-vis the deutsche mark, which the market has in fact not ratified: the Belgian franc–deutsche mark relationship within the snake stayed on average at the same level as before the realignment. After this October operation, leads and lags were reversed, we recovered the reserves that had been spent during the tension, and monetary policy could be relaxed. The policy of pegging the franc to the deutsche mark meant an effective appreciation of the franc during 1976. This, together with a slowing down of wage increases, enabled us to decrease our inflation rate to 7.5 percent between December 1975 and December 1976 and thus decrease substantially the difference in inflation rates between Belgium and West Germany.

I think this case and simple arithmetic would show that, if we had followed the generally accepted view of the need for exchange rates to follow market forces, we would be much worse off today. Our inflation rate would be much higher, since imports are equivalent to about half of GNP and wages are fully and almost immediately indexed.

Our resistance to market pressures also had an additional psychological benefit that should not be underestimated. Those who speculated against the Belgian franc in fact lost substantial sums, both in high interest rates paid to finance leads and lags and in actual exchange losses (indeed they bought foreign exchange when the Belgian franc was weakest against the deutsche mark, and after the realignment the Belgian franc was stronger vis-à-vis the deutsche mark). This is a lesson that will not be lost in the future and will lead many to greater prudence in the future.

This example illustrates three points:

1. Authorities in various countries may have different interpretations of basic underlying factors.
2. The VC theory has important elements of validity, especially in small, open, wage-indexed economies. (I would recognize also that there are limits to this theory and that it cannot be applied blindly to any economy. I stressed, for instance, that Belgium continued to have a favorable basic BOP position.)
3. The snake is an essential element in the stabilization efforts of the smaller European countries participating in it.

To draw some lessons from the case just outlined, I would not accept Balassa's recommendation that "it would seem desirable to allow for the possibility of more frequent exchange-rate changes among snake countries." Minisnake countries have shown that, contrary to the Bretton Woods practices, they were able to adjust when required. I see no need for more flexibility of the snake itself or a priori for more frequent changes.

I have some doubts about applying the target zone concept to the snake countries as a group. First, from a technical point of view, the setting of a single effective exchange rate for the whole snake seems to me to raise difficulties. Calculations by means of weighting the movement of the exchange rate in the various countries do not seem to lead to meaningful results. Second, there is the rather simplistic but valid consideration that the snake mechanism has on the whole functioned well. There has been no overshooting upward of snake currencies. The problem we try to address with target zones is basically how to avoid excessive depreciation, overshooting of some of the weaker currencies in the EEC. So we should apply the target zone concept to the currencies in the EEC that are floating freely.

One answer to that argument is that politically there should be some symmetry in obligations. To that one can say in turn that EEC countries can choose either the snake mechanism or the system of target zones. Those who opt for the snake mechanism accept tight obligations. Those who opt for target zones accept for good and realistic reasons less tight exchange-rate obligations. I can see nothing wrong with such a system.

In his section on the European financial markets I believe Balassa dismisses too rapidly a type of capital control: the system of a dual exchange market. He gives as his only argument, "it appears that relatively small differences in rates on current and capital account transactions provide inducement for evasion." As I have tried to indicate, our experience, including the recent one with a dual exchange market, shows that this system constitutes for us an important and useful safety valve in periods of tension. In 1976 the difference between the Belgian franc on the free market and on the regulated market ranged between 4 and 5.5 percent. Thus when tension develops, part of it is absorbed by the free market.

I would apply the target zone concept only to nonsnake currencies. I basically support the proposals put forward by Oort, which are also developed in Balassa's paper. This system of target zones offers flexibility but indicates clearly the targets of the authorities. To be credible, of course, this system should be accompanied, as the authors have stressed, by measures to increase convergence of the European economies, particularly in the fields of monetary and fiscal policy.

As the proponents of the system have insisted, it would provide the necessary framework for meaningful discussion in the community. It would provide the country concerned and the EEC with the opportunity for a more conscious assessment of the extent to which actual economic developments and policies should give rise either to adjustment of the target zone or to a reorientation of national policies. Thus, as Balassa and Oort have correctly emphasized, the proposals are primarily intended to serve as a trigger for consultation and for coordination of economic policy in general.

Let me say parenthetically that I do not share the overpessimistic view of some participants that no measures have been taken that should ensure greater convergence among EEC countries. I might agree that little has been done in an EEC framework, but we should not forget important efforts made by countries either in broader international forums such as the IMF or on their own. The fact that some of these important measures have been taken in a broader framework than the EEC is relatively easy to understand. I would compare this phenomenon with the reluctance many of us would have to go to a doctor who is a close member of our family. The other main reason is that large credits accompanying such operations are more easily gathered in a wider forum. That does not mean that we should not try to get at some discipline and convergence within the EEC. Nor should recent improvements in convergence be ignored because they are negotiated in a broader forum than the EEC.

Let me conclude in the broad framework of this useful conference on U.S.-European monetary relations. I am sure we all agree with the general objective for exchange rates stated in the amended IMF articles, which is to "promote a stable system of exchange rates." Clearly the foremost means of ensuring this stability, as emphasied in article IV, is for each member to "endeavor to direct its economic and financial policies toward the objective of fostering orderly economic growth with reasonable price stability." Undoubtedly the return to exchange-rate stability can best be ensured by promoting a return to stability of all our economies.

But I hope we would all agree that the management of floating rates can and should be improved. It seems to me that it would be useful to work toward a better international harmonization of policies directly affecting exchange rates. Experience has shown us that floating does not relieve the authorities of the need to take measures to counteract exchange fluctuations not warranted by underlying economic conditions. It is not necessarily a question of intervening more extensively in the foreign exchange markets but rather of making more active use of the other instruments that can enhance stability, especially interest-rate policies. In some cases control of capital movements could also play a role.

Finally, let me hope that, partly as a result of this conference, there will be a better understanding of the efforts of European countries to develop regional arrangements aimed at promoting greater stability of the economies and the exchange rates. In particular, I hope that the merits of the snake will be better understood, as well as the efforts to reduce the gap between snake and non-snake currencies in Europe.

Hubertus Müller-Groeling

In his paper Balassa advocates the introduction of target zones for exchange rates, but at the same time he carefully spells out the problems of exchange-rate determination (and forecasting) in the short run and gives a description of the consultation and negotiation process necessary for fixing and changing the target zones. In doing this, he has produced a truly dialectical paper, in the sense that it would not be difficult to argue from his very balanced exposition that (under present circumstances and with the past experience with monetary union) the target rate approach to exchange-rate union is not a viable proposition.

This is emphasized by his remarks on short-run exchange-rate formation. To fix target rates for any reasonable span of time, one would have to take into account the "expected future behavior" of the economic system, including labor costs, business cycles and their synchronization (or lack of it), and the BOP effects of economic policy measures. The less than satisfactory record of the profession when it comes to such projection is too well known to need much stressing. However, it may not be superfluous to remember the margin of error (if it can be called that) in some of the most elaborate BOP forecasts.[1] And it is no secret that, for instance, the proponents of flexible exchange rates (and of revaluations before they were introduced) in West Germany erred by a very wide margin in their estimates of where the exchange rate would move (or by how much the deutsche mark would have to be revalued).[2] I really do not believe that there would be much disagreement with the author about the general difficulty of the task of calculating (defining) proper target zones.

In arguing against the introduction of target zones for exchange rates, I do not mean to imply that a reduction in exchange-rate varia-

---

Note: The author has greatly benefited from suggestions made by Gerhard Fels, Reinhard Fürstenberg, and Frank Weiss, who are, however, not to be held responsible for the views expressed.

[1] See, for instance, Willett's paper.

[2] Admittedly their task was very difficult after a prolonged period of distortions in exchange rates.

tion, especially in the EEC, is undesirable. On the contrary, for obvious reasons, as much exchange-rate stability as is attainable by a harmonization of economic policies in the EEC is very welcome.

After the experience with the fixed-exchange-rate system, however, and with the attempts at forming (or reviving) a European exchange-rate union, it does not seem advisable once again to "put the cart before the horse" by first fixing (or quasi-fixing) exchange rates and then trying to force the policy harmonization on the European governments. What else is the suggestion of target rates or zones if not a very sophisticated attempt to reintroduce—however slowly and cautiously—the adjustable peg system through the back door?[3] What could and should be attempted is exactly the opposite: to try first to harmonize economic policy in the EEC as far as is acceptable to (and attainable by) the various governments. This would help eliminate some of the most important causes of exchange-rate fluctuations and divergences.

Such a renewed attempt at harmonization should be both cautious and ambitious: cautious in the sense that one goes back to piecemeal engineering, advancing step by step and not wishing to do too much at once; ambitious in that such an attempt at harmonization would center on one of the most crucial variables. One need not be a monetarist in the strict sense of the word to believe that monetary policy would be a serious candidate for any attempt at harmonization.

Fiscal policy, even though it may well have a short-run influence on the price level and on the balance of payments, seems to be singularly unsuitable as a target for harmonization efforts. First, fiscal policy is determined in many countries, especially in West Germany, by a number of parliaments at national, regional, and local levels; by administrations at all those levels; and, especially in times of inflation, by varying numbers of government enterprises at all those levels. Whether harmonization is feasible is subject to much doubt. In any case, the West German experience with trying to form an internally coordinated anticyclical fiscal policy is anything but encouraging.

Second, fiscal policy is usually an instrument lagging behind overall developments in the economy. This would probably not be serious for automatic, induced changes in fiscal policy, which tend to operate after a relatively short lag and can even be exempted from

---

[3] Since Balassa did not state as explicitly as Oort did in his paper that the only purpose of target zones is to trigger consultation, I interpret this as meaning that he is not as firm in this matter as Oort. If Balassa were ready to accept this interpretation (which he does not seem to be), his position would appear to be the more logical one, since what good would the elaborate process of fixing target zones be if it served only as a trigger for consultations (and for speculation about their results)?

harmonization; but it is a serious objection to discretionary fiscal policy measures.

Third, fiscal policy already has to accomplish a large number of tasks. It is the vehicle for redistribution programs, for economic development programs, and for anticyclical policy.

Fourth, and most important, fiscal policy is the central core of the sovereignty of the nation-state, and it seems to be quite clear from recent experience that it would be a great mistake to overestimate the willingness of governments to make concessions in this area. For all these reasons, fiscal policy seems totally unsuitable as an instrument to be harmonized, even if national governments were acting in good faith.

From these negative properties of fiscal policy follow some simple principles for choosing an adequate instrument for harmonization:

- The instrument must actually be in the hands of institutions promising to exercise control.
- The instrument should be one that leads economic activity, particularly prices and exchange rates.
- The instrument must be truly negotiable among countries.

Such an instrument is monetary policy. While not all European central banks have equally independent control over national monetary policy, with some assistance from their governments they could have such control. Of course, differing institutional arrangements among countries impinge on the methods applied. As the West German Council of Economic Experts states in its most recent report, the instruments of monetary policy are fairly similar in Europe, although preferences in the use of specific instruments differ.[4] If anything is negotiable, it should be monetary policy with its less direct and less visible effects on the relative income positions of different groups in society. I do not wish to go into detail about the appropriate money aggregate to take as a basis for the harmonization efforts. As I see it, in deciding on the money aggregate one would have to weigh the advantage of close bank control over the aggregate chosen (money base), as in the suggestion of the Council of Economic Experts, against that of closer short-run connection with the level of economic activity and prices, as in the aggregate suggested by Balassa. It may well turn out, however, that in the medium run closer control over the aggregate will be more important. Once harmonization of monetary policy has been introduced, short-run arguments will lose some of their weight.

---

[4] Sachverständigenrat zur Begutachtung der Gesamtwirtschaftlichen Entwicklung (Council of Economic Experts), *Jahresgutachten 1976/77*: (Stuttgart, Mainz, 1977), pp. 493–503.

What is suggested here as a viable policy option is not the total equalization of growth rates of the monetary aggregate but the negotiation of preannounced, though nationally different, monetary growth rates, which should take into account the growth rate of the productive capacity of the economy and, at least for the time being, existing under-utilization of capacity. It is hoped that this would also lead to a lowering of inflation rates in Europe and a narrowing of their range. In all probability, it would also take much "noise" out of the exchange-rate markets, leaving exchange-rate changes to take care of the more gradually working forces of change in competitive positions and, per-haps more important, to take care of disruptive events. It is not sug-gested here that this harmonization effort be supported by target zones for exchange rates or any other form of fixing or quasi-fixing. With the introduction of a harmonized, steady monetary policy (in terms of preannounced target growth rates of money aggregates) in the partici-pating countries, the differentiation between the short-run and the long-run effects of fiscal and monetary policy that Balassa gives as one reason for the need to harmonize fiscal policy may lose much of its weight.

Admittedly there is not much room left in such an arrangement for institutions like the snake (or what is left of it). But it may well be that the existence of the snake tends to stand in the way of a more fundamental and more promising approach to European monetary integration. By this approach I do not mean only the attempt at an increasingly closer harmonization of monetary policy but, over and above such a measure, the introduction of a European parallel currency of stable purchasing power, as suggested in the *Economist* Manifesto.[5] This is a serious effort, in Vaubel's words, "to bring about currency union *without* passing through the stage of exchange-rate unification."

Of course, if a European parallel currency is made too attractive relative to national currencies, and if a purchasing power guarantee is a very strong advantage because of the degree of inflation, governments might not accept the parallel currency. If there is anything to be learned from recent European history, however, it is that there is no substitute for the readiness of European governments (and their elec-torates) to give up sovereign rights in favor of European union.

---

[5] Giorgio Basevi and others, "The All Saints' Day Manifesto for European Monetary Union," *The Economist* (London), November 1, 1975, pp. 33–38. The signers were Giorgio Basevi, Michele Fratianni, Herbert Giersch, Pieter Korteweg, David O'Mahoney, Michael Parkin, Theo Peeters, Pascal Salin, and Niels Thygesen.

F. Boyer de la Giroday

The first thing I should like to say is that last Monday the Council of Ministers of the European Communities concluded its rather long study of the so-called Duisenberg proposals, which as you know covered a much larger field than exchange management. One of the conclusions of the Council of Ministers was that focusing the exercise on exchange management on the model of the target zone scheme was relatively premature and therefore that one had better consider a wider field of consultation to be held regularly, bearing not only on exchange matters but on various other fields connected with exchange rates, namely, the whole range of short-term economic policies.

I hope this venture is going to develop into a more effective process of consultation than has been the case heretofore. There is, of course, some danger that it will be drowned in cumbersome procedures that may fail to elicit adequate responses on the part of the countries chosen for some scrutiny. The council's decision may not correspond to a "grand design"; but grand designs, as Oort told us in the beginning of his paper, have produced only accidental successes, and perhaps modest designs will one of these days produce grand achievements.

It would be too rash to hope that this will happen soon. We are not near the sort of grand shock that Vaubel, quoting from Uri, says might bring a big leap forward into a single currency for Europe. In fact, as we have heard today, shocks have been extremely detrimental to plans for monetary integration in Europe.

This new exercise will continue to be mainly the responsibility of the Commission of the European Communities, and it will be up to this institution to present cases in as effective a way as possible. This still has to be devised and put into practice.

It has often been said that human beings or groups can be prodded toward progress by two instruments, one the carrot and the other the stick. In this connection one ought perhaps to add: "provided that these instruments are used at the right ends of the body." In the present state of affairs, the commission has little carrot and hardly any stick at its disposal. And this, as Kafka said, is true not only of the commission but of the community as a whole and of international institutions in general. Let us hope that so-called moral suasion and the general will to achieve something worthwhile will lead us into a better position than we are in now.

Since I will probably be sharing in the preparation of these consultations, let me say to Balassa that the advice he gave us and the policy options he discusses in his paper have been very useful. Given the political parameters under which we will be working, there will be no automatic trigger of any kind, and although many indicators will be used, perhaps not the same indicator of unit labor costs that Balassa propounds in his paper. The experience of the staff of the commission in this connection has gone exactly in the same direction as that of the Optica group. Although in theory indexes of unit labor costs have many virtues in comparing competitive positions of currencies and appear to be a very useful reference for helping to move exchange rates correctly, they are not so in practice because statistics on such costs are not very reliable and their supply involves tremendous delays. Perhaps we should try to improve on that, but for the moment such is the situation.

Of course, in preparing these consultations, we will bring in monetary and fiscal policies and monetary targetry, which are so much in fashion these days. I do not believe too much in it myself, but it can do no harm, and it may do some good in the sense that it may induce governments to think twice before transgressing too grossly the limits they have assigned themselves in the creation of money.

We have already had much consultation on budgetary policies—even ex ante consultation—in the Common Market, although this may not be widely known. There is in fact an exercise every year to set limits to budget deficits. This is done in accordance with a secret procedure. I hesitate to give an opinion why this procedure is secret. Is it for the same reason that the British chancellor of the exchequer cannot possibly divulge what is contained in the famous "red box"—so as not to give clues to speculators? Or is it—and this is more likely—because governments are afraid of not being able to stick to the targets agreed upon within the community, as happens too often in practice, and fear that repeated and gross failures may put them in a rather delicate position?

There has just been a discussion of the meaning of target zones. For my part, my concept of them derives, like most of what has been produced on the subject, from the IMF guidelines for floating. When I read them the first time, I did not realize as much as I do today that, perhaps because they were the product of difficult international negotiations, they were marked by a kind of nostalgia for stable rates. That is what characterizes the guidelines when one reads them today.

Whatever may have been the thrust of the efforts of those who participated closely in the demise of the Bretton Woods system, the whole concept of target zones must be interpreted as belonging to the family of stable rates. I think that an experiment along these lines— even in the Common Market, marked as it is by pervasive economic interdependence and great intensity of trade—would be premature at this time because it would impose constraints on the member countries that at present would be unbearable. When target zone commitments are made, a country may not be obligated to defend the rate at a certain margin, but a country is expected to do just that.

Therefore, it is much more rational not to focus on intervention obligations in the field of exchange rates as such but to bring into the consultation process the whole gamut of economic policies that influence exchange rates. In fact, that is the message delivered by the Rambouillet communiqué (in paragraph 11, I think); and that is the main message contained in recent texts of the IMF, such as the draft article IV and the proposed decision on surveillance of exchange rates. At the moment I fail to see why we should go over this field once more; it has been explored from all sides. In the Common Market the performances of national economies are as divergent as those of countries outside the Common Market. Why should exchange rates be considered the main test of coordination in such a state of affairs?

For one thing, we do not know what an equilibrium rate is, even though the IMF guidelines for floating would advise us to consider such a rate and to devise a path that over a period of some four years would bring us to it. This, I think, is utopian, especially in a period that can be characterized by the very interesting quotation from Dick Cooper in Balassa's paper about the impossibility of integrating trade unions across frontiers. Since trade unions cannot be integrated and unions in various countries behave in an economically irresponsible way, and since national governments and central banks have no other course but to create the money needed to finance excessive wage claims, how can partner countries be protected from imported inflation except by floating rates? Where would a system of target rates take us in such conditions?

The process cannot avoid being progressive, and we are doing something in the Common Market, by small steps, to get trade unions to give more serious consideration to the imperatives of economic stability than they do today in most countries. Horst Schulmann, who is at this conference, is very much occupied with an attempt to bring the social partners together and get them to talk about medium-term and short-term targets, as well as about economic policy in general. I hope he will choose to say a few words on this. He knows much more about it than I.

I would also mention—this is no mere joke—the emerging Eurocommunism movement that may help. Berlinguer in Italy seems convinced of the necessity of organizing Europe in a framework that would protect it from Soviet domination. The communist leaders in Spain and France are gradually moving toward the same position. Interesting news on this subject appears in an article by George Kennan in a recent issue of the British magazine *Encounter*.[1] This trend may prove very important in tackling the as yet intractable task of integrating trade unions.

Although I have already mentioned my high opinion of Balassa's paper, the third section, about financial organization, I think has been given more attention than it deserves. I wish it had been replaced by another subject. From the perspective of monetary union, which may be a little theoretical now, the kind of argument he develops there may be useful. But given the state of affairs today and the possibilities for tomorrow, I think the emphasis on financial organization and control of the Euromarket and on freedom of movement of capital in the Common Market is very premature.

Even if one does not place too much faith in exchange controls, they may have a restraining influence on short-term capital movements in certain circumstances. Belgium is one example of a generally liberal country where a modicum of exchange control as an adjunct to an appropriate monetary policy—in this case a very courageous monetary policy—proved capable of offsetting financial flows and preventing them from drowning the whole banking and monetary system.

I feel something is lacking in Balassa's paper as well as in all the papers prepared for this conference. When I was told that there was going to be a conference on U.S.-European monetary relations, I expected to participate in debates on, and to read papers about, the famous "asymmetry" between the dollar and other currencies. Attempts were made to solve this problem during the doomed attempt to reform the international monetary system. My expectations were reinforced when I learned that Fred Bergsten was going to exercise important responsibilities in the new administration. I immediately ordered his latest book and read it. This book confirmed what had become clear to many observers—that the American economy had shrunk relative to the world and that the economic bases of the dollar were no longer sufficient to bear all the burden associated with the role of single key international currency. Asymmetry, once perhaps an unavoidable fact of life, had become a very dangerous way of living.[2]

In fact, before Fred Bergsten, Ronald McKinnon had written a brilliant essay, that contained similar findings and gave a recipe for

---

[1] "From Containment to Self-Containment: A Conversation with George F. Kennan," *Encounter*, September 1976, especially part 8.

[2] C. Fred Bergsten, *The Dilemmas of the Dollar* (New York: New York University Press, 1975).

action.[3] Now Lamfalussy comes to about the same conclusion when he says that Europeans would be well advised not to forget the role played by the dollar crisis in wrecking their hopes of monetary union.

It is hard to imagine even an approximate stability of intra-European exchange rates without continued confidence in the dollar or, to put it more pointedly, without a fair degree of stability in the dollar–deutsche mark rate. We cannot put too much faith in the present "nonsystem" to produce a state of affairs that will ensure effective stability between these two currencies. Moreover, I am told that Bergsten's academic views on the subject may not be awarded a very high order of priority by the new administration.

This conference seems to be tending to the conclusion that the implementation of a scheme for common exchange management in the Common Market would be extremely difficult, if not outright premature or otherwise impossible, and that the results would at best be problematic. This leaves a pretty narrow choice for action in this field in Europe.

The only possibility I can see is the development of the Europa that is the subject of the papers Thygesen, Basevi, and Vaubel will present later. In my opinion, the Europa should be at the center of a conference on U.S.-European monetary relations. I find it very strange that these three authors have given ground to the criticism that Thygesen recalls in the last paragraph of his paper. He says that American observers of the European monetary scene have often been struck with the inward-looking nature of the debate on this subject.

We have been speaking about monetary problems from a purely internal European point of view. But it has another dimension, which is precisely the lack of a possibility of having something different from what we had in the past in the international framework. Of course, we have fluctuating rates now. But they will not protect us from commotions that—as we have been warned by Lamfalussy—may derive from policies regarding the dollar on which we Europeans have nothing to say.

Cairncross said that the European Monetary Cooperative Fund (EMCF) was rather useless. I do not agree at all. I am surprised that van Ypersele didn't mention that, during the perturbations of 1976, recourse to the facilities of the EMCF was of great importance to the countries that were suffering from speculation, that is, Belgium and Denmark. I don't remember exactly the sums involved, but they were

---

[3] Ronald I. McKinnon, "A New Tripartite Monetary Agreement or a Limping Dollar Standard?" Princeton Essays in International Finance, no. 106 (October 1974).

enormous, running into billions of units of account. This is useful because, however short the "very short-term credit" can be, it provides at least six months' respite to a hard-pressed currency, and for part of this time for an unlimited amount. For a currency like the Belgian franc, which was very hard pressed, to obtain a six months' access to such credit was of considerable importance.[4] Central banks, however, may not wait for the moment when the period of grace lapses; when the current market trend is reversed—and the very short-term credit helps them to do just that—they may prefer to buy back the currency they have had to sell in the market and repay earlier than they have to. I therefore think the scheme is very useful.

In fact, the importance of an international institution is not to be measured by the amount of money it wields. Money is a very important factor, but it is not the only one at work. If we were to press the point, we would be coming very close to the argument about the Pope's legions. Not long ago I read the proceedings of the annual meeting of the American Economic Association, which, all would agree, is a serious and respectable body. In that meeting a very respectable economist compared the IMF to an empty shell. He described a time when the fund, though provided with more money than now, wielded so little authority because of the demise of the Bretton Woods system that various voices were heard calling for its merger with the World Bank. Depending on the points of view and circumstances, these things can change very quickly. These days, when politics play a very important part in monetary and economic matters, the effectiveness of an organization is not measured only by the amount of money it can spend on a country, precisely because the money may be used in a way that is gratifying to the politicians, but not necessarily to the economists.

---

[4] An intervention from the floor offered a correction: "Six weeks, not six months!" In response Boyer de la Giroday said, "Six weeks, yes, as far as unlimited credit is concerned, but the credit can be renewed up to a certain quota for a period not exceeding six months."

PART
FOUR

NEXT STEPS IN EUROPEAN INTEGRATION

INTRODUCTION AND SUMMARY
OF OPTICA PROPOSALS

Niels Thygesen

The latest several steps in the economic integration of the European Community have not been in a forward direction. Europe of the 1960s presents in retrospect a picture of stability and slowly progressing integration. It is ironic that the optimism that these experiences generated at the political level found expression only at the very end of the decade —at the Hague summit in December 1969—just before irresistible centrifugal forces began to eat away at its foundations. From the Hague summit and the elaboration of the concept of economic and monetary union in the so-called Werner plan of 1970 there is a remarkable descent to the present level of what is thought feasible. A few points will suffice to illustrate the main trend in economic policy coordination.

The major decisions of the Council of Ministers in March 1971 and March 1972 to establish firmer rules for exchange market interventions did not stick. The pound sterling and the lira have been floating individually and with increasingly dramatic movements since June 1972 and March 1973 respectively and the French franc since January 1974 (with an interruption during part of 1975–1976). The remaining snake

Note: *Towards Economic Equilibrium and Monetary Unification in Europe* (Optica 1975) and *Inflation and Exchange Rates: Evidence and Policy Guidelines for the European Community* (Optica 1976) were published by the Directorate General for Economic and Financial Affairs of the Commission of the EC in January 1976 and February 1977 respectively. The reports were prepared by a group of independent economists consisting of Giorgio Basevi (Bologna), who acted as our chairman throughout; Emil-Maria Claassen (Giessen and Paris) during Optica 1975; Paul de Grauwe (Leuven) during Optica 1976; Pascal Salin (Paris); Hans-Eckhardt Scharrer (Hamburg) during Optica 1976; and Niels Thygesen (Copenhagen). The opinions expressed in the reports remain the sole responsibility of the group and not of the commission and its services. The work of the group was greatly assisted by Hermann Burgard and Francis Woehrling during Optica 1975 and by Michele Fratianni and Horst Schulmann during Optica 1976. I am also grateful for critical comments made at the Washington conference, in particular by Bela Balassa, Stephen Marris, Conrad Oort, and Roland Vaubel. The responsibility for any errors and obscurities in the present introduction and summary rests solely with the present author. The paper was revised in June 1977, but has not been updated to take into account developments in 1978, notably the adoption of the European Monetary System.

has not imposed any closer explicit policy coordination and the cross-rates between the currencies in this enlarged deutsche mark zone have had to be adjusted on several occasions. There has been no common facing up in the community to the problem of sharing the overall external deficit, made unavoidable by the explosion of oil prices in 1973 and 1974; two member countries (West Germany and the Netherlands) have been in sizable current surplus, most of the others, like other European countries, in large deficit. The common agricultural policy is in deep crisis because of the refusal of governments to accept the domestic price adjustments required by the exchange-rate changes. Restrictions on capital movements have expanded in recent years. The community members and institutions have played a secondary role in financing the external deficits of the most exposed members.

The list is long enough. Even though useful habits of cooperation have developed—for example, in concerted interventions and other technical matters among the central banks and in the consultations before global meetings such as the IMF and North-South dialogue—the overall picture is hardly modified. The most positive statement that can be made is that a liberal trade system continues to operate. However, as countries come to realize that their external imbalances do not respond much to exchange-rate changes, they become increasingly ready to consider protectionist initiatives to modify an external constraint they find imposing unpalatable consequences on them.

The change in mood since 1970 is even more striking. The time horizon is short, and the impatience with more ambitious and longer run ideas is considerable. To take an example, the Council of Ministers has never carefully reviewed the report submitted at the end of 1975 by Prime Minister Tindemans on possible lines of evolution for the community. The proposal made in July 1976 by the Dutch finance minister, then president of the Council of Finance Ministers, to formulate target zones for exchange rates has not yet reappeared from the technical scrutiny to which it was subjected in the EC Monetary Committee, in particular.

How can one talk in a hopeful tone about the "next steps in European integration" in a climate where (1) previous steps have been backward or, at best, sideward, (2) few ideas reach the policy makers, and (3) the few ideas that do are shelved or given a dusty answer? The scope for making a constructive contribution is clearly limited.

One must give credit to the Commission of the EC for continuing in these unfavorable circumstances to explore with the cooperation of independent experts new approaches to European monetary union and the reasons the earlier attempts failed. Starting in 1973 several such groups, consisting largely of university economists, have been drawing up reports. The two Optica reports, of which Basevi and I are co-authors, are only the most recent of those specializing in possible new initiatives in monetary and exchange-rate cooperation.[1] Other lines of specialization, for example, fiscal integration and the community budget, might in retrospect have been more productive.

It is important to realize that in this conference on U.S.-European monetary relations we shall be discussing proposals at three different levels for the next steps in European integration. I am here abstracting from the level of immediate political realities, where the next steps—as I have argued above—are hardly being discussed seriously at the present time.

The paper presented by Vaubel to the conference represents the most ambitious level of proposals. It is an approach that embodies gradual monetary unification and monetary reform in Europe through the introduction of a parallel currency with highly attractive features as a unit of account and a store of value. This parallel currency would gradually replace national currencies, making exchange-rate changes between them irrelevant, or indeed impossible, and it would bring within reach the considerable welfare gains in having only one money.

The least ambitious of the three levels of proposals is that represented at this conference by the papers of Oort and Balassa. I do not say this in any derogatory sense, because their proposals are still very advanced relative to current official thinking. They consist of the introduction of target zones (or reference rates) for the effective exchange rates of the individually floating EEC currencies and for the snake in order to trigger consultations on policy coordination among member countries. They also introduce a wider use of a parallel currency based on the European unit of account (EUA).

In this hierarchy of proposals the Optica report occupies the middle ground. We combine constraints on the use of exchange rates—thereby going well beyond the discretionary and informal arrangements envisaged by Oort and Balassa—with the introduction of a parallel currency of an intermediate kind: not as strong as the fully indexed one, but more attractive as a unit and store of value than the EUA.

Occupying the middle ground is not a comfortable position, because one is likely to be under double attack. From the side of Vaubel we are attacked for sacrificing what economic logic requires in favor

---

[1] Two precursors pursuing a broader approach to integration are *Report on Economic Integration and Monetary Union* (October 1973) and *Report of the Study Group "Economic and Monetary Union 1980"* (March 1975). Both documents have appeared in stenciled form from the Commission of the EC.

of political expediency. To use his phrase, the Optica reports are "teeming with political realism." From the side of Oort we are criticized for being overambitious and politically counterproductive in proposing exchange-rate management by objective indicators. Unfortunately, both our critics may be right; we cannot take comfort in assuming that these criticisms cancel each other out. Nevertheless, with that risk in mind, let me summarize our report and proposals.

Summary of Some Main Points Raised in Optica 1975 and 1976

It is natural to deal with the two reports as a whole. The 1975 report is largely theoretical, putting forward propositions and hypotheses for testing, while the 1976 report is partly empirical, partly normative. All references in the following are to the 1976 report.

The analysis of the Optica group may conveniently be summarized under the three chapter headings of the 1976 report: (1) Origins and consequences of exchange-rate changes; (2) Enforcing purchasing power parity (PPP) in the exchange markets: A rule for the convergence of inflation rates at a low level; and (3) The attractiveness of a European parallel currency (EPC).

Inflation and Exchange Rates. On the subject of the origins and consequences of exchange-rate changes our work starts from the general notion that *monetary union can be viewed as an institutional organization among countries aiming at economic union such as to minimize the inefficiencies inherent in the use and control of money within the union.* Welfare considerations, to which we shall return in dealing with the EPC, arising from the uses of money as a unit of account, a means of payment, and a store of value, point toward the adoption of a single currency or at least of irrevocably fixed exchange rates among currencies in the economic union. But minimizing the inefficiencies in using money by going this far implies the unification of monetary policy at the union level. This implication will be undesirable if national control of monetary variables (the money stock and the exchange rate) adds in an important way to the possibilities of influencing real variables (employment, output, and the terms of trade). The crucial question, then, for striking a proper balance in the design of a monetary union between these potentially conflicting considerations is to what extent and over what time horizon exchange-rate changes have an impact on real variables.

There is no doubt that there has been a significant difference between the views of policy makers and their immediate advisers on the one hand and a growing number of outside economists on the other. Policy makers would stress the need for exchange-rate flexibility to exploit rigidities in price and wage formation and obtain some real effects. Outside economists would argue that these effects are short-run and hardly worth exploiting. There would be general agreement that a country may be prepared to have an inflation rate different from the average inflation rate of the union to which it belongs and that exchange-rate flexibility is necessary to preserve this option. There will be additional scope for influencing the wealth and income distributions between debtors and creditors and between the money-issuing authority and the money users (the "inflation tax"). Recognition that countries exhibit different "national propensities to inflate"[2] does not ensure agreement between the two groups, because the outside economists tend to regard such differences as predominantly "political"—linked to differences in national views of unemployment-inflation trade-offs and in monetary-fiscal policies pursued—rather than as necessary consequences of differences in economic structure. As arguments for exchange-rate flexibility, they are on a different footing from the central issue whether exchange-rate changes have real effects in the sense defined above or whether they are caused by differences in structure. The distinction is crucial also to the proposal for exchange-rate management that we develop.

In the first chapter of Optica 1976, we aim to place this debate at the empirical level where is belongs.[3] We draw on three types of evidence: (1) conformity of observed changes in bilateral or effective exchange rates with differentials in national inflation rates, (2) a brief review of national mechanisms for transmitting imported inflation (depreciation and/or a rise in "world market" prices), and (3) a more detailed study of the effects of depreciation in the United Kingdom and Italy. The evidence supports the general view that the effects of exchange-rate changes tend to become very largely nominal after a rather short time span and that this pattern is becoming clearer as one moves into the recent period.

Our review of the conformity of exchange-rate changes with PPP is based on several possible price indexes and base periods and on both bilateral and effective rates. Some of our main results for a longer time

---

[2] A term introduced by Giovanni Magnifico, *European Monetary Unification* (London: Macmillan, 1973), pp. 62–81.

[3] In the same spirit as Vaubel, who also applies the distinction between political and economic motives for preserving exchange-rate flexibility inside the community; see Roland Vaubel, "Real Exchange-Rate Changes in the European Community: The Empirical Evidence and Its Implications for European Currency Unification," *Weltwirtschaftliches Archiv*, no. 3 (Tübingen, 1976), pp. 432 ff.

FIGURE 1
INFLATION DIFFERENCES AND CHANGES IN DEUTSCHE MARK AND EFFECTIVE EXCHANGE RATES
(compound average annual rates)

Inflation Differences and Changes in Deutsche Mark Exchange Rates 1961–1975

Inflation Differences and Changes in Effective Exchange Rates 1963–1975

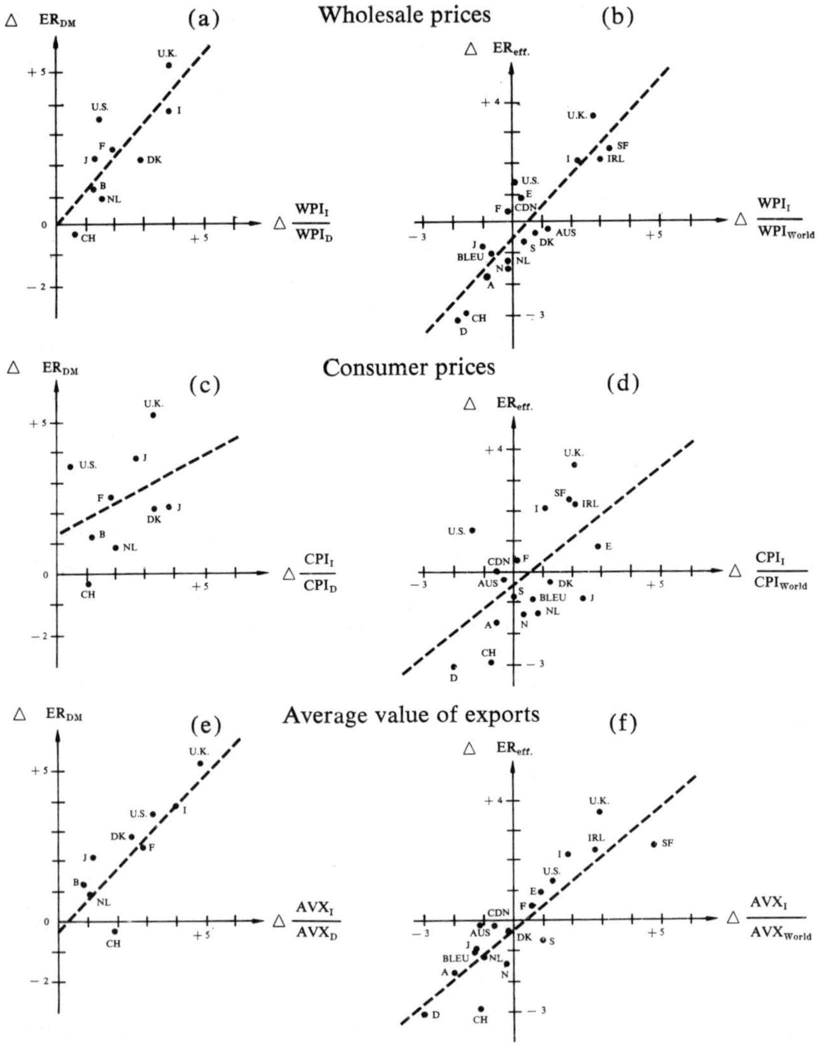

NOTE: Effective rates are doubly weighted by export shares.

SOURCE: *Inflation and Exchange Rates: Evidence and Policy Guidelines for the European Community* (Optica 1976) (Brussels: Commission of the European Communities, 1977), p. 12.

span are those presented in Figure 1. We find, as have other studies, that regressing changes in exchange rates on inflation differentials "explains" the major part of observed rate changes when either wholesale price or average export value indexes are used to measure inflation differentials. The correspondence is greatly weakened when consumer price indexes are used. This is, indeed, what earlier studies and the notion of "productivity bias," originally introduced by Balassa, would lead us to expect. Consumer price indexes cover a far larger group of nontraded goods and of services than do other measures of price and cost trends, and price changes for such goods and services are much less effectively aligned with a common international trend. The productivity bias casts severe doubt on the usefulness of testing PPP by means of consumer prices, even among a fairly homogeneous group of countries.[4]

More interesting than these fairly standard results are three further conclusions that emerged from our calculations:

- Conformity with PPP is considerably better when effective rather than bilateral—vis-à-vis the deutsche mark—exchange rates are used.
- Conformity with PPP is no worse for a broad sample of sixteen to eighteen industrial countries than for the members of the community.
- Wholesale prices serve nearly as well as export prices in the PPP tests.

The first point is of considerable practical importance because it has a direct bearing on how rules for exchange-rate management might be formulated in the community. There are several possibilities here: effective rates, bilateral rates vis-à-vis the single most important currency (deutsche mark) or the rate vis-à-vis some average of other community currencies, such as calculated in the European unit of account. Our calculations suggest that if, in guiding exchange markets, one wants to use the long-run equilibrium relationship embodied in PPP, it is the effective rate version that should be used. This raises certain complications in relation to the snake, which is a bilaterally

---

[4] For this reason we feel uneasy about interpreting departures from PPP of national consumer price indexes as a measure of "real exchange rate changes" as suggested by Vaubel, ibid. We think such departures should be seen as caused—apart from differences in the composition of national indexes—mainly by productivity bias. We recognize, however, that the aim of Vaubel's work was different from ours, namely, to study the implications for national inflation rates of adopting a fixed exchange-rate system for the EEC.

oriented system; we return to these matters in our proposals for exchange-rate management in chapter 2 of the 1976 report.

The second point may appear surprising since the interpenetration of the European economies could be expected to have led to more nearly parallel cost and price trends between them than in a wider area. That this expectation is not fulfilled may be seen most clearly in calculations for the post-Smithsonian period. In Optica 1976 (p. 62), we compare the effective rate and PPP of the deutsche mark vis-à-vis the currencies of sixteen to eighteen other industrial countries with the trade-weighted exchange rate and PPP of the deutsche mark vis-à-vis (1) six other community currencies, (2) the snake currencies including the French franc, and (3) the snake currencies excluding the French franc. Nowhere is the conformity with PPP over the four years following the Smithsonian agreement as close as for the average of sixteen to eighteen currencies; it is least close for the minisnake currencies (excluding the French franc) where the deutsche mark appeared undervalued by the end of 1975 and by the end of 1976, which is not shown in our graphs. Clearly we could not expect PPP to apply to exchange-rate relationships that are fixed through central bank interventions as in the snake; but the calculations serve as an illustration that the mechanisms that align national inflation rates measured in a common *numéraire* in a flexible rate system have worked more efficiently than the mechanisms that align national inflation rates measured in domestic currency when exchange rates are largely fixed. Put differently, there are no obvious economic grounds in past experiences for confining proposals for PPP-based management of exchange rates, such as those made later in Optica 1976, to countries in the EEC.

The third point is surprising since the pressure to keep national prices in line when measured in a common *numéraire* should be at a maximum for export goods and somewhat weaker for the broader range of goods covered by wholesale price indexes. However, the quality of national indexes of average export values is more uncertain than that of other price series.[5] These statistical defects and the more comprehensive information contained in wholesale prices made us concentrate on the latter. It is possible that further experimentation would have been warranted, for example, with a weighted average of the available cost and price indicators along lines used in some OECD presentations. Yet the virtue of simplicity will become evident if the PPP calculations have an operational purpose in guiding exchange-rate management.

---

[5] This also applies to unit labor cost (ULC) indexes. We report several calculations with ULC data in an annex to Optica 1976, but the irregularities appeared too great to base any further analysis on a ULC-based formulation of PPP.

In view of the evidence we have collected on the conformity of effective exchange-rate changes with PPP as calculated from wholesale prices we disagree with Balassa and others who have argued that indexes of relative costs and prices are notoriously unreliable as possible quantitative indicators for exchange-rate decisions.[6] In the cross-section study of the effective exchange-rate changes for eighteen currencies from 1963 to 1975 reported in Figure 1 we found that 80 percent of the variability of rate changes was "explained" by differential movements in wholesale prices. The relationship is an excessively simple one, and it does not give any insight into the causal mechanisms at work. Yet it seems to us too good to be overlooked as a prime objective indicator for exchange-rate adjustments. Over longer periods one would not be upsetting equilibrium relationships by forcing exchange-rate movements to conform to PPP; such conformity *is* the long-run pattern in a system of flexible rates. But there may be costs of abandoning the freedom to deviate from this pattern in the short run. To study these issues we require an analysis of the shorter run effects of moving the exchange rate.

We have approached this problem mainly through econometric models of the economies of the United Kingdom and Italy, the two countries that have inflated and devalued the most. This may give our conclusions a bias, since it is not obvious that they apply symmetrically to countries that have inflated less than the average and have revalued.

We had hoped to base our comparative work more broadly—and to develop also more of a feel for the role of openness, the criterion used by McKinnon[7] in defining an optimal currency area—in determining the effectiveness of exchange-rate changes. In view of the shortage of comparable and comprehensive models, such a study of the transmission of inflation did not prove feasible. We do report, however, some preliminary results based on 1970 input-output tables for the community countries, which suggest that they are not very different in their degree of openness. The share of traded goods in total output appears to be fairly uniform; and the elasticity of consumer prices with respect to a change in the effective exchange rate is close to one-half in all the countries, rising to two-thirds if one assumes full indexation of wages on consumer prices. Thus the direct price effects, even in the absence

[6] Bela Balassa, "Monetary Arrangements in the European Common Market," *Banca Nazionale del Lavoro Quarterly Review*, Rome, December 1976. Balassa also argues that available price indexes do not pay attention to prices for services and that they may be misleading indicators if capital movements are important.

[7] Ronald I. McKinnon, "Optimum Currency Areas," *American Economic Review*, vol. 53 (December 1963), p. 717.

of indexation, are strong.[8] They are compounded by factors neglected in the simple input-output framework, notably derived demand and monetary effects.

In analyzing the experiences of the United Kingdom and Italy we focus on three aspects of the impact of exchange-rate changes: (1) the time profile of the current account, (2) the assertion that an external impact depends upon sustained changes in the government accounts, and (3) the time profile of costs and prices.

In the case of the United Kingdom the report draws on three recent econometric studies of increasing comprehensiveness.[9] In the case of Italy, the group was able, with the help of Professor Basevi, to perform a number of simulations, similar to those for the United Kingdom, on a large-scale econometric model of the Italian economy.[10] The evidence is not easy to summarize briefly, but these are the main conclusions we have drawn:

The first of the three United Kingdom studies concludes that devaluation has historically had favorable effects on the current account after a brief initial worsening (J-curve effect). Artus's work on the effects of the 1967 devaluation is, however, of a partial-equilibrium nature; fiscal policy is assumed to be adjusted so as to keep aggregate demand unchanged. The second study, by Burns and Warburton, also leaves some scope for a drawn-out impact of devaluation on the current account, particularly at less than full employment and if bolstered by a pay pause. But in the long run the expenditure-switching effects of devaluation disappear, and the only way an improvement of the current account may be sustained is through the expenditure-reducing effects of non-index-linked government transfer payments— an uncertain and unlikely mechanism.

The third study, using the London Business School model, is the closest approximation to a general equilibrium model available for the

---

[8] Indexation has become more widespread in labor markets, and the time lags in the triggering of allowances have shortened. While this emerges clearly from a survey in an annex, it is difficult to detect any correlation between the inflation rate of individual countries and the degree of formal indexation. For example, Italy and the United Kingdom have in the past used indexation far less extensively than, say, Belgium or Denmark.

[9] J. R. Artus, "The 1967 Devaluation of the Pound Sterling," *IMF Staff Papers*, November 1975; T. Burns and P. J. Warburton, "International Aspects of the UK Inflation: Some Preliminary Empirical Results," unpublished, London Business School Econometric Forecasting Unit, 1975; and R. J. Ball, T. Burns, and J. S. E. Laury, "The Role of Exchange-Rate Changes in Balance-of-Payments Adjustment: The United Kingdom Case," *Economic Journal*, March 1977.

[10] Università di Bologna, *Il modello econometrico dell'Università di Bologna: struttura e simulazioni* (Bologna, 1976).

United Kingdom; it treats the government budget, though not the money supply, as endogenous. We have reviewed a number of simulations of the impact over the years 1975–1980 of a 20 percent devaluation at the beginning of 1975. There is a deterioration of the current account for five quarters (J-curve effect), which is absorbed only after ten quarters. Ultimately the improvement of the current account corresponds to 0.7 percent of GNP; there is a similar improvement in the government accounts.

For Italy we have looked at two simulations for six-year periods—1963–1968 and 1975–1980—and the answers are somewhat different. In the early period there is, after a sharp deterioration in the first year and only a modest improvement in the second, a steady strengthening of the current account because of an incomplete transmission of the devaluation into domestic costs and prices. In the 1975–1980 period this positive effect has nearly vanished; for every percentage point devaluation of the effective exchange rate for the lira, the current account at the end of the 1975–1980 period improves by only 0.12 percent of the sum of exports and imports as against 0.68 percent at the end of the 1963–1968 period, illustrating vividly the diminishing effectiveness of exchange-rate changes.

The assertion that any improvement in the current account is linked to a strengthening of government finances is associated with the "New Cambridge School" in the United Kingdom. It is broadly confirmed by the simulations with the London Business School model, in which, as reported above, devaluation generates a parallel improvement in the current and government accounts. If the latter are constrained to show no improvement, the deficit being kept at the level of the control simulation, the strengthening of the current account also vanishes, and the model leaves us with the short-run deterioration as the only likely effect of the devaluation.[11] Thus the New Cambridge School position finds support; however, there is no causal relationship from the government budget to the current account, rather a reminder that some movements in both have a common cause—devaluation and inflation.

In the London Business School model, domestic inflation in the long run—that is, at the end of the five- to six-year simulation period—fully offsets devaluation. After two years three-fourths of the devaluation has shown up in export prices, more than 60 percent in wages and consumer prices. Very similar conclusions are found in the Italian model

---

[11] The Italian model is not equipped to throw light on the New Cambridge School hypothesis; the government accounts are largely exogenous, and the simulations cannot adequately capture how the additional inflation generated by devaluation affects government expenditure and revenue.

for the 1970s, whereas in the 1963–1968 period the response of domestic costs and prices was slower and less complete, with wages and consumer prices rising ultimately by only 60 to 70 percent of the devaluation. This is, of course, the counterpart to the permanent improvement in the Italian current account reported above.

The Optica group's review of selected empirical evidence on the origins and consequences of exchange-rate changes has confirmed the view that a country's exchange rate is, in the European economies in the late 1970s, very largely a nominal phenomenon. On the one hand, its movements in a system of flexible exchange rates tend to offset the differential between domestic and foreign inflation rates, appropriately measured. On the other hand, the more detailed review of the British and Italian experiences suggests that sizable downward movements of the effective rates for the pound and the lira have been offset to a large and increasing extent by more rapid inflation, leaving only few traces on the current account and on domestic real variables. While the impact on real variables is not completely negligible over short periods—and may be enlarged by government action on prices and incomes—the usefulness of exchange-rate changes in effecting macroeconomic adjustments seems more limited than is generally believed. Particularly as regards external adjustment, the time between the initial change in the current account in the "wrong" direction (the J-curve effect) and the ultimate phase when domestic costs and prices have fully embodied the exchange-rate change appears to have shortened so much as to make such changes undesirable.

Policy Guidelines for Exchange Rates. If one accepts the conclusion that exchange-rate changes in European economies in the late 1970s have become largely unsuitable for purposes other than that of permitting different national inflation rates, three main policy implications may be drawn. One may wish to:

1. introduce policy measures and structural changes designed to restore to the exchange-rate mechanism a greater degree of effectiveness in bringing about real adjustment
2. subject the divergences in national inflation rates to a careful cost-benefit analysis, aiming to show that by far the larger part of the divergence of inflation rates in the mid-1970s is due to divergent monetary and fiscal policies, which have done little to facilitate the attainment of high and stable activity levels; or, to take a stronger line, argue that adjusting to a common and low inflation rate and a high degree of fixity of exchange rates would entail lower costs and higher benefits than is generally believed

3. accept that national inflation rates will continue to differ for a
long time because the costs of adjusting to a common rate are
important, but restrain the use of the exchange-rate changes in
the short run to their nominal role of offsetting inflation differentials in the long run.

Much national policy discussion centers on position 1. Governments have been aiming, particularly through direct interventions in
wage and price formation, to lower inflation rates and obviate the need
for exchange-rate adjustments. When such adjustments have taken
place, incomes policies have been introduced to "make devaluation
stick." There is not much evidence that they have been successful
except in a very transitory sense. In fact, national inflationary mechanisms have become faster and more comprehensive over the past
decade; it seems unlikely that a sizable measure of exchange-rate
illusion could be reintroduced after a period when these illusions have
been so effectively dispelled. The Optica reports do not pursue this
approach despite its topicality in some countries.

The group has not pursued the second approach either, despite
a basically sympathetic view of this position, which is the logical
opposite of the first. In explicit and practical terms, it leads to
recommendations of strong policy harmonization, particularly in the
monetary field, and to the introduction of a parallel currency attrac-
tively designed to reduce the role of national currencies rapidly. With
these pressures from both sides, the issue of exchange-rate changes
would fade into the background; with the main common cause of
inflation differentials and exchange-rate changes—divergent monetary
and fiscal policies—under surveillance and the role of national currencies reduced, adjusting exchange rates would become both unnecessary and ineffective. This approach was taken in the *Economist
Manifesto*,[12] which was signed by, among others, three members of the
Optica group.

Positions 2 and 3 are not irreconcilable, and support for both
should not be regarded as evidence of schizophrenia. In the Optica
reports we have deemphasized the longer run approach taken in the
second position, not on grounds of economic logic but because it

[12] Giorgio Basevi and others, "The All Saints' Day Manifesto for European
Monetary Union," *The Economist* (London), November 1, 1975, pp. 33–38. The
signers were Giorgio Basevi, Michele Fratianni, Herbert Giersch, Pieter Korteweg,
David O'Mahoney, Michael Parkin, Theo Peeters, Pascal Salin, and Niels
Thygesen. For an elaboration of this approach, see also Michael Parkin, "Monetary
Union and Economic Stability in the EEC," *Banca Nazionale del Lavoro
Quarterly Review*, Rome, June 1976.

seemed too far removed from what is feasible. It would not be a "next step in European integration" but would be seen by governments as a giant leap; the negotiations leading to it might not get started at all. This is a case of the best being the enemy of the good. The Optica group advocates the third approach, that is, the PPP rule in exchange markets combined with an attractive European parallel currency, as the handmaiden to progress toward the goal of a European monetary union, which we share with advocates of the second group.

Since Basevi has in his paper explained the design of the rules for exchange-rate management that we propose, it is possible to confine the present summary to very general remarks. The proposal is inspired by two elements in addition to the evidence on conformity with PPP described above: the phenomena of overshooting, instability, and "vicious circles" in exchange markets observed particularly in 1976, and new thinking on asymmetrical invention systems and "reference rates" as developed in papers by Ethier and Bloomfield, Williamson, and Oort.[13]

The first of these sources of inspiration is the experience that causation in the inflation–exchange-rates nexus may at times run from the latter to the former rather than the other way, as discussions of PPP usually imply. As in the case of the pound and lira depreciations in 1976, exchange rates have at times moved quite a bit further than could be justified in the light of past inflation differentials. Such temporary departures from PPP will tend to justify themselves, as the depreciation feeds into domestic costs and prices through the rise in the prices of traded goods and derived inflationary effects. It is possible to check some of these effects by a more restrictive monetary policy but, since wages and prices are not sufficiently flexible, only at considerable short-run costs in unemployment.

It is possible that exchange-market operators have moved ahead of PPP because of a basically correct view of the policies likely to be followed in the devaluing country. In that case they may just be accelerating a process without necessarily affecting the long-run outcome. But it is a very real possibility that they will overreact because of incomplete information and, particularly, that they will, on their interpretation of past experience, fail to register a change in policy attitudes. When such overreactions take on important dimensions, it

---

[13] W. Ethier and A. I. Bloomfield, "Managing the Managed Float," Princeton Essays in International Finance, no. 112 (October 1975); John Williamson, "The Future Exchange Rate Regime," *Banca Nazionale del Lavoro Quarterly Review*, June 1975; and C. J. Oort, "Exchange-Rate Policy in the European Communities," *Common Market Law Review*, August 1976.

seems well justified to check them through interventions in exchange markets. Such interventions will reinforce, or indeed make possible, noninflationary monetary policies.

It would take us too far here to check to what extent the vicious circle hypothesis, which has gained some ground in the analysis of inflation trends, is empirically founded.[14] The view of the Optica reports is (1) that the vicious circle—interpreted as an additional and partly independent source of inflation rather than as a self-perpetuating movement—has been sufficiently important to warrant special action and (2) that the proposed PPP rule provides an operational, though admittedly crude, additional way of breaking the circle.

The other inspiration is the asymmetrical intervention obligations contained in the "reference rate" proposals developed over the past three years by several economists. In relation to the present proposal, the asymmetry comes in by regarding inflation differentials as the upper limit for exchange-rate changes. Thus no country would be allowed to depress its own depreciated currency by selling or push up its own appreciated currency by buying when it is valued at PPP. However, actions to keep the movements in exchange rates narrower than PPP would suggest are possible.

It is difficult to assess the prospects for the adoption of the proposals. They may, indeed, look naively specific and rigid in light of the present tendency in the EEC and the IMF to move away from objective indicators for exchange-rate adjustments and toward vaguer and more discretionary criteria. What we claim for our proposal is (1) absence of long-run distortions and (2) simplicity and automaticity. The proposal is indeed at a lower level of intellectual ambition than the solution of a multilateral exchange-rate model carried out at the IMF and the OECD in preparation of the exchange-rate adjustments of the Smithsonian agreement in 1971. But we cannot pretend to know as much about what an equilibrium rate structure is as we thought we knew in 1971; external equilibrium seems consistent with a range of exchange-rate constellations.

In any case simplicity and automaticity are real virtues. PPP

---

[14] See, for example, Bank for International Settlements, *Annual Report 1975/76* (Basle, June 1976). For a critical view of the hypothesis, see T. Willett's paper in this volume. What may be overlooked by opponents of this critical view is that, even when market operators hold rational expectations, shifts in the supply and demand functions for financial assets denominated in a certain currency will cause the exchange rate of that currency to overreact; see, for example, W. H. Branson, "Asset Markets and Relative Prices in Exchange-Rate Determination," *Institute for International Economic Studies Seminar Papers*, no. 66 (Stockholm, 1976).

comparisons have implicitly or explicitly formed the basis for most of the exchange-rate evaluation in recent years, in the snake and in the community as a whole. The proposed PPP rule will not, therefore, appear so unfamiliar to officials as to ban it from consideration for that reason.

The operation of a PPP rule based on effective exchange rates creates problems in relation to the snake, which fixes bilateral rates. Technically, the neatest solution would be to manage each snake currency according to the PPP rule, thus creating symmetry between all community currencies. It would clearly be unrealistic, however, given the political commitment to the survival of the snake. And to propose the abandonment of the snake would be inconsistent with the aims of breaking the depreciation-inflation circle, of stabilizing exchange rates, and of harmonizing inflation rates at a low level. The Optica group envisages the continuation of the snake, but with either its dominant currency, the deutsche mark, or the weighted average of snake currencies conforming to the PPP rule. This might not make a great difference relative to past practice, since the deutsche mark has on the whole conformed well to PPP, but it would no doubt induce stronger pressures for policy coordination inside the snake.

The proposed intervention system may look permissive, in that it permits national inflation rates to continue to differ. Yet we feel justified in saying that the proposal would tend to harmonize inflation rates at a low level. The scheme would help to check vicious circles, and the intervention obligations would be conditional on the observance of certain minimum standards in domestic monetary policies, in particular nonsterilization of external imbalances. We see the intervention rules as a desirable complement to closer harmonization of monetary policies, not as an alternative to such harmonization. We have not felt able to make detailed suggestions for domestic monetary policies, since this presupposes better empirical knowledge about the monetary interactions of the European economies.[15]

A European Parallel Currency. The idea of a European parallel currency (EPC) has reappeared many times over the past six years. In Optica we have left aside those versions that confine the EPC to official use or to purely accounting functions. In terms of welfare and efficiency

---

[15] The Commission of the EC has recently launched an empirical study of the interdependence of money and credit markets in the community. This work, to be coordinated by M. Fratianni, may provide some of the background for developing the domestic monetary policy counterparts to the type of exchange-rate rule proposed here.

the attractions of a common full-scale money for private use are considerable. The introduction of money in a barter economy frees resources previously engaged in finding "appropriate" exchange rates between goods. The gains from a common money in Europe, freeing the sizable resources now engaged in exchange-market activity in a broad sense, are of the same nature, though obviously quantitatively less significant. In particular, the efficiency of money as a unit of account and standard of value has been gravely impaired in the environment of the past decade of inflation and exchange-rate flexibility.[16]

The nature of the welfare gains to be achieved depends, of course, on the characteristics of the new monetary asset. But there is a trade-off: the more attractive the EPC, the more rapidly it is likely to replace national currencies. The parallel currency would become the single money, forcing a premature monetary unification. It is more likely, however, that the process would not be allowed to run very far but that governments would wish to retain for some time their limited scope for managing their own money.

Optica 1975 reviewed a range of options for the EPC ranging from the existing European unit of account (EUA), which is a fixed-weight basket of all community currencies, to the fully indexed Europa proposed in the *Economist* Manifesto. It settled, mainly on grounds of political expediency, for an intermediate version to be discussed briefly below. But a few remarks on the options on either side may be helpful.

The EUA is currently in official use in the European Development Fund, the European Coal and Steel Community, and the European Investment Bank. The commission is preparing the ground for using it in the community budget, which would be a major step. There are no current plans for introducing it for accounting and settlement purposes in the European Monetary Cooperation Fund (EMCF) or in the common agricultural policy; nor are there any plans to extend its use into the private sector. The interest among banks in denominating loans in EUA has been minimal, even though it has been adopted in official uses by the community. As an average of the EEC currencies, it does lower exchange risk in a European perspective. But in an environment of high and divergent inflation rates, it is unattractive as a store of value relative to the least inflation prone of the currencies,

---

[16] The most penetrating analysis of the case for an EPC is Roland Vaubel, "The Parallel-Currency Approach to European Monetary Unification and the Search for a New European Unit of Account," prepared for the Commission of the European Communities study group, Unité Monétaire Européenne (Brussels, 1976).

notably the deutsche mark. While this could be compensated for by a higher interest rate, it is unlikely that, for example, West German residents would wish to hold EUA assets or enter into contracts denominated therein. The private use of an EPC with the characteristics of the EUA would probably remain limited.

The EPC proposed in the *Economist* Manifesto is a basket of currencies, in which the weights are adjusted to take account of both exchange-rate changes and national inflation rates. In summary, it is indexed on an average of European consumer prices, which greatly increases its attraction as a store of value and a unit of account.[17] If residents of community countries were given the option of converting their national currency assets into such an EPC, there is reason to believe that they would wish to do so on a substantial scale. For assets that do not serve as a means of payment, interest rates both in national currencies and in the inflation-proof EPC would have to adjust to reflect the expected appreciation of the EPC. Optica 1976 contains some calculations of the interest rate on assets denominated in one national currency (French francs) which would have been required just to offset ex post the appreciation of the EPC–French franc rate.

One main argument against the fully indexed EPC is that it might penetrate national financial markets too quickly for governments to be prepared to take the risk of allowing their residents to use it. This argument is less than fully convincing. In addition to the possibility of offsetting interest-rate movements, governments would have powerful means of influencing the speed of penetration of the EPC. If all transactions with public authorities, notably tax payments, had to take place in national currencies, this would put a strong brake on the penetration of the EPC into private uses; an exchange-rate risk would work against it. Obviously such measures by the authorities would diminish the efficiency gains from the EPC.

In Optica 1975 we were impressed with the idea that governments would not be ready to face the risks of a fully indexed EPC. We therefore outlined an alternative and intermediate version of the EPC in Optica 1975 and performed a number of computations to illustrate its properties together with those of the fully indexed EPC in Optica 1976.

In this intermediate version, the EPC offers protection against that part of national inflation that exceeds the national minimum inside the community. This amounts to creating an EPC with characteristics similar to the "strongest" EEC currency from the starting date of the

---

[17] For an example of how an indexed EPC works, see the *Economist* Manifesto.

scheme.[18] This currency need not be the same at all dates, although for the past decade the performance of West Germany as the least inflationary EEC economy has been without serious contender.

This particular definition of the EPC might therefore in practice become a complicated way for the community to move to a deutsche mark standard.[19] Such a step would have obvious efficiency advantages; the deutsche mark is a currency in which the potential users and holders would have confidence, which would ensure rapid penetration in other economies if the process were not checked. But it has drawbacks: control of the European money supply by one country would be acceptable neither to the other countries nor to the West German monetary authorities, who have shown no signs of welcoming the trend for the deutsche mark to become a reserve currency. It is unlikely, in other words, that the conflict between an expanding external role for the deutsche mark and the conduct of West German monetary policy could be reconciled. This prompts a reconsideration of moving toward a genuinely European money, managed in the long run by a European institution.

The fully indexed EPC would have these qualities (though it would initially be "managed" by the national central banks as they stand ready to exchange the national-currency assets of their residents against the EPC). The calculations made in Optica 1976 of the performance of the indexed-basket EPC did not substantiate our initial fears that the EPC would be so attractive as to flood the central banks with requests to move out of the national currency. Possibly the main problem would lie not so much with the European residents as with the potentially important role of an indexed EPC as an international reserve asset. It seems likely that the appearance of the EPC might cause large upsets in the international monetary system as official and private holders of dollars wanted to shift into the new asset. This is unfortunately not a problem discussed in the Optica reports or in the *Economist* Manifesto; nor are there any comments on how the international reserve role of the EPC could be restricted to acceptable proportions.[20] Such restrictions could hardly avoid curtailing the econ-

---

[18] Historically, "strength" has two dimensions. It may be defined as the currency that has experienced the least domestic inflation or as the currency that has appreciated the most. To the extent that PPP does not apply, the internal and the external indicators diverge; if the PPP rule suggested above is enforced, they will converge. The PPP rule would also make the complicated basket formulas for the EPC unnecessary; any national indexation formula would lead to the same result.

[19] This and the following paragraph contain some personal reflections on the rereading of Optica 1976 rather than a summary of the report.

[20] Some tentative remarks may be found in Balassa, "Monetary Arrangements in the European Common Market."

omies of scale and other efficiency gains of having the EPC, and rationing the supply of the EPC would also make it impossible to control its value according to the indexed-basket formula. These considerations leave a question mark hanging over the definition of the EPC: how to reconcile the need to make the new currency acceptable in European markets with the requirement not to upset the desired composition of international reserves too strongly.

The Next Steps

Over the past few years a number of formal or informal groups have made suggestions for the next steps to be taken in European integration. The Optica reports are the result of the efforts of one such group. Evidence on the inability of exchange-rate changes to bring about significant real adjustment has led us to our PPP rule for managing exchange rates so as to confine them to their nominal role also in the shorter run. We want to complement this with closer monetary and fiscal policy coordination and to reinforce integration by early issue of an attractive EPC.

In most of this, the Optica recommendations do not differ in basic approach from the policy recommendations made by several other groups or institutions.[21] We have chosen to be fairly specific because we have been disappointed with the vagueness and the large element of discretion that continue to mark discussions at the official level. By being more specific on indicators for exchange-rate management and on the definition, we hope to have injected a useful note, though one that will appear more vulnerable to critical comments.

It is important not to overlook in all the differentiated products available the common concern that new steps forward in European monetary cooperation are vital. There has been a constant bias in national official views in recent years, overstating the gains from having some freedom in managing national monies and their exchange rates and understating the welfare gains of monetary harmonization and of access to a less inflationary and more stable unit of account and store

---

[21] It would be natural to point to the recommendations of the group that has been meeting during 1976 under the chairmanship of the Earl of Cromer; see, in particular, the article in the *Times* (London) of July 26, 1976, in which the group recommends smoothing exchange-rate fluctuations, coordination of domestic policies, and issue of an EPC based on the EUA. The recent report of the West German Council of Economic Experts, *Zeit zum Investieren* (Stuttgart, November 1976), also contains a discussion of European monetary cooperation with many viewpoints similar to those in Optica, though with heavier emphasis on coordination of money supply (central bank money) targets.

of value. Official views are changing, but there is much scope for prodding them to reduce and eliminate this bias.

American observers of the European monetary scene have often been struck with the inward-looking nature of the debate. Such a comment might also be prompted by a reading of Optica. Yet it should be kept in mind that many of its conclusions apply at a broader level than that of the community. The reason for proposing European rules for managing exchange rates and a European parallel currency is not that the community is so closely linked as to be qualitatively different from other groupings. What does single out the community is the existence of habits of coordination and of institutions that make the launching of new initiatives of the kind envisaged here conceivable. If the next steps are successful, as we hope they would be, other countries may want to take them and should be encouraged to do so by the community.

A EUROPE-WIDE PARALLEL CURRENCY

Roland Vaubel

This paper deals with three aspects of the Optica reports: (1) the relationship between the snake approach and the parallel-currency approach, (2) the attractiveness and prospective speed of penetration of a European parallel currency (EPC), and (3) the implications and desirability of attempts to restrict real exchange-rate changes between the currencies of members of the European Communities. The paper cannot go into the details of how the parallel-currency approach could best be implemented, because fundamental adherence to the fixed-exchange-rate philosophy has hindered the Optica group in the prior task of presenting the full case for the parallel-currency approach to European monetary unification.[1]

A European Parallel Currency and/or Exchange-Rate Unification?

According to the Optica group, the exchange-rate system in the European Economic Community (EEC) should, for the time being, remain flexible to some extent but "evolve with the process of monetary unification to attain fixity in a final state."[2] In this final state, "the member countries could still decide whether or not they wished to introduce a single common currency."[3] The group hopes to attain "the benefits . . . of a fixed exchange-rate system or, in its extreme formulation, of a single European currency . . . through progressive harmonisa-

---

Note: The author thanks Harmen Lehment and Jürgen Roth for helpful comments on the first draft.

[1] See Roland Vaubel, "The Parallel-Currency Approach to European Monetary Unification and the Search for a New European Unit of Account," prepared for the Commission of the European Communities study group, Unité Monétaire Européenne (Brussels, 1976), pp. 15–66; and Vaubel, *Strategies for Currency Unification: The Economics of Currency Competition and the Case for a European Parallel Currency*, Kieler Studien, 156 (Tübingen: J. C. B. Mohr, 1978).

[2] Study Group on Optimum Currency Areas (Optica Group), *Towards Economic Equilibrium and Monetary Unification in Europe* (1975 Report) (Brussels: Commission of the EC, 1976), p. 40.

[3] Ibid., p. 25.

tion and reduction of national inflation rates";[4] it rejects the suggestion of abandoning the snake, "for it would be inconsistent with the aim of breaking the vicious circle of depreciation and inflation [*sic!*] so as ultimately to stabilise nominal exchange rates and harmonise national inflation rates at a low level."[5]

The role of the European parallel currency in this strategy is twofold: (1) During the transition to "a fixed exchange-rate system with the possibility of introducing a single currency,"[6] the EPC is to reduce "the problems arising from . . . flexibility [of exchange rates] . . . in international transactions."[7] (2) The EPC is to "impose some measure of discipline in the fight against inflation on the countries with the highest rates of inflation,"[8] although "in case of too high a divergence in national inflation rates, [it] should only circulate within those countries which have approximately the same inflation rate (for instance among the 'snake' countries)."[9]

The group envisages the creation of the European parallel currency not as a substitute for the Werner approach, but as a complement to it. The same concept underlies the parallel-currency proposal that the Commission of the EC submitted to the Council of Ministers in June 1975.[10] The *Economist* Manifesto, in contrast, rejected the fixed-exchange-rate philosophy of the Werner approach and advocated the creation of an EPC of stable purchasing power that would displace the national member currencies gradually but completely.[11] As the Manifesto had to be very short on this issue, this section explains in some detail why the enlargement or maintenance of the snake does not recommend

---

[4] Ibid., p. 41.

[5] Study Group on Optimum Currency Areas (Optica Group), *Inflation and Exchange Rates: Evidence and Policy Guidelines for the European Community* (1976 Report) (Brussels: Commission of the EC, 1977), p. 91.

[6] Optica Group, *1975 Report*, p. 42.

[7] Ibid., p. 40.

[8] Ibid., p. 30.

[9] Ibid., p. 42.

[10] "Alternative methods do not, therefore, have to be sought: it is more a matter of deciding which new measures could be added to those already adopted" (The Commission of the EC, "The European Union," *Bulletin of the European Communities*, Brussels, supp. 5/75, para. 39). The common-currency method "would in no way render obsolete the Community 'snake,' and the ultimate objective of stable exchange relationships within the Community would be retained" (ibid., para. 41).

[11] "The case for a monetary union is not a case for fixed exchange rates in a world of many monies. It is rather a case for the replacement of all national monies with one common unit of account, medium of exchange and store of value" (Giorgio Basevi and others, "The All Saints' Day Manifesto for European Monetary Union," *The Economist* (London), November 1, 1975, Conclusion III).

itself over any time horizon and why the crucial advantage of the parallel-currency approach consists precisely in its ability to bring about currency union *without* passing through the stage of exchange-rate unification. The analysis starts with some of the traditional arguments against fixed exchange rates but then proceeds from static to dynamic optimization. By contrasting the parallel-currency approach with the Werner approach, it identifies the criteria for choosing between them and thus may lay the foundations for what might be called a theory of the optimum currency unification process.

Exchange-Rate Unification with Intervention. Among the traditional objections to a snake-type system, two concern the practice of foreign exchange intervention.

The first argument against foreign exchange intervention is that it involves avoidable interference with the monetary policies of foreign central banks. If a central bank sells (buys) foreign currency that it has not held (does not deposit) with the private banking system and if the foreign central bank affected does not manage (in time) to neutralize the effect of the intervention on its money supply, intervention implies export of inflation (or deflation). Even if the principle of "no intervention without notification"[12] were strictly observed and if neutralization could take place with a short lag, the intervening central bank would still force the other central bank to bear the transaction cost (however low) of internal money supply adjustment. Thus foreign exchange intervention can be said to give rise to "negative externalities." It is incompatible with the principle that everybody has to bear the full consequences of his actions; it runs counter to the notion of individual responsibility that is a necessary condition for the market's feedback mechanism of incentives and disincentives. In a monetary system that permits mutual interference, responsibility for national *and* overall monetary policy tends to get lost.

Second, if the surplus countries are obliged to buy and hold the currencies of the deficit countries on their own account or to lend to those countries at a rate of interest that falls short of the market rate, the policy of foreign exchange intervention involves an incentive to inflate: it encourages competitive monetary expansion and competitive inflation. The most obvious example of such subsidized borrowing facilities are the IMF's special drawing rights. According to the interest-rate rule introduced in July 1976 the interest rate payable on activated

---

[12] See Herbert Giersch, "IMF Surveillance over Exchange Rates," in *The New International Monetary System,* Robert A. Mundell and Jacques J. Polak (eds.), (New York: Columbia University Press, 1977), pp. 53–68.

SDRs amounts to only three-fifths of the weighted average of short-term market rates of interest in the United States, United Kingdom, France, West Germany, and Japan.[13] Subsidization of borrowers is also implicit in the rules for the settlements of balances through the European Monetary Cooperation Fund (EMCF), although it is not as large and is more difficult to discover. Interest has to be paid at the (leveled-down) average discount rate, which, in most snake countries, tends to fall short of the market rate (the relevant standard of comparison is the market rate for four-month credits).

It follows a fortiori that the commission's repeated pleas for an expansion of the EMCF and for the gradual establishment of a European reserve pool are even less consistent with an anti-inflationary strategy. Indeed, since a pooling of reserves would encourage the more inflation-prone member countries to adopt even more divergent economic policies, it is self-defeating from the point of view of monetary policy coordination. The commission likes to depict all transfers to deficit countries as acts of community aid and solidarity. It ignores the moral hazard that indiscriminate help tends to create.

The incentive to inflate could be eliminated by charging a market rate of interest for official borrowing. This raises the question why central banks should borrow at all from each other rather than in foreign private money and capital markets. If foreign exchange is obtained through public sector borrowing in private markets (as is increasingly the case),[14] neither the moral hazard nor external effects with regard to foreign money supplies arise. In these circumstances, a central bank's attitude vis-à-vis foreign exchange intervention will depend on whether it considers it less costly to reduce the domestic monetary base by selling foreign exchange borrowed at the foreign market rate of interest or by selling government debt bearing the domestic market rate of interest (that is, through open-market operations). If capital markets are fully integrated internationally, it is difficult to see why central banks should find foreign borrowing more attractive than domestic borrowing through open-market operations.

Even if foreign exchange reserves are borrowed and held in the

---

[13] See International Monetary Fund, *Annual Report 1976* (Washington, D.C., 1976), pp. 49 ff. Borrowers were also subsidized under the more complicated interest-rate rule in force from July 1974 to June 1976 (see, for example, Jacques J. Polak, *Valuation and Rate of Interest of the SDR*, IMF Pamphlet no. 18 [Washington: International Monetary Fund, 1974], pp. 1, 19 ff.). Before July 1974 interest on acquired SDRs was 1.5 percent.

[14] According to OECD sources, the Eurocurrency market has become the most important source of international liquidity since 1974, relegating the U.S. balance-of-payments deficit to the second rank.

159

market, however, intervention has external effects. It may not, it is true, affect the supply of foreign base money, but it does involve a change in the demand for the foreign money and hence a change of its velocity and ultimately of the rate of change of the foreign price level. For example, a central bank that purchased foreign exchange in intervention and deposited it with the private banking system would still interfere with the foreign central bank's monetary policy because the given supply of foreign money would meet an increased demand and consequently imply a lower price level than without the intervention.

Exchange-Rate Unification without Intervention. One way of dealing with the problem of externality and the moral hazards created by the snake arrangements is to rule out all foreign exchange intervention and to maintain fixed exchange rates through continuous adjustments of domestic monetary policies.[15] However, such a nonintervention system cannot work without an agreement about who is to adjust to whom: it requires a "hegemonial" or "dominant" currency. In the context of the Bretton Woods system, this has become known as the "redundancy problem," the "nth currency problem," or the "key-currency problem." There seems to be general agreement that, if the intervention rules of the snake are given up, the fixed exchange-rate system cannot be maintained without conferring the "exorbitant privilege" of pivot currency status on one of the member currencies. As in the case of a private price cartel or oligopoly that faces frequent unpredictable shifts in demand for its products, there is a need for explicit or implicit price leadership by one of the participants.

If a formal agreement is not reached, the hegemonial-currency role is likely to be performed by the currency of the largest economy in the region (the dollar in the international monetary system of Bretton Woods and the deutsche mark in the snake) for two reasons. The largest economy and its currency tend to account for the largest share in international trade and capital transactions, so that, for most other countries, it is the most useful pivot to which to link their own currencies. The largest economy tends to be least open vis-à-vis the rest of the world, so that it can best afford to adopt a purely passive exchange-rate policy ("benign neglect").

---

[15] This is not to ignore that, in conditions of capital mobility, domestic open-market operations also have external effects on foreign inflation (or real output) through their impact on foreign interest rates and velocity. However, since exchange market intervention (with foreign exchange reserves not held with the private banking system) is equivalent to a combination of domestic and foreign open-market operations of opposite sign, the external effect of a domestic open-market operation only is bound to be smaller than the external effect of a foreign exchange intervention. (I owe this point to Harmen Lehment.)

In terms of welfare economies, this choice can be viewed as the result of an asymmetrical mutual externality (or public good). While the microeconomic benefits of exchange-rate constancy accrue to the users of both currencies between which the exchange rate is held constant (positive external economies of scale through adaptive monetary policy), the internalizable part of the benefit of adjustment has a much larger weight for the small than for the large economy.

Once it is realized that exchange-rate unification must be based on the hegemony of the most important economy, it becomes apparent that —however voluntarily this hegemony may be accepted by the smallest countries—there are strong political reasons for expecting that it will not prove acceptable to the EEC. Moreover, there is empirical evidence that, even from a purely economic point of view, the deutsche mark is not likely to be an acceptable pivot for a snake of the nine present members of the EEC (see Table 1, col. 4). If the real exchange-rate developments since 1970 can be extrapolated, price stability in West Germany (of course, as measured by the consumer price index)[16] would require considerable and persistent deflation in Italy (3.8 percent per annum), the United Kingdom (3.1 percent), and Ireland (2.9 percent) if the latter countries adopted the monetary policies required to keep the exchange rates of their currencies constant vis-à-vis the deutsche mark.[17] Indeed, no EEC country is likely to commit itself permanently to a perfectly adaptive monetary policy unless it receives assurances as to the course of monetary policy that the hegemonial-

---

[16] The Optica group's somewhat critical references to my 1976 article are highly misleading and reveal a serious misunderstanding (see Optica Group, *1976 Report*, pp. 8–10, 64). The purpose of my paper was not to test the PPP doctrine, let alone to find the price index that affords the best predictions of exchange-rate changes. It aimed at establishing a new, comprehensive, operational criterion for judging the economic cost of currency unification in a monetarist world. It identified this cost as the community variance in national rates of inflation or deflation that members would have to accept in a currency union whose average price level is kept stable. Since the target of price-level stability is formulated first or even exclusively with regard to the CPI (and certainly not export or wholesale price index), for my purpose real exchange-rate changes had to be measured with respect to the CPI (see Roland Vaubel, "Real Exchange-Rate Changes in the European Community: The Empirical Evidence and Its Implications for European Currency Unification," *Weltwirtschaftliches Archiv*, no. 3 [Tübingen, 1976], p. 444). Thus it cannot be said that my "results have been much influenced by [my] choice of price index" (Optica Group, *1976 Report*, p. 64)—it was Hobson's choice.

[17] The Optica Group (*1976 Report*, p. 17) believes that the inflation-rate range within a European currency union may be narrowed to 1 percent because, as I have shown ("Real Exchange-Rate Changes," pp. 449–455, 462 ff.), real exchange-rate changes tend to be smaller within currency unions than between them. Given that the deutsche mark has not been subject to the largest real exchange-rate appreciation in the EEC, this conjecture seems extremely optimistic.

TABLE 1

INCOME ELASTICITIES OF DEMAND FOR MONEY AND REAL EXCHANGE RATES IN THE EUROPEAN COMMUNITIES

Country	Income Elasticities of Demand for M_2			Real Exchange-Rate (RER) Changes in the EEC			
	Elasticity in 1950s and 1960s (quarterly estimates)[a] (1)	Elasticity 1970–1975 (annual estimate)[b] (2)	r^2 1970–1975 (annual estimate)[b] (3)	Annual compound average RER change (CPI) vis-à-vis EC average, 1970–1975[c] (4)	Variance of annual RER change (CPI) vis-à-vis EC average, 1970–1975[c] (5)	r^2 between deutsche mark exchange rate and PPP (CPI) 1961–1975[d] (6)	r^2 between deutsche mark exchange rate and PPP (WPI) 1961–1975[d] (7)
West Germany	0.97–1.35 (2)	2.06	0.79	+0.90	21.91	—	—
France	1.18 (1)	1.84	0.97[e]	+0.54	24.08	0.82	0.88
United Kingdom	0.45–2.47 (11)	3.14	0.89[f]	−2.22	22.01	0.91	0.90
Italy	1.92 (1)	2.52	0.86[f]	−2.96	4.74	0.81	0.92
Netherlands	0.80–0.99 (2)	1.43	0.96[e]	+2.54	5.98	0.81	0.49
Belgium	n.r.	1.07	0.87[f]	+1.12	2.80	0.65	0.58
Denmark	n.r.	0.85	0.90[f]	+1.48	7.87	n.r.	n.r.
Ireland	n.r.	0.70	0.46	−2.01	16.70	n.r.	n.r.

n.r. = Not reported.

a SOURCE: M. M. G. Fase and J. B. Kuné, "The Demand for Money in Thirteen European and non-European Countries: A Tabular Survey," *Kredit und Kapital*, 1975, 3, pp. 414–416. The figures in parentheses indicate the number of estimates from which the indicated extreme values could be chosen. The periods of observation differ. Most equations contain an interest variable as well.

b My own calculations. The elasticities were estimated from the constant-elasticity function $ln(M_{2t}/P_t) = ln\,a + b\,ln(Y_t/P_t)$, where M_{2t} is money plus quasi-money at the end of year t, Y_t is GNP (or the country's equivalent) in year t, and P_t is the price index of Y_t. The estimate thus incorporates a rigid built-in recognition and reaction lag of six months. A quarterly analysis was not undertaken because the proponents of the combined approach envisage annual agreements on rates of domestic monetary expansion and because, for several member countries, recent GNP data are not available on a quarterly basis. A relatively short period of observation has been chosen to avoid concealing recent differences in elasticities through long-term averaging. Being based on only six observations, the estimates are necessarily crude, but they have the crucial advantage that they are based on the same period of observation and method of estimation.

c SOURCE: Vaubel, "Real Exchange Rate Changes," pp. 460, 464. A detailed description of the method of calculation can be found there.

d SOURCE: Optica Group, *1976 Report*, p. 53, table I.A.2.

e Significant at the 1 percent level.

f Significant at the 5 percent level only.

currency country intends to follow. An "irrevocable" fixing of exchange rates requires an "irrevocable" ex ante agreement on money supply rules to be observed by the hegemonial-currency country. This leads us to a further option that has repeatedly been advocated by R. I. McKinnon and that the West German Council of Economic Experts has recommended in its latest report.[18]

Exchange-Rate Unification with Intervention and with ex ante Agreements on Rates of Domestic Monetary Expansion. The third way of solving the problem of externality and the moral hazards—and one that avoids the hegemonial-currency problem—is to combine the commitment to a set of fixed exchange rates with an ex ante agreement on the rates of domestic monetary expansion to be followed in *each* member country.[19] According to McKinnon, the national member governments or central banks would:

- predetermine jointly the rates of domestic monetary expansion[20] for each of the member countries that they (unanimously?) expect to lead to identical rates of change (or stability) of their wholesale price indexes and hence to exchange-rate constancy
- agree to correct for any errors that became apparent by maintaining the agreed exchange rate through symmetrical foreign exchange intervention
- consent to accept the deviations from the predetermined money supply targets that the foreign exchange intervention entails (nonsterilization commitment).

A combined exchange-rate and money supply agreement that comes very close to this proposal was concluded by the community in October 1972. The Resolution of the Council of Ministers of October 31, 1972, stipulated that in 1974 the annual rates of growth of M_2 in each member country were to be held to the estimated rate of growth of its real GNP

---

[18] Ronald I. McKinnon, *A New Tripartite Monetary Agreement or a Limping Dollar Standard?* Princeton Essays in International Finance no. 106 (October 1974) (see the summary of his proposal in P. de Grauwe, D. Heremans, and E. van Romony, "Vers une relance de l'union monétaire européenne," *Idées et Etudes*, no. 305 [Brussels: Ministère des Affaires Etrangères, du Commerce Extérieur et de la Coopération au Développement, 1975], pp. 47 ff.); and Sachverständigenrat zur Begutachtung der Gesamtwirtschaftlichen Entwicklung (Council of Economic Experts), *Jahresgutachten 1976/77* (Stuttgart, Mainz, 1977).

[19] The Optica group also wants to combine fixed exchange rates within the snake and the preannouncement of monetary targets, but it does not envisage community agreements on those targets.

[20] Domestic monetary expansion is here defined as an increase in money supply not originating in foreign exchange intervention.

(that is, not the rate of growth of productive potential) plus the common target rate of inflation, which was fixed at 4 percent and related to the CPI. Why did it fail? What are the objections to this combined approach?

The suggested approach is not vitiated by the externality problem cr the moral hazard. Since rates of domestic monetary expansion are agreed on in advance, the individual member country is not free to inflate in order to pass the international needs test for subsidized credits and hence to exert external effects on the monetary conditions in the lending countries. While the combination of exchange-rate commitments and ex ante agreements on domestic monetary expansion would thus be a considerable improvement on the present system of the snake, it nevertheless suffers from a number of drawbacks.

It is a high-friction approach. In McKinnon's and the Council of Economic Experts' "brave new world," member governments or central banks would have to enter each year into money supply negotiations that promise to be at least as lengthy, painful, and unproductive as the annual EEC farm price reviews. Political friction is maximized by this approach for two reasons. First, conflicts between the national price-level preferences are given maximum publicity so as to arouse nationalist feelings and hinder political compromise. If credits are subsidized, agreement is made even more difficult because the probability that, by borrowing, a member country can participate in the others' seigniorage depends on the relative rates of domestic monetary expansion agreed upon.

Second, econometric estimates of what sets of domestic monetary expansion are consistent with exchange-rate fixity are not particularly reliable, and such uncertainty (risk) tends to make agreement all the more difficult. To determine the rates of growth of money supply that produce approximate exchange-rate constancy, one has to know the future rates of growth of real GNP, the real-income elasticities of demand for real balances,[21] and the prospective real exchange-rate changes in the community. Errors in predicting real GNP are often large (as in 1975). The real-income elasticities of demand for real money and quasi-money (M_2) not only differ widely within the community (these differences could, of course, be allowed for) but also

---

[21] The demand for real balances may also be affected by other factors, such as the rate of inflation, the real rate of interest on substitute assets, and the stock of wealth, but neglect of their influence may be justifiable if the monetary aggregate (like M_2) constitutes the closest substitute for non-interest-bearing currency and demand deposits, namely interest-bearing quasi-money. Moreover, estimates of the elasticity of the demand for real M_2 with respect to, say, long-term interest rates would be useful in determining money supply targets only if the size of these interest rates could be predicted.

165

depend crucially on the period of observation and the estimating equation (see Table 1, cols. 1–2). The predictive power of the more recent estimates is significant at the 1 percent level for only two member countries; in the majority of cases it is less than 90 percent (col. 3). Admittedly, the elasticities would probably have been more stable if money supply targets had been formulated and announced, but it may be doubted that this improvement would be significant. Real exchange-rate changes, as measured by the CPI, have been not only large (col. 4) but also highly variable (cols. 5–6), and the 1961–1975 time series results given in the Optica report for individual member countries (vis-à-vis the deutsche mark) indicate that in most cases wholesale price indexes were an even worse predictor of exchange-rate changes than consumer price indexes (cols. 6–7).[22]

Since the variability of the income elasticities of demand for money and the variability of real exchange-rate changes need not be cumulative, it must be admitted that this evidence is not entirely conclusive. Only the empirical work on the monetary approach to exchange rates that is under way in several places can give a final answer (the preliminary and unpublished results I have seen are not encouraging). However, since the proponents of the combined approach base their suggestion on the assumption of very stable income elasticities of demand for money and high real exchange-rate stability, the evidence that has been presented is relevant and throws doubt on the feasibility of ex ante agreements on money supply targets.

The relatively high variability of these five key parameters has important implications for the prospective durability of any money supply agreement that might, in spite of these difficulties, be concluded. As the example of the agreement for 1973 has shown, the joint formulation of target rates for monetary expansion need not mean that the targets will be attained and that exchange rates will remain fixed. If a member government, for example, realizes that the agreed targets turn out to imply more inflation and subsidized lending for its country than was expected and is considered tolerable, exchange-rate union (unlike currency union) always leaves it the option to withdraw and disappoint the expectations it has nurtured or to resort to restrictions of trade and convertibility, which is probably even more harmful for economic integration. The danger that one of these options will be exercised is

---

[22] Only if the six EEC countries whose deutsche mark exchange rates have been studied by Optica 1976 are taken together, do the wholesale price indexes perform better than the consumer price indexes. Note that correlations between effective deutsche mark exchange rates and trade-weighted PPP are not reported by the group for individual EEC countries, although for various country groups this method yielded higher coefficients of determination.

166

the more serious as the time horizon of the exchange-rate commitment will tend to exceed the time horizon of the money supply agreement if the latter is not (yet?) renewed. The obvious way to avoid this danger is to confine oneself to fixing, announcing, and, as far as possible, harmonizing rates of monetary expansion and to refrain from freezing exchange rates. However useful the announcement of money supply targets is in stabilizing expectations and notably in restraining wage bargains, it does not seem to permit the attainment of specific exchange-rate targets with a sufficient degree of precision.

The crucial weakness of the combined approach, as of all other variants of exchange-rate unification, is its lack of automaticity. This problem manifests itself in four ways:

1. There is no way of ensuring automatic ex ante consistency of price targets (exchange rates) and quantity targets (money stocks).
2. Since the participants retain their power of discretion and the instruments to exercise it, there is no automatic mechanism that prevents them from violating the agreement.
3. A fortiori, there is no way of ensuring that the agreement will automatically be renewed.
4. Again a fortiori, there is no automatic process by which national discretion (the possibility of opting out) is reduced over time.

In all four respects, exchange-rate unification resembles the attempt of private producers to establish and maintain a cartel in the face of unpredictable changes in total demand and of shifting particular interests.[23] Even if the price cartel is combined with a quantity cartel, collusion is usually short-lived because price and output targets soon become inconsistent. No such problems arise in the case of monopolization (currency merger): since there is only one producer, there is no need to formulate ex ante targets for the distribution of output (money); in a currency union, money moves automatically from regions that grow slowly to regions that grow fast, so as to equalize the opportunity cost of holding money in all member regions.

As far as particular interests are concerned, a cartel of central banks is likely to be even less stable than a cartel of private producers. While private cartels are a means of increasing prices and profits above the level that would prevail under competition, the central banks as regional monopolists in the production of money *lose* by joining the international cartel. They lose the freedom to maximize seigniorage in

---

[23] The analogy with private cartels was first drawn in Norbert Walter, "Europäische Währungsintegration: Kartell-Lösung versus Euro-Währung," *Die Weltwirtschaft*, no. 1 (Tübingen, 1972).

the country in which they are monopolist because exchange-rate unification sets an end (or at least a limit) to spatial price discrimination. Such disincentives can be avoided only if the national monopolists are offered participation in a larger, more profitable monopoly absorbing also total monetary demand for international intracommunity transactions (currency union) or if the process of currency unification is left to those who stand to reap the efficiency gains from it—the private users of money.

Since exchange-rate unification lacks automaticity and consistent incentives, it fails to make exchange rates predictable. The economic cost of such unpredictability stands out most clearly if exchange-rate unification is contrasted with currency unification.

Currency Unification versus Exchange-Rate Unification: The Case for Predictability. With regard to economic integration, many economists evaluate the difference between exchange-rate unification and currency unification mainly in terms of money-changing and information costs. These costs may be considered relatively small. Probably more important is that only currency unification can eliminate the risk of convertibility restrictions, which acts as a barrier to international capital mobility and thus prevents both a more efficient allocation of long-term capital and a smoother financing of temporary payments imbalances through short-term borrowing. These drawbacks that distinguish exchange-rate unification from currency unification would remain even if the member central banks offered free forward cover for all maturities at the fixed parity. In the absence of such cover, the risk of sudden large parity changes acts as an additional disintegrative force; for, in a world of imperfect foresight and uncertainty, both the "irreversible convertibility" and the "irrevocable fixing of parities" that the council resolution of March 1971 envisaged are a logical impossibility. The failure to give guidance to expectations is also the key to the domestic drawbacks of exchange-rate unification, which arise regardless of whether coordination is merely to be maintained ("static optimization") or is still to be attained ("dynamic optimization").

From both a static and a dynamic point of view, any strategy that makes it easy for member governments to opt out tends to be self-defeating because it leads trade unions and entrepreneurs to assume that the national authorities will yield to their pressure. Wage and price setting then becomes inconsistent with the government's international commitments, national monetary policy accommodates to avoid a rise in unemployment, and the exchange-rate target has to be abandoned. This, in turn, strengthens the public's expectations of even more government compliance, wage and price setters feel even more autonomous, and so on: a vicious circle develops.[24] Since the maintenance of national currencies has such obvious economic disadvantages compared with currency union, the public's expectations can be regarded as entirely rational. It is difficult to see why exchange-rate unification could ever be preferred to currency unification by national governments if they were unconditionally committed to exchange-rate fixity. They do not dare to undertake unconditional commitments because they have experienced a "need" for accommodation in the past, not realizing that this "need" was the result of their failure to commit themselves unconditionally in the first place. Hence, in a strategy of exchange-rate unification, the authorities themselves tend to become an integral part and victim of a self-perpetuating circle, which cannot be broken by them unless they realize its circularity. Currency unification, by contrast, being as irreversible and credible as any unification can be, tends to be self-fulfilling: economic agents know what to expect and what to adjust to, and they will find it in their interest to avoid a collision.

From a dynamic point of view, it is important, furthermore, to consider how maladjustment of expectations can be avoided if a group of countries that aims at monetary integration starts from a position of monetary policy "disequilibrium." This question seems to be particularly relevant to the community's present situation, which is characterized by high, very different, and uncoordinated rates of inflation in the various member countries. Since exchange-rate unification requires the assimilation of inflation rates but the member countries with the lower rates of inflation are unlikely to accept an acceleration for the sake of community conformity, the more inflation-prone members will have to adopt a strongly disinflationary policy. Indeed, as has already been mentioned, consumer price inflation in Italy, the United Kingdom, and Ireland has to be reduced below the rates prevailing in the other member countries if nominal exchange rates are to remain constant; for the historical evidence shows that Italy, the United Kingdom, and Ireland have a permanent need for real exchange-rate depreciation (defined in this way). As the Optica reports also emphasized,[25] the downward harmonization of monetary rates of expansion and of inflation is likely to produce temporary reductions in the level of employment because inflation

---

[24] This is even more likely if the exchange-rate commitment relates not to the current spot rate but to the spot rate at a future date and, by implication, to the current forward rate for that date (as suggested in Wolfram Engels, "Verschiedene Wege zu einer europäischen Währungsunion," unpublished, Frankfurt University, 1971, para. 27); this is because each instance of government accommodation may be excused as a purely transitory deviation from the announced path.

[25] Optica Group, *1975 Report*, p. 40; *1976 Report*, p. 2.

expectations are slow to adapt (and cannot be made entirely irrelevant through indexation). No such cost of transition arises if, instead of being stabilized, the inflating national currencies are replaced by a new currency that does not suffer from a record and expectations of inflation and that, as long as it remains a parallel currency, can be made subject to a value guarantee that can be enforced with precision through currency conversions. Deeply entrenched inflation expectations are the reason that, many times in history, governments have preferred currency reform to currency stabilization. If the new currency is the same for all member countries, currency reform coincides with currency unification: instead of nine currency reforms there would be only one.

Gradual Currency Unification: The Parallel-Currency Approach. Currency union can be brought about at one stroke or gradually. In choosing between these alternatives, both political and economic considerations are relevant.

From a political point of view, it has been argued (for example, by Pierre Uri) that only an external shock can induce all member governments to accept currency unification at the same time and that their willingness to accept it, which will be short-lived, must be exploited at once and completely. The political objection to this view is that it is too categorical. The possibility cannot be excluded that, as money illusion and exchange-rate illusion are eroded, governments may gradually come to realize that, except over the very short term, monetary and exchange-rate policy is not an effective means of raising the level of employment and hence that, except with regard to seigniorage, currency unification does not involve a loss of economic sovereignty. Governments might be willing to accept an approach by which the common currency, defined as an indexed basket of member currencies, would spread first among those economic agents who are most aware of the inflation of their national currency, that is, where national monetary policy has lost most of its real effects anyway. If the community confined itself to waiting for the day on which a political crisis in Europe might permit the "big leap forward," it might fail to keep pace with the monetary-policy disillusionment of governments and their increasing willingness to accept piecemeal unification engineering. In addition, it would ignore the fact that even those politicians who have no objections to *uno actu* currency unification tend to prefer a gradual process of transition that does not maximize the provocation to, and hence resistance from, the nationalist or conservative constituency.

From an economic point of view, a gradual process of currency unification has the crucial advantage that it facilitates the adjustment of expectations, contracts, and accounting. As for expectations, gradualism reduces the probability and size of errors in predictions because, with given lags in expectation adjustment, the divergence between anticipated and actual outcomes is reduced. It is important to avoid errors about currency unification because they lead to misallocation of resources. In particular, investment should anticipate the implications of currency union for international transactions and regional restructuring. No doubt these considerations were also an important reason that the European Common Market was not set up at once and that the reduction of tariffs and of other trade barriers was spread over many years.

The adjustment of contracts, by contrast, is a problem peculiar to currency unification. That is because only currency unification requires the disappearance of the means of payments agreed on in existing longer term contracts and hence the disappearance of a market exchange rate at which obligations fixed in the national currencies could be converted into the common currency. That is why currency reforms are invariably accompanied by the stipulation of legal conversion ratios for old debt. But the fixing of such a ratio is bound to distort the intentions of contract partners because it involves a judgment about the purchasing power that the old currencies had been expected to have at maturity and because those expectations tend to differ between contractors. A gradual transition to currency union that leaves the old currencies in circulation for a number of years reduces the danger of arbitrary interference with private contracts.

From an accounting point of view, gradualism has the advantage of permitting a more uniform use of the resources devoted to the adaptation of business machines and habits of thinking.[26] On the other hand, it can be objected that the coexistence of a common currency with the national currencies will involve costs of transactions, portfolio management, and accounting during the period of transition (diseconomies of small scale) that can be avoided by *uno actu* unification. However, the sustained growth of the share of foreign-currency balances suggests that, even for many nonbanks, dealings and calculations in more than one currency do not constitute a serious obstacle.[27] Moreover,

---

[26] This is also how, for example, the British government has justified the long changeover period for decimalization. See Chancellor of the Exchequer, *Decimal Currency in the United Kingdom* (London: Her Majesty's Stationer's Office, Cmnd. 3164, December 1966), para. 64.

[27] I estimate that, since the sudden reversal in 1971, nonbank foreign-currency deposits have been growing faster than nonbank domestic-currency deposits and that they have reached a record share. Among nonbank demand and time deposits denominated in the seven main Eurocurrencies and held either in the Eurocurrency market or with commercial banks in the country of the currency, the share of foreign-owned deposits in total deposits has, according to my calculations

171

if the users of money are given a free choice whether and when they accept the parallel currency and whether, for themselves, they prefer a gradual transition or a big leap, it could at least be made sure that the creation and penetration of the EPC would represent an improvement on the previous situation at any moment in time.

To summarize the argument of this section, the parallel-currency approach possesses nine characteristics of an optimal currency unification process:

1. It operates without foreign exchange intervention and hence without international externalities and moral hazards or international ex ante agreements on national rates of growth of the money supply.
2. It triggers an automatic mechanism that works without political discretion and leads to currency union in a predictable and self-fulfilling process.
3. It provides a common standard of value, means of payment, and store of value at a very early stage, thus facilitating market integration while leaving control over national monetary policies with the member governments.
4. It has all the political and economic advantages of gradualism.
5. It permits the speed and pattern of currency unification to be determined by the needs of the market and the degree of money disillusionment.
6. It avoids the temporary unemployment created by the downward harmonization of inflation rates under exchange-rate unification.
7. It does not encourage competitive inflation but, through competition, tends to discourage it.
8. It avoids national rivalries and hegemony.
9. It gives the member governments a consistent incentive to accept and desire currency unification.

The Optica group mentions only three of these criteria (3, 4, and 7). Its uncritical attitude with regard to exchange-rate unification prevents it from being sufficiently persuasive in advocating the parallel-currency approach. Exchange-rate unification does not qualify on any of these counts except one (4). The parallel-currency approach is needed because exchange-rate unification does not qualify for adoption.

(based on Bank for International Settlements and national data), developed as follows (end-of-year estimates): 1967, 2.5 percent; 1968, 2.8 percent; 1969, 3.6 percent; 1970, 3.6 percent; 1971, 3.0 percent; 1972, 3.1 percent; 1973, 3.4 percent; 1974, 4.3 percent.

The Prospective Speed of EPC Penetration

The speed with which the EPC will displace the national currencies depends, in the absence of exchange controls, on the value guarantee that is offered to EPC holders (and on the interest that may be paid on the EPC reserves held by commercial banks). The Optica group wants to link the EPC to the strongest member currency (as measured from the date of EPC introduction). It admits that the indexed-basket formula suggested in the *Economist* Manifesto may be superior from an economic point of view, but it believes that an EPC of stable (weighted) EEC purchasing power would be too useful and hence too attractive to economic agents to be politically acceptable to the national member governments. The Optica reports are teeming with "political realism," but the authors' quest for short-run political acceptability does not seem to be successful on this point: an EPC linked to the strongest member currency not only would be an arbitrary standard of value and a store of value whose price (opportunity cost) exceeds its marginal cost of production by a larger margin than can be justified on economic grounds but also would suffer from the serious political disadvantage that it could not start to displace all national member currencies at the same time. In terms of the previous analysis, the Optica proposal can thus be criticized for failing to solve the hegemonial-currency problem.

Chapter 3 of Optica 1976 presents abundant evidence on how the indexed-basket EPC would have performed vis-à-vis the deutsche mark (that is, the Optica EPC), the French franc, French franc bonds, and Eurodollar deposits had it been introduced in 1967. My own simulations, which assume that in March 1971, instead of adopting the Werner approach, the Council of Ministers had decided on the introduction of an indexed-basket EPC,[28] provide some additional information (Figure 1).

The following points are worth noting:

- While the indexed-basket EPC ("Eurostable")[29] of course appreciated vis-à-vis the deutsche mark in the five years from 1971 to 1976, this rate of appreciation is small compared with the

---

[28] Unlike Optica, I assumed that the composition of the initial basket would have been the same as the composition of the new standard-basket European unit of account (EUA) introduced by the community in March 1975.

[29] The name Eurostable was first suggested in Jacques Riboud, "Pour une monnaie européenne stable," *Combat*, December 7, 1974, pp. 8–9. However, the indexed-basket formula originated with Herbert Giersch, "Final Remarks," in Commission of the EC, Study Group on Economic and Monetary Union, *European Economic Integration and Monetary Unification* (Brussels, 1973).

FIGURE 1

EXCHANGE-RATE MOVEMENTS OF THREE CURRENCY UNITS (SIMULATED) AND FIVE EEC CURRENCIES VIS-À-VIS THE U.S. DOLLAR

(Monthly Averages; March 1971 = 100)

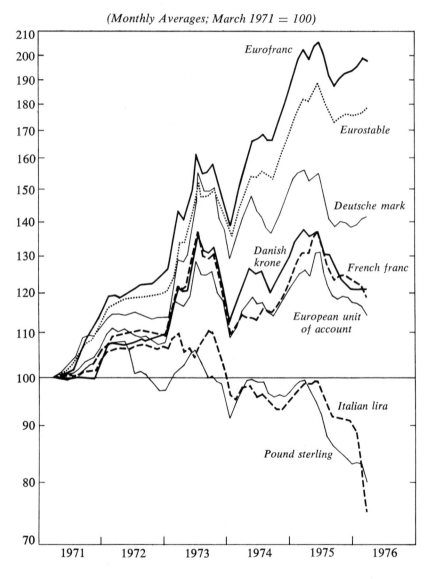

SOURCE: Calculated from *Federal Reserve Bulletin; IMF International Financial Statistics;* and *Bulletin de Statistique*, Institut National de Statistique, Brussels.

appreciation of the deutsche mark vis-à-vis sterling and the lira. Thus the choice between the indexed-basket EPC and the Optica EPC makes relatively little difference for the speed with which the weaker member currencies are displaced, but it is decisive for determining whether the deutsche mark can be displaced.

- Even though the indexed-basket EPC appreciated vis-à-vis the deutsche mark over the full period from March 1971 to March 1976, there are some stretches (notably the second and third quarters of 1971 and the first and second quarters of 1973) over which real exchange-rate changes (as measured by the CPI) produced the reverse result. Thus if the EPC's competitive edge over the strongest member currency is not to become even more discontinuous, it must not be made weaker than the indexed basket.

- An EPC of constant Brussels purchasing power ("Eurofranc")[30] would have appreciated even more than the indexed-basket EPC, owing to real exchange-rate appreciation of the Belgian franc as measured by the Brussels CPI. Although its exchange rate is easier to calculate, it is always subject to the risk that, owing to even larger real exchange-rate changes, it may cease to be representative of average community purchasing power.

- A fixed-basket EPC as proposed by the Villa Pamphili group[31] (EUA) would, over the whole five years, have appreciated vis-à-vis the dollar but depreciated even vis-à-vis the French franc and the Danish krone, which, alternately, kept the median position in the community. Within the EEC, the EUA would have appreciated only vis-à-vis the lira and the British and Irish pound and, unless its greater stability in terms of exchange-rate fluctuations had proved to have considerable attraction for risk-averse users of money, it could have made inroads into these three currencies only.

While the simulations are useful in determining the yield differentials for non-interest-bearing assets in these currencies and the income tax differentials for interest-bearing assets denominated in them,[32] they

---

[30] The proposal to revalue the EPC vis-à-vis the Belgian franc by the rate of increase of the Brussels CPI and to give it the name Eurofranc was made in Walter, "Europäische Währungsintegration."

[31] Villa Pamphili Group, "Monetary Arrangements in the Common Market," *Banca Nazionale del Lavoro Quarterly Review*, Rome, December 1976. A short version appeared in the *Times* (London), *Le Monde, Die Welt,* and *La Stampa* on July 26, 1976.

[32] In several member countries capital gains are not taxed or not as highly taxed as interest income. Since strong-currency assets offer higher capital gains and smaller interest income than weak-currency assets, the former are more attractive from an income tax point of view, if yields before tax are equal.

do not permit a conclusion as to whether the process of EPC penetration would be slow and gradual. They indicate whether and to what extent the users of money have an incentive to prefer the EPC, but not how fast they will respond to it. To test the gradualism hypothesis, it was therefore necessary to measure the extent to which currency preferences have been determined by exchange-rate changes and inflation in the past.

An extensive regression project was undertaken that analyzes changes in the composition of total foreign-currency deposits, nonbank foreign-currency deposits, official foreign-exchange reserves, foreign currency bonds, and changes in the share of unit-of-account bonds, purchasing-power bonds, indexed deposits, indexed wage bargains, and other indexed contracts. Only the most significant results can be reported here.

A market-share analysis with regard to total foreign-currency deposits in seven currencies yielded rather heterogeneous results.[33] On the average of the seven currencies, however, it was striking that the explanatory power (β-weights) of the transaction cost variables[34] and the seasonal dummies[35] is far higher than the explanatory power of the return and exchange risk variables.[36]

Perhaps the most interesting results were obtained in explaining

---

[33] The seven main Eurocurrencies used were the dollar, the deutsche mark, the Swiss franc, the French franc, the British pound, the lira, and the Holland florin. However, the shares refer not only to those Eurocurrency deposits that, according to a prior estimate, are denominated in a currency foreign to the depositor but also to all foreign-currency deposits held in the country of the currency. The data are quarterly (first quarter of 1966 to fourth quarter of 1974) and were obtained from the BIS and national sources.

[34] The following proxies were successfully used to capture the transaction motive: (1) GNP shares; (2) export growth shares; (3) the share of the countries' exports and imports (each adjusted for invoicing habits) and gross issues of bonds denominated in each of the currencies; (4) the share of the square roots of the exports, imports, and bond issues (as defined in 3); and (5) the differential between the countries' cumulative basic balance since 1960 (inertia hypothesis). The cubic-root hypothesis with regard to the precautionary demand for money was not confirmed.

[35] The seasonal pattern shows very clearly that the dollar is the preferred end-of-year window-dressing currency.

[36] The return variables included: covered interest ratios (0); covered interest ratios net of 0.15 percent transaction cost (0); uncovered interest ratios (1); ratios of bond yields to maturity (substitution effects) (1); ratios of forward exchange-rate factors (plus or minus forward premia/discounts) (2); CPI deflator ratios over one and four years (2 for one year); and cumulative basic balance differentials as exchange-rate expectation proxies (2). Three exchange-risk proxies were used: ratios of past squared percentage changes of nominal exchange rates (3); ratios of past squared percentage changes of real exchange rates (1); and ratios of deviations of current spot rates from past forward rates (1). Note: the figures in parentheses indicate the number of final equations (out of seven) in which the variable could be included.

changes in the ratio of foreign-currency deposits held by nonbanks in all seven currencies to own-currency deposits held by nonbanks in those currencies (fourth quarter 1967 to fourth quarter 1974). The following equation offered the highest coefficient of determination adjusted for degrees of freedom (R^{-2}), that is, the highest probability that the equation's explanatory power is not zero:

$$\log(\Sigma D^{FC}_{NB} / \Sigma^7 \, {}^{DC}_{NB}) = \begin{array}{cc} -1.43 & +0.746 \log(X/\text{GNP}) \\ (6.79^*) & (10.25^*) \end{array} \; \begin{array}{c} +6.34 \log CiR \\ (3.70^*) \end{array}$$

$$-0.013 \log ERR \quad -0.039 \log ERF$$
$$(1.76) \qquad\qquad (4.05^*)$$

$$-0.127 \, CCSM \; -0.042 \, S_2 \; -0.0768 \, S_4$$
$$(2.30^+) \qquad (1.66) \qquad (3.15^*)$$

Where: X/GNP is the ratio of total exports by the seven countries to the sum of their GNPs

CiR is the ratio of the weighted-average covered interest on foreign-currency deposits to the weighted-average covered interest on domestic-currency deposits[37]

ERR is the ratio of weighted-average expected exchange risk as approximated by real exchange-rate changes over the last year (linearly declining quarterly weights)

ERF is the ratio of weighted-average expected exchange risk as approximated by the deviation of the current spot rate from the rate predicted by the ninety-day forward rate ninety days ago

$CCSM$ is a capital control dummy that is set at 1 in third quarter 1971 only, which allows for the numerous restrictions that European governments imposed on short-term capital inflows from August 1971 to the Smithsonian agreement in December 1971[38]

S_2 and S_4 are seasonal dummies for the second and fourth quarter respectively.

---

[37] Interest rates on foreign-currency deposits were calculated as a weighted average of ninety-day Eurodeposit rates and of interest on ninety-day deposits held with the national banking system of the foreign currency.

[38] Several other capital control dummies were tried but could not be included.

Given some simplifying assumptions that have been shown to be rather realistic with regard to international trade,[39] the estimated coefficient of the ratio variable CiR can be interpreted as the covered-interest elasticity of currency substitution. The t-values are indicated below the coefficients and are marked * or + when significant at the 1 percent or 5 percent level, respectively.

The estimate confirms the conclusion of the market-share analyses that foreign-currency preferences are in the first place determined by transaction needs (the β-weight of log $[X/GNP]$ is 41.4 percent). The inclusion of the return variable CiR indicates that nonbank holders are very sensitive to covered-interest differentials. Moreover, inspection of the simple correlation coefficients indicates quite clearly that there is also a preference for currencies wth a low-inflation record.[40] The results for the two exchange-risk variables ERR and ERF (they account for 21.8 percent of the equation's explanatory power!) show that nonbanks are averse to exchange-rate risk and are deterred not by nominal exchange-rate changes but by real exchange-rate changes and deviations from past forward rates. Moreover, the fact that a dummy for exchange-rate flexibility proved to be nonincludable shows that it is not exchange-rate flexibility but unpredictable exchange-rate change that deters nonbanks from holding foreign-currency deposits. The highly significant negative coefficient of S_4 demonstrates that nonbanks do not like to show foreign-currency deposits in their end-of-year balance sheets (window-dressing effect).

The analysis of central banks' currency preferences relates to the quarterly changes in the ratio of dollar to sterling reserves from first quarter 1966 to second quarter 1974 (IMF data). Various functional forms and also a longer period were tried. The results can be summarized as follows:

- There is clear confirmation that central banks' currency preferences tend to follow the private pattern of transactions and hence the private choice of transaction currencies.
- The currency composition of foreign exchange reserves is sensitive

---

[39] See J. D. Richardson, "Beyond (but Back to?) the Elasticity of Substitution in International Trade," *European Economic Review*, December 1973, pp. 384–87.

[40] The simple correlation coefficients between the log of the dependent variable and the log of the CPI deflator ratios are −0.839 over the short term (past year) and −0.689 over the longer term (past four years). Nevertheless, these variables could not enter because of their high negative collinearity with log (X/GNP), whose correlation with the log of the dependent variable is even closer. The negative collinearity seems to indicate that, in a system of delayed parity adjustment—as was typical of most of the period of observation—high-inflation countries tend to be least competitive in export trade.

to bond yields, especially if these are adjusted for past inflation. At the short end of their portfolio, however, central banks tend to buy weak currencies and do not even shy away from financing the *basic* balance deficits of reserve currency countries.

- Central banks are averse to exchange risk, but, unlike private depositors, they evaluate it purely in terms of nominal exchange-rate changes (that is, they are subject to more exchange-rate illusion than private economic agents).

The analysis of the currency composition of gross issues of bonds denominated in a currency foreign to the issuer (quarterly OECD and World Bank data, first quarter 1967 to fourth quarter 1974 for dollar, deutsche mark, and Swiss franc) demonstrates very clearly that foreign-currency bonds tend to be denominated in those currencies that have suffered the smallest loss of purchasing power over several years. Exchange-rate changes have very little, if any, effect on the currency composition of bond issues. The abandonment of parities, however, reduces the bond-market share of the currency in question. Thus, while exchange-rate *variations* seem to affect short-term rather than long-term exchange-rate expectations, (nominal) exchange-rate *variability*—which makes little difference for short-term assets such as deposits—is interpreted as a sign of increased long-term exchange risk by the bond market. The analysis of gross issues of unit-of-account bonds as a proportion of foreign and international bond issues shows that the market reacts to increasing exchange-rate flexibility by enlarging the share of unit-of-account bonds but that this reaction is not very marked (first quarter 1970 to fourth quarter 1974).

The analysis of the market's choice of index clauses had to be confined to four types of contracts in four countries (annual data from national sources): bank deposits in Finland (1955–1967), bonds in Finland (1952–1967) and Israel (1957–1966, 1969–1973), major wage bargains in the United States (1956–1974), and nonfinancial, nonwage contracts in West Germany (1966–1974).[41]

The results can be summarized as follows:

- The market propensity to use index clauses can satisfactorily be explained by the experience of inflation. However, in different markets different inflation variables prove to be most relevant: for bonds, the rate of change of inflation; for deposits, the rate of

---

[41] A detailed description of the analysis is contained in Roland Vaubel, "The Case for Indexed Financial Instruments," in *The Development of Financial Institutions in Europe*, J. E. Wadsworth, J. S. G. Wilson, and H. Fournier (eds.) (Leyden: Sijthoff, 1977).

179

inflation and its variance over the last twelve months; for wages, again inflation variance; and for nonwage, nonfinancial contracts, the rate of inflation.[42]

- The typical lag with which the share of indexed contracts reacts to the most relevant inflation variable ranges from zero to two quarters for bonds to two to four quarters for deposits and wage bargains.[43]

- Changes in the regulations governing the permission of index clauses (West Germany) and, in Finland, tax exemptions for indexed deposits and houses (as substitutes for purchasing-power bonds) had a marked impact on the share of indexed contracts.

- In Finland the reaction conformed to a Gompertz curve rather than a normal linear function,[44] indicating that the reaction weakened as saturation levels (for bonds outstanding, 80 percent) were approached. Moreover, the Gompertz functions obtained and the positive constant terms in the linear regressions imply that some contracts are indexed even if the price level has been stable. This "hard-core" demand for indexation is largest for long-term contracts because, for the long term, recent price-level stability is least relevant as a predictor of future developments.

The econometric results that have been summerized confirm essentially three hypotheses with regard to the prospective speed of EPC penetration: (1) The EPC's expansion as a deposit, bond, official reserve, and general contract currency will be faster, the faster the national currencies lose purchasing power. (2) The EPC's expansion as a deposit, bond, and official reserve currency will be faster, the

---

[42] There are at least two ways of explaining the fact that the rate of inflation and the rate of change of inflation have had more influence on the public's evaluation of purchasing-power risk than the instability of the rate of inflation. In the first place, the inflation rate may have been used as a proxy for inflation-rate variability in order to save information costs. Alternatively, however, the closer (positive) correlation of the extent of indexation with the rate of inflation and notably with the rate of change of inflation may indicate that the public has not yet understood that a rapidly falling rate of inflation involves just as much purchasing-power risk as a rapidly rising rate of inflation.

[43] While the long indexation lag for depositors, among them many small savers, should be attributed to a recognition and a decision lag, the long lag for wage bargains would rather seem to comprise a decision and a negotiation lag. Trade union leaders require some time to secure agreement on wage claims within their own organizations; furthermore, some time elapses until the presentation of wage claims leads to a wage bargain. Bond issuers, on the other hand, are hierarchic institutions, which react (if at all) without much of a decision or negotiation lag and possess enough financial expertise to be free of a recognition lag.

[44] In all other cases, normal linear functions gave the best fit (also a better fit than semilog or double-log functions).

larger the variations and variability of exchange rates between the national currencies. (3) Since inflation and exchange-rate risk are of less importance for the choice of a deposit currency than the size of the transaction domain, real demand for EPC deposits will expand relatively slowly and gradually.

Restricting Real Exchange-Rate Changes?

I do not wish to intrude into Oort's domain, but a brief comment on Basevi's proposal to establish gliding target zones for real exchange rates (as measured with respect to the wholesale price index) may be permissible. It seems necessary because, according to Optica 1976, it is "unrealistic to retain as the *main* approach to European monetary unification the launching of an EPC" and because the new "main approach" is even claimed to be "a prerequisite for the eventual launching of an EPC."[45] Essentially, I have three objections to the scheme.

First, it may delay necessary adjustments in the terms of trade. Assume that a series of sizable oil price increases affects the member countries differently, depending on the scarcity of substitute energy, such as natural gas, from which each country suffers. Suppose, for example, that a considerable and cumulative real exchange-rate depreciation of the deutsche mark is called for that cannot be accommodated over several years within the proposed bands of 1 percent and through the proposed crawl. To prevent the real depreciation of the deutsche mark, the Bundesbank would have to support it through intervention, that is, it would have to reduce the supply of deutsche marks. As a result the domestic price level would fall (or rise less than without the scheme), so that the real depreciation of the deutsche mark would only be delayed. Since the real exchange rate is not permitted to adjust except for a limited proportion, in the next period the adjustment backlog would imply further intervention, reductions in deutsche mark money supply and the deutsche mark price level (increase) in addition to any new adjustment need that might arise. Thus the real exchange-rate disequilibrium and the volume of intervention per period would increase cumulatively until the speed at which new adjustment requirements for real exchange rates arose fell below the maximum speed of the Optica reference-rate crawl. The example shows that attempts to restrict real exchange-rate changes have far more serious consequences than attempts to restrict nominal exchange-rate changes because intervention (money supply adjustments) removes only nominal, but not real, exchange-rate disequilibrium.

---

[45] Optica Group, *1976 Report*, p. 2.

The Optica group's proposal of a 1 percent band around a reference rate, equal to the gliding average real exchange rate over the last four quarters, limits the maximum real exchange-rate adjustment vis-à-vis the pivot currency or unit of account to less than 2 percent if, for example, all quarters receive the same weight. And, according to its Table I.A.6, the deviations from WPI purchasing-power parity (vis-à-vis the deutsche mark) exceed 5 percent in 52 percent of all quarters from 1961 to 1975 (unweighted average of six member countries). The Optica group therefore concedes that "there may be a residual need for real exchange-rate changes in the case of individual Community currencies."[46] However, if exceptions from the proposed rule are easily granted in case of "residual need," one may wonder whether the scheme would have any sizable effect at all.

My second objection is that the need for WPI real exchange-rate changes may arise not only relatively continuously as a result of real changes (terms of trade) but also temporarily because monetary policy affects wholesale prices with a longer lag than international asset equilibrium and hence the nominal exchange rate. This is acknowledged by the Optica group and explains why the largest real exchange-rate variability was obtained for financially open countries like the United Kingdom and the United States (WPI) and Switzerland (average value of exports).[47] The implication is that the Optica proposal would prevent a participating country from returning to price-level stability considerably faster than the other members. It is difficult to see how such a constraint could be justified as long as the most inflation-averse country pursues a steady and preannounced policy on money supply.

The third objection is that since real exchange-rate depreciation can be engineered through a particularly expansionary monetary policy and since attainment of the lower intervention point establishes the right to receive subsidized credits from the other members, the moral hazard is not solved. The Optica group, it is true, proposes that "over the whole year . . . the foreign-exchange intervention should be nil" and that medium-term aid should continue to be conditional on the borrower's compliance with a collectively agreed standard of behavior,[48] but the unconditional short-term credit facilities of the EMCF (up to four months) would fail to be eliminated.

To summarize this section, implementation of the Optica proposal is likely to be harmful unless margins are widened so drastically that they would rarely be attained. The aim of the proposal, the reduction

---

[46] Ibid., p. 17.

[47] Ibid., p. 88; see also tables A8 and A1 and appendix, p. 57.

[48] Ibid., pp. 86, 90.

of inflation and of exchange-rate fluctuations, can best be attained by fixing and announcing disinflationary rates of expansion of money supply in all member countries. The case for the EPC does not in any way depend on the Optica scheme; on the contrary, the indexed-basket EPC is a substitute for it because it offers protection against intra-community real exchange-rate changes.

Conclusion

Although a large part of my paper has been devoted to a critique of proposals that should not be adopted, five suggestions for increasing monetary integration in Europe have emerged:

- The parity system of the snake should be abandoned.
- The EMCF and IMF facilities for subsidized central bank borrowing should be abolished.
- Central banks should abstain from foreign exchange intervention (except, perhaps, in a once-and-for-all operation to fund existing net foreign exchange reserves).
- The central bank of each member country should fix, announce, and, of course, attain a moderately disinflationary quantitative target for its rate of monetary expansion and, if possible, harmonize it with the targets of the other members.
- The EEC should offer conversion of the national currencies into a European parallel currency of guaranteed constant-weighted EEC purchasing power and let it be used freely in all member countries.

To say that these are the next steps to be taken, unfortunately, is not to say that they are near.

SUMMARY OF THE OPTICA 1976 PROPOSALS FOR EXCHANGE-RATE MANAGEMENT

Giorgio Basevi

Introduction

In the year that has passed since the first Optica report was published,[1] progress toward European monetary and economic integration has been blocked and, indeed, set back by a succession of crises in exchange markets. The reaction to these crises has been a reintroduction of foreign exchange controls and of more or less disguised trade restrictions. These, if maintained, threaten to destroy the little that remains of European economic union. Firmer cooperation on exchange rates is of prime importance in the present situation and a prerequisite for the eventual launching of a European parallel currency along the lines that were proposed in the Optica 1975 report.

This is the background to the Optica 1976 proposal for the management of exchange rates. The evidence assembled in the report indicates that it would be desirable to limit the movement of exchange rates in line with the difference in an average of recently observed inflation rates at home and abroad. This is far less ambitious than many other schemes that have been proposed in the past. It gives concreteness to broad ideas that have recently been put forward in official circles, which would probably not be operational in their original form because they leave too much discretion to national authorities in defining exchange-rate targets. As a minimum, the Optica proposal would check the type of positive feedback between exchange markets and domestic inflation witnessed in 1976. Its objectives are the stabilization of expectations and the reinforcement of the kind of monetary guidelines that are increasingly being adopted in community countries. But it recognizes that differences in national inflation rates can be eliminated only very gradually.

---

[1] Study Group on Optimum Currency Areas (Optica Group), *Towards Economic Equilibrium and Monetary Unification in Europe* (1975 Report) (Brussels, Commission of the European Communities, 1976).

Justification for the Proposal

If all wages and prices were set in competitive markets, full employment would be ensured by the flexibility of the wage and price structure: monetary policy (under floating exchange rates) or exchange-rate policy (under fixed but adjustable rates) would take the role of determining a given rate of inflation for each country relative to the rest of the world. In reality, however, prices and wages are not perfectly flexible, so that a given growth in the money stock under floating rates (or a choice of an exchange rate under a fixed-exchange-rate system) does not ensure a desired rate of inflation over the short run. Thus over the same period, the pace of inflation, together with the level of employment, depends on the price-setting behavior of trade unions and producers in the labor and product markets as well as on how all economic operators anticipate future changes in the price level. In this situation, control of the money stock under flexible exchange rates is no longer sufficient to ensure a predetermined rate of inflation consistent with full employment. The feedback from exchange-rate changes leads to cost increases that, if ratified by monetary policy, give further impetus to the inflationary mechanism and possibly lead to a spiral of ever-increasing inflation. While it is clear that this mechanism can only continue so long as monetary policy is accommodating, price and exchange-rate expectations play a fundamental role in the process, and their formation may not be uniquely determined by monetary policy. Thus quantitative rules on money and credit supply, even though essential, are not enough. They may not be credible, particularly when the social and political struggle can find an acceptable resolution only through a validating monetary policy. In these cases quantity rules for monetary policy should be reinforced by ceilings placed on government expenditures and thus on budget deficits, by guidelines on factor input remuneration, and, last but not least, by rules for managing the exchange rates.

In the recent past there has been a gradual shift in official thinking about the importance of announcing specific targets in the domain of monetary policy. Some central banks have experimented with setting rules of conduct for periods up to a year. However, sizable departures of exchange rates from their PPP value occur typically over the short run. When for exogenous reasons the external value of a currency falls, its effects in raising the prices of imported inputs and the cost of living are quickly incorporated into the wage- and price-setting mechanism. Traditional guidelines for incomes policy do not help here, since the problem is not one of income distribution between wages and profits but rather of income distribution between foreigners and nationals. While this problem should in the first instance be dealt with by modifying the automatic indexation mechanism built into the cost-of-living clauses, its inflationary potential can be reduced by smoothing short-run exchange-rate changes through some rules for managing the foreign exchange markets.

Clearly, any rule that requires central bank intervention in the foreign exchange market comes into conflict with the maintenance of a money supply target. In fact, intervention on the foreign exchange markets, unless successfully sterilized, implies a one-to-one creation or destruction of domestic base money or central bank money. However, although the two sets of rules appear contradictory when viewed as simultaneous, they may become complementary in sequence.

A Proposal for a New Exchange-Rate Agreement for the European Community

The Optica 1976 report contains a proposal for a new agreement among EEC members whereby exchange rates are managed in relation to reference rates that crawl on the basis of the relative performance of countries in terms of their wholesale price indexes. The proposal can be summarized as follows:

1. The reference rate for each country participating in the arrangement is defined in terms of an effective exchange rate. The reference rate is subsequently expressed in European units of account (EUA) for purposes of standard measurement.
2. An effective PPP index is calculated for each participating country by dividing a country's wholesale price index by a weighted average of the wholesale price indexes of its competitors, the weights being the same as those entering into the formula of that country's effective exchange rate.
3. A country's reference rate is changed periodically (at least quarterly) in proportion to the change of a moving average of the country's effective PPP index. The length of the moving average and the weights to be attached to the individual time elements in the average should be the same for all countries in the arrangement.
4. The authorities are to set margins around the reference rate.
5. At the beginning of each period (month or quarter) the authorities ascertain, on the basis of the computation described in (2) and (3), whether their country's reference rate has appreciated or depreciated relative to the preceding year. In the case of an appreciated currency, the authorities intervene by selling their currency on the spot market if the market rate tends to exceed the lower bound of the band. Conversely, in case of a depreciated currency, the

authorities intervene by buying their currency on the spot market if the market rate tends to exceed the upper bound of the band.

6. The authorities are not to sterilize the monetary counterpart of their foreign exchange intervention in the spot market.

7. The mechanism of intervention and reserve borrowing currently in use among members of the European Monetary Cooperation Fund (EMCF) should be extended to make this scheme operational. Borrowing countries are to pay a positive real rate of interest on the outstanding loans. Borrowing privileges are reduced or completely abolished if a country contravenes (5) and (6).

8. Snake countries can keep their present arrangement but at the same time would need to coordinate their economic policy so as progressively to align their exchange rates with their implied PPP values.

Implementation of the Scheme

Concerning proposals (1), (2), and (3), the use of country-specific effective exchange rates and effective PPP indexes implies a uniform and consistent intervention. However, it does not enforce a correspondence between changes in bilateral exchange rates and in bilateral PPP. Such a feature is an advantage of the proposal, since bilateral PPP performs statistically worse than multilateral (effective) PPP. Alternatively, however, the scheme could function by aligning reference exchange rates measured in a common-basket *numéraire* (EUA) with PPP indexes based on the same weighting scheme of the basket. Neither the length of the moving average nor the weights to be given to each element in the average should make the crawling parity unduly sticky. They should simply smooth seasonal and exceptional elements that might otherwise push exchange rates away from their recent trend, for example, by using a moving average of the last four quarters. The length and the time of the weighting scheme must be identical for all participating countries to avoid the emergence of inconsistent reference rates.

Concerning points (4) and (5), the proposal envisages intervention, if any, in only one direction for a given currency during every period. Relatively depreciated currencies are not permitted to depreciate more than is indicated by their purchasing power (plus the margin), but they are free to appreciate if the market so indicates. Conversely, relatively appreciated currencies are not permitted to appreciate more, during every period, than is implied by their purchasing power (plus the margin), but they can depreciate if the market so indicates. The rationale for this one-sided intervention scheme can easily be understood.

On the one hand, the scheme aims at avoiding the buildup of

exchange-rate–wage-price spirals in devaluing countries. It does not aim, however, at preventing those countries from doing better on the exchange-rate front than is indicated by their past performance on the inflation front, if the market so esteems. On the other hand, the scheme aims at avoiding too rapid appreciation of strong member currencies but allows them to appreciate by less than seems granted by their past relative price performance, if the market so esteems.

On the whole, the scheme puts the emphasis on stabilizing expectations in the exchange markets and on harmonizing inflation rates among member countries. Such a goal, however, is not sought through the imposition of a straitjacket in the form of shrinking margins of fluctuations. Inflation rates will continue to diverge among member countries for as long as they do not harmonize their incomes and monetary policies. The proposal only aims at preventing inflation rates from diverging even more as the consequence of exceptional disturbances in the foreign exchange markets. The scheme in no way implies that low-inflation countries would be induced to raise their inflation rates.

To appreciate the importance of (6), our proposal should be seen as a supplement to monetary policy. Otherwise, we would commit the error of expecting from rules governing the exchange rate results that can be obtained only by more fundamental policies. To clarify, consider the following example. Assume that a yearly money supply target is set at a 5 percent growth level; it may still happen that the target is temporarily overshot and that this or other exogenous factors push the exchange rate upward (a devaluation) during a quarter. Intervention to slow down such a move will require destruction of base money at a rate that may restore the growth of money supply to the target or temporarily reduce it below 5 percent. Over the whole year, however, if the exchange rate is smoothed on the PPP path implied by the yearly target for money supply, the foreign exchange intervention should be nil, so that the evolution of the exchange rate would indeed be determined by the target of money supply relative to the demand for it.

On the other hand, if the smoothing rule on foreign exchanges were not followed, excessive departure of the exchange rate from the PPP trend implied by the yearly target for money supply might feed back into prices and wages to such an extent that the authorities' capacity to keep aiming at the yearly target of money supply might lose credibility. In fact, abiding by the money supply rule in the face of the unexpected inflationary push (implied by the unexpected devaluation) means a more stringent credit squeeze or a reduction of the central bank's willingness to finance the government deficit, both of which may be politically unacceptable.

The scheme should make it easier to set a given money supply target on a short-term basis, even though the magnitudes on which these targets are set usually span longer (yearly) periods. The scheme should also make it easier to adjust the money supply target when the real magnitudes on which it has been based turn out to have been incorrectly estimated.

As for the first claim, since money supply targets are difficult to enforce on a short-term basis, temporary deviations from the target may be reflected in unexpected changes in the exchange rate, which, if allowed to manifest themselves and be transmitted into price expectations, may make it more difficult for the authorities to stick to their preannounced money supply target. By requiring the authorities to smooth the excessive depreciation of a devalued currency (or, less likely in this example, the excessive appreciation of a revalued currency), the scheme as proposed here puts a brake on their abnormal money creation. It thus constitutes a built-in stabilizer for the short-term conduct of their monetary policy.

As for the second claim, it may very well happen that the authorities wrongly estimate the variables on which they base their money supply target. The demand for a money whose currency area tends to increase (such as the deutsche mark) may be underestimated by the authorities that supply that money (such as the Bundesbank). As a result, their money supply target may turn out to be deflationary and tend to provoke an appreciation of their currency that is unexpected on the basis of past inflation performance. By requiring the authorities to intervene to slow down the appreciation of their currency, the scheme here proposed would compel them to create more currency (which they sell against foreign exchange) than they had planned on the basis of their estimates— which is indeed what is required, given the unexpectedly larger demand for their money. Thus again the scheme provides a built-in stabilizer, which in this case takes the form of correcting inaccurately set targets, rather than the short-term adaptation of actual quantities to correctly set targets (as in the previous example).

Clearly the stabilizing features of this scheme also have some drawbacks. While on the whole the scheme has the advantage of making it difficult for devaluing countries to accelerate their money supply too rapidly, it makes it difficult for revaluing countries to decelerate their money supply too rapidly. In other words the scheme puts a premium on monetary convergence. This difficulty should not be too great, however, especially if allowance is made for the moderate length of the moving average (a year), the frequent periodicity in resetting the reference rates (every quarter or month), and the margins applied to the reference rate.

In conclusion, how effective these constraints will be depends, among other things, on the width of the margin beyond the crawling parity, the length and weights of the moving average formula, the periodicity of the crawl, the lags between money and prices, and whether expectations in foreign exchange markets are formed on the basis of adaptive processes or of rational behavior. In particular, the way expectations are formed is crucial in reconciling the use of the proposal in a market system.

With respect to (7), the danger of excessive use of EMCF resources should not be exaggerated. Since the scheme does not require realigning initial reference rates on the basis of the current level of absolute purchasing power but simply crawling from those reference rates on the basis of changes in purchasing power from the initial period, it is unlikely that the weak currencies—if indeed currently undervalued —will put too much pressure on the working of the scheme. Nor, for that matter, is the converse likely for strong currencies if—as it appears at present—they are overvalued in terms of purchasing power.

Despite the Optica group belief that the use of EMCF resources required to sustain the scheme would indeed be modest—particularly as the exchange markets become familiar with its modalities and incorporate them in the formation of expectations—it is possible that the initial skepticism of the countries that see themselves as likely creditors will be considerable. To overcome this understandable attitude, supplementary features are underlined in the proposal: (1) It would be expedient to begin with relatively wide margins around the parities, thus limiting the need for intervention; margins could be narrowed substantially after an initial period of, say, one year. When the system has reached normal operation, margins should be narrow to make effective the automatic corrective pressures on domestic monetary management that the scheme is designed to introduce. (2) While it is essential that the scale of lending facilities be adequate to strengthen the credibility of the reference rate structure, automatic drawings would be repayable over a short period, as they are at present in EMCF. To the extent that drawings could be repaid only by mobilizing short- and medium-term credit facilities, access to the latter would be conditional on the borrower's compliance with collectively agreed behavioral standards, as is already the case in the community. In the proposed scheme these standards are points (5) and (6) on intervention rules and absence of sterilization.

Since the reference rates in the proposed scheme are formulated in effective rate terms, the choice of a medium of intervention is left open. The national monetary authorities in their concerted intervention may choose to defend a particular reference rate by intervening in one or more community currencies or in dollars, and the choice will no doubt vary from time to time. Claims and debts arising out of intervention should be denominated in European units of account (as for the reference rates). This will spread exchange risks more fairly than in the present EMCF rules, where they are assumed by the debtors. But borrowers should be charged a positive real interest rate on their drawings.

The Optica proposal for exchange-rate management was inspired by the experiences of 1976 for the individually floating currencies. At first we did not specifically envisage any changes in the management of the five community currencies that (with two noncommunity currencies) constitute the snake. It is obvious, however, that adoption of the proposed scheme would present problems for the snake currencies.

First, enforcing PPP on the non-snake currencies would raise the question why it should not also be enforced on the others. If it is recognized that members of the snake do not meet the requirements for maintaining fixed nominal rates bilaterally, that is, parallel inflation trends and coordinated monetary policies, would it not appear logical to apply the same principle as proposed for the individually floating currencies?

Second, preserving the snake creates technical problems in managing the PPP rule when intervention to operate the rule takes place in snake currencies. It is obvious that these problems would be easier if each snake currency were managed according to the PPP rule—a symmetry of treatment that would no doubt be suggested in preparatory negotiations by the countries now floating individually.

Notwithstanding these objections, the Optica group has not proposed the abandonment of the present snake; it would be inconsistent with the group's aim, which is to present a proposal for breaking the vicious circle of depreciation and inflation so as ultimately to stabilize nominal exchange rates and harmonize national inflation rates at a low level.

MANAGED FLOATING
IN THE EUROPEAN COMMUNITY

C. J. Oort

The course of monetary events in Europe since the late 1960s is marked by grand designs, utter despondency, accidental successes as well as failures, and generally a complete lack of a clear, common, and consistent strategy. Blocked by their failure to think and act alike, the countries of the European Economic Community have stumbled through the international monetary crises without a common sense of direction and hence without any real influence on the course of events. The objective story is told by Table 1 and Figures 1 and 2. What stands out is the adventures of the "snake," for only the snake represents a specifically European experience.

In what follows I want to color the objective picture with my personal interpretation, based on subjective opinions and possibly tinted also by my national background and experience. The Netherlands has adhered to the snake from the start and has never left it. We tend to think of the European monetary scene as consisting of the snake and of errant outsiders. Others may well interpret the present situation quite differently: as a group of individually floating currencies—the deutsche mark, the pound sterling, the French franc, and the Italian lira—and some satellites that have hitched their exchange rates to one of the majors. Has the snake in fact become a deutsche mark bloc? Could it again become the common exchange-rate arrangement for the EEC as a whole? If not, or if not in the foreseeable future, what other arrangements can we devise? Or is the present situation satisfactory for the time being?

Those are some of the questions that we ask ourselves in the EEC today. In commenting on them, I shall pay special attention to the proposals now being discussed in the community to set up a system of "rules for floating" based on the concept of target zones for effective exchange rates. These proposals are part of the Duisenberg plan to reactivate the coordination of economic policies generally.

First, I want to present a brief description and a personal view of the snake, followed by a review of various suggestions that have been made to improve the present snake arrangement.

The European Snake Arrangement

A Brief History of the Snake. The snake was conceived as part of the grand design for European monetary union in 1980.[1] The whole terrain in which the snake grew up is well known. The history of the Werner plan is a fascinating story that deserves careful analysis by students of many disciplines, not least of political science. Occasionally we still hear echoes of the battle between the so-called economists, who claimed that coordination of economic policy has to come first, the so-called monetarists, who believe in the feedback from irreversible monetary commitments, and the so-called institutionalists, who focus on the decision-making machinery. But the main combatants have become weary, disillusioned, and even cynical. The plan for monetary union has been virtually abandoned, in fact if not officially, as a practical policy objective for the foreseeable future.

But the snake has survived, if badly amputated and divorced from its background. Its original purpose was to serve as an instrument for bringing about full monetary union. Since exchange rates would be completely frozen in the final stage, it was thought that the margins of fluctuation should be gradually reduced during the interim. The strategy now appears somewhat naive. What was the use of reducing those margins, as long as countries retained their national autonomy with respect to the far more important decision to adjust the parity—the central (cross-) rates in modern terminology—of their currency? And what was the economic case for reducing margins that were then only 3 percent for the cross-rates of European currencies?

In my view the snake would have remained an insignificant monetary gimmick if the world scene had not changed radically before the poor animal was set loose. It had to fend for itself in the cold world that was rapidly evolving from the quasi-security of fixed parities to the free-for-all of floating rates. The emergence of the snake as an instrument of common exchange-rate management was perhaps inevitable given the monetary events in the world at large, but its association with European monetary union was, I believe, an historical accident.

When the ministers of the Group of Ten major industrial countries decided at the Smithsonian conference, in December 1971, to increase the margins on the dollar from 1.5 percent to 4.5 percent, the countries of the European Economic Community would have been faced with a

---

[1] Most of the official documents on the European Economic and Monetary Union can be found in a *Compendium of Community Monetary Texts*, published by the Office for Official Publications of the European Communities (Luxembourg, 1974). The so-called Werner plan was published as a supplement to the November 1970, *Bulletin of the European Communities*.

total margin of 9 percent on their cross-rates if they had not been able to put the snake mechanism into operation almost immediately.[2] In March 1972 they decided to limit the margin of fluctuation on their cross-rates to 4.5 percent, these margins to be maintained by intervention in one another's currencies: the "snake in the (dollar) tunnel" was born.

The snake became potentially even more important when the EEC countries decided to float their currencies against the dollar in March 1972.[3] The snake enabled the EEC to act as a monetary unit in a floating world. At the time it appeared to us that the par-value system had died in Washington, only to be revived in the European framework with one major new feature: the multilateral intervention system of the snake arrangement.

But the decline of the snake as a communitywide mechanism had already set in before it assumed its new role. The United Kingdom and Ireland left in June 1972, and in February 1973 Italy dropped out. France decided to leave temporarily in January 1974, returned briefly in July 1975, and left again on March 15, 1976 (see Table 1). What remains today is the small central core consisting of West Germany, the Benelux countries, and Denmark, that is, only five of the nine EEC countries, with Norway and Sweden as associates, Austria as a de facto participant, and Switzerland as a reluctant suitor.[4]

The snake started out as a community affair, embedded in the ideal of full monetary union. It has evolved into something that now looks like a deutsche mark zone, not in the technical sense that countries use the deutsche mark as their main reserve asset—West German payments surpluses, the lack of suitable paper, and the resistance of the West

---

[2] For many reasons I shall never forget the Smithsonian conference: its atmosphere of drama, the solemn pronouncements by the high priests of Bretton Woods, the computer spewing out effective devaluations and revaluations in two decimal points, the efficient badgering by the chairman and his clever deputy, the ponip and circumstance surrounding the president's solemn speech—all of it cut down to very small size by what happened shortly afterward. In contrast, the decision to increase the margins was taken in a rather offhand manner, without preparation of any kind and determined as an average of the U.S. desire for even wider margins and the European wish to go less far. Hence the rather curious figure of ±2.25 percent.

[3] Or, as we insisted at the time, when the dollar started to float against those currencies that maintained their formal parity. The matter was of some importance then in connection with the valuation of the SDR.

[4] The difference between the four groups is that the associates, though participating fully in the multilateral intervention system, do not take part in the short-term credit mechanism of the EEC; Austria has no formal ties with the arrangement at all but aligns its exchange rate with that of the deutsche mark by unilateral action; and Switzerland appears to align its exchange rate with the deutsche mark as much as possible without always succeeding.

194

TABLE 1

BIOGRAPHY OF THE SNAKE

Date	Event
May 1971	Deutsche mark and Dutch guilder floated.
August 1971	Convertibility of the dollar into gold "temporarily" suspended.
December 1971	Smithsonian agreement.
March 1972	EEC finance ministers decide to set up the snake mechanism.
April 1972	Snake mechanism becomes operational.
May 1972	United Kingdom, Ireland, Denmark, and Norway join the snake.
June 1972	United Kingdom and Ireland leave the snake. Denmark leaves but rejoins soon after.
January 1973	Swiss franc floated.
February 1973	Dollar devalued by 10 percent. Italy leaves the snake.
March 1973	The snake leaves the tunnel (joint float). The United Kingdom, Ireland, and Italy continue to float independently. Sweden joins the snake. Deutsche mark revalued by 3 percent.
June 1973	Deutsche mark revalued by 5.5 percent.
September 1973	Dutch guilder revalued by 5 percent.
January 1974	France leaves the snake.
July 1974	France rejoins the snake.
March 1976	France leaves the snake.
October 1976	Deutsche mark revalued by 2 percent. Norwegian and Swedish kroner devalued by 1 percent, Danish krone by 4 percent.

German authorities have so far prevented that development—but in the sense that countries are strongly dependent on the West Germany economy and have chosen to define their exchange-rate policies in relation to the deutsche mark. It is tempting to interpret the monetary history of Europe in the last ten years as a failure to establish a fixed-but adjustable par-value system among major countries and as a success of that same system within an emerging deutsche mark zone. Every time the cross-rates of the smaller countries' currencies vis-à-vis the deutsche mark were considered out of line, they did adjust their central rates. Every time the relation between the major currencies of the community had to be adjusted, the weaker partner dropped out.

The only exception to the latter proposition was the deutsche mark revaluation in June 1973; but it can be argued, and I believe correctly, that at the time we had not yet fully understood the truly multilateral character of decisions to adjust the central cross-rates within the snake. The 1973 revaluation of the deutsche mark was basically a unilateral action, regarded by the others (which then still included France) as an adjustment of the deutsche mark vis-à-vis the rest of the world, affecting the other snake countries only to the extent that their terms of trade with West Germany were revised. This would have been true if the snake had still been in the dollar tunnel, as it was until two months earlier: the fixed dollar rate of the other snake currencies would not have been affected by the revaluation of the deutsche mark. But, in a floating world, the relation between the snake as a whole and the dollar is codetermined by the dollar–deutsche mark rate as established in the market; a deutsche mark revaluation within the snake implies an effective devaluation of the other currencies with respect to the entire world. In other words, the decision to adjust the central rate of a major currency within the snake affects the other members far more than was the case for individual actions in the Bretton Woods system. Decisions to adjust central rates within the snake are necessarily multilateral.

This elemental truth was brought home to the snake countries in March of last year, when France demanded an adjustment of the deutsche mark–franc central rate.[5] For precisely the sort of political reasons that prevented prompt adjustment of par values in the Bretton Woods system—national pride on the one hand and reluctance to antagonize commercial interests on the other—the two major countries proposed to split the difference: West Germany would revalue the deutsche mark a bit, and France would devalue the franc to about the same extent. It was not realized until the finance ministers and central bank governors of all the snake countries met that the proposed solution would work only if the smaller countries would agree to act as the zero line with respect to which the revaluation of the deutsche mark and the devaluation of the French franc would have to be defined. It was actually a surprise to the major partners when the smaller countries pointed out that the position of the zero line within an agreed deutsche mark–franc adjustment was primarily their concern and their decision. The discussion was a fascinating lesson in formal logic and political maneuvering.

It all proved once again, not that politicians are irrational, but that devaluation and revaluation are still emotional matters in the public mind, however they are labeled (and many cleverly euphemistic labels

---

[5] I reported on this incident in a speech at the University of Edinburgh in May 1976, published in *Common Market Law Review*, August 1976, especially pp. 305 ff.

were proposed). In the end France decided to pull out rather than adjust.[6]

In contrast, the minisnake's mini-Smithsonian of October 18, 1976, came off without a hitch, all countries agreeing on the size of the relative adjustments and on the definition of the zero line (which is significant only for the common agricultural prices in the EEC). The case is an interesting exercise in "managed crawling peg," for the adjustments of central rates were such that the new margins overlapped the previous ones. In fact, market rates hardly changed at all after the realignment even though the gurus of the exchange markets had almost unanimously condemned the adjustment as "too little, too late." But "the market" had been outsmarted all along. Instead of giving in to the strong upward pressure on the deutsche mark in the summer, which policy makers considered exaggerated in terms of fundamental economic developments, the smaller countries first intervened very heavily in the exchange markets to contain the cross-rates within the prescribed margins and then squeezed their money markets until the very high short interest rates choked off the speculative capital flows.[7] Once the storm was over, central rates were adjusted, the capital flows were reversed, and the intervention debts were largely repaid out of reverse intervention.

The European monetary experience of the last decade provides us with two case histories: one of failure, one of success. The European snake has disintegrated, but the minisnake has survived and has even drawn in several noncommunity associates. What factors are responsible for the difference, and what lessons can we draw from the European experience?

Lessons of the Snake. The history of the snake reflects and repeats much of world monetary history of the last ten years. The main lesson of that period would appear to be that a par-value system is not capable of dealing with strongly divergent economic developments. In theory, par

---

[6] There was a persistent and inspired rumor at the time that the French decision was prompted by the Dutch refusal to agree to a limited revaluation of the guilder as part of a total package that would be so complex as to blur the political significance of revaluations and devaluations. The somewhat dramatic late evening exit of the Dutch minister to consult with his cabinet colleagues in The Hague (the dramatic effect mitigated by a heaping plate of delicious Belgian sandwiches provided by a kind Treasury official for the long drive home) may have added to these rumors, which were just not true. The French announced their decision to leave the snake before Duisenberg called back from The Hague.

[7] At one point interest rates on one-month interbank loans reached levels of about 26 percent in the Netherlands. In a public speech that created some commotion at the time (September 1976), I made an estimate of the rather substantial interest and exchange losses that the market incurred by its rather silly speculation against the guilder.

values (or central rates) could be adjusted promptly, in small steps, and as frequently as divergent economic developments require. In practice, however, a system that relies on frequent adjustment by government decisions simply does not work. I argued this point at some length in a paper I gave in 1974 for the Per Jacobsson Foundation, and nothing that has happened since has given me any reason to change that opinion.[8]

What about the inner circle that has stuck with the snake since 1972 and that seems to have managed to run a reformed Bretton Woods system rather successfully?

One explanation is that economic developments, particularly in-flation rates, have not diverged as much between the members of the minisnake as they have between the minisnake as a whole and the other countries of the EEC. That is certainly part of the answer, but I do not believe it represents the total picture. A reduction in differential rates of inflation to at most the range observed in the minisnake is un-doubtedly a necessary condition for the survival of a maxisnake, but I doubt that it would be sufficient. The minisnake has experienced no less than seven revaluations and devaluations among the six currencies involved within the course of only five years (see Table 1). I submit that a maxisnake, encompassing all community currencies, would not have survived the number of realignments needed to keep it together.

Why this difference? Apart from the trivial but in practice quite important fact that decisions among nine (the seven independent currencies of the community plus the two associates) are exponentially more difficult than among six, the main reason for my statement is that the present minisnake is qualitatively a different animal from a European maxisnake. The present minisnake has one vital feature that keeps it together: it contains only one major currency, the deutsche mark. It seems to me that history provides abundant evidence for the proposition that a currency area consisting of one dominating currency and several minor currencies can survive where similar arrangements among major currencies would fail. The minisnake may not be a deutsche mark zone in the traditional sense that the participants hold their international reserves largely in deutsche marks, but it is so in all other relevant respects.

The general argument is based on the old and obvious proposition that small countries, which generally have relatively open economies, have strong economic incentives to maintain fixed, if adjustable, ex-change rates with their closest trading partner or partners. Put in other

---

[8] Conrad J. Oort, "Steps to International Monetary Order," Per Jacobsson Lecture, International Monetary Fund (Tokyo, 1974), pp. 12–13.

FIGURE 1
EXCHANGE RATES OF EEC COUNTRIES AND
PERCENTAGE DEVIATIONS FROM CENTRAL RATES

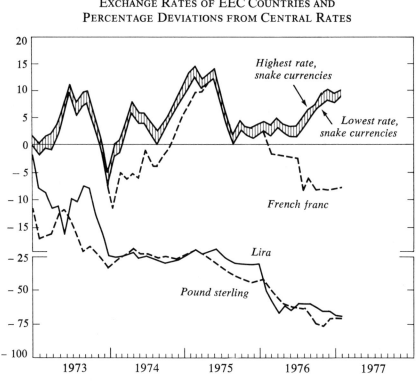

SOURCE: European Communities.

terms, their national currency areas are so clearly suboptimal that they are more willing than larger and less open countries to adapt their national policies to those of their major trading partner.

The case history of the snake seems to bear out these propositions. The larger countries of the community have all shown themselves luke-warm toward the snake. All but West Germany have left the arrangement. Even France, the champion of fixed exchange rates, left the snake in 1974 and 1976 rather than adjust the central rate of the French franc when it was under market pressure (see Figure 1).

The same picture emerges when we look at the coordination of economic policies. It is sometimes said that the minisnake has been able to coordinate national economic and monetary policies more successfully than the EEC as a whole. That may be true, but the implied notion that the methods or the mores of the smaller group are somehow superior to those of the community as a whole reflects, I believe, an incorrect

199

interpretation of the actual situation. As I see it, the smaller countries have been willing to align their policies, in particular their monetary policies, with those of West Germany, while West Germany has set its own national targets without regard to the policies of the snake partners.[9] The declared objectives of monetary policy in the different snake countries are clear evidence of this. West Germany has declared a quantitative target for the growth of its domestic money supply (the *Zentralbankgeldmenge* or "central bank money"), whereas the smaller countries have declined to set such targets with explicit reference to the fact that their monetary policies must be geared to the requirements of the exchange markets and in particular to their commitments in the snake. The asymmetry is obvious and reflects what I believe to be the true nature of the minisnake: that of a deutsche mark zone dominated by the strong West German economy and held together by the need of the smaller countries to keep as close a tie with the West German economy as possible, even at the expense of some of their monetary autonomy.

The asymmetry is also inevitable: where there is such inequality of economic interest, there cannot be equality in the give-and-take of policy coordination. Since it is always difficult to maintain the shifting balance between near-equals, the minisnake may well be a more stable arrangement than a maxisnake of the entire EEC, provided the dominant partner in the minisnake does not abuse its power—as West Germany has not done—and provided it leads rather than lags in economic performance—as West Germany clearly has done, particularly with regard to inflation.

Stable the minisnake may be, but it is not a very satisfactory arrangement in the long run from anybody's point of view. The EEC lacks a coherent exchange-rate system; the countries with individually floating currencies feel excluded from the "inner circle of strong economies." It should not be surprising, therefore, that several ideas have been proposed to set up a communitywide system of exchange-rate management. Essentially two approaches have been suggested: (1) adapting the present snake arrangement to enable countries that now have a floating currency to join, and (2) creating a looser framework

---

[9] This statement sounds like a reproach but it is not meant to be. As long as West German monetary policy is more successful in reducing inflation than the policies of its partners, one can hardly object to the kind of discipline that West German policy imposes on its partners through the snake. The statement also sounds more negative than perhaps it should. Although the major targets of West German economic and monetary policy have not, as far as I know, ever been amended as a result of discussions in the snake, the timing of intended policy measures has occasionally been geared to the requirements of the snake.

of rules for floating to apply to all community currencies, the minisnake being maintained as it is. The second part of this paper will briefly comment on the first approach; the third part will focus on the second.

These two sets of proposals need not be considered mutually exclusive. They may each be relevant for different stages in the development of the EEC. I would submit that no modification of the snake that retains its essential characteristics—the obligation to maintain cross-rates within prescribed, relatively narrow margins—will enable all countries of the community to join such an arrangement under present circumstances. The snake, however modified, will be a realistic option for the community as a whole only when we have succeeded in reducing present differences in economic development, in particular rates of inflation and balance-of-payments positions. Until such time we need a different strategy if we wish to establish a coherent exchange-rate system for the community as a whole. The proposals to be presented in the third part deal with that immediate future, while the next part will focus on the next stage of European monetary integration, when an all-community snake will again be conceivable. It will deal with several proposals that have been made to improve the snake mechanism or to modify it so as to enable present outsiders to join at an earlier date than would otherwise be possible.

Proposals to Modify the Snake

In the more than five years since the snake came into being, many proposals have been made to modify the agreement. The most comprehensive set of proposals was presented in 1974 and again in 1975 by Jean-Pierre Fourcade, then French minister of finance. To make it easier for all members of the EEC to join the agreement, he proposed a number of modifications of the snake arrangement, which implied a relaxation of the intervention rules, an increase of the volume and a lengthening of the maturity of the credit available under the agreement, and the development of a common dollar policy.

It is curious that, at least on the policy-making level, not one proposal has been made to deal with the major flaw of the par-value system and hence also of the snake arrangement—the reluctance of governments to adjust par values (central rates) promptly and adequately. The tenor of my comments has been to show that the European snake has in fact been incapable of keeping major currencies together for any length of time, precisely because countries outside the minisnake group have failed to adjust their central rates promptly. Periodic rate adjustments will be required as long as rates of inflation and other determinants of the balance of payments continue to diverge in the different countries of the community—which, I am afraid, will be the case for some time to come. If that is true, the mechanism of central-rate adjustment is a vitally important issue that requires far more attention than it has received, at least in official circles. For that reason I shall devote this part of my paper to that point only and ignore the other important issues.

First I would like to comment on credit arrangements. Ever since Anthony Barber, then chancellor of the exchequer, demanded "unlimited credits, for unlimited periods, at low rates of interest" as a condition of British participation in the snake, credit has been a somewhat emotional issue in the community. Barber may not have been serious in presenting his demands, but potential creditors were not amused. And sensitivity has grown since then. Potential creditors regard credit arrangements, particularly if they are not subject to strict and strictly enforced economic policy conditions, as habit-forming drugs that keep deficit countries from putting their house in order. Potential debtors, on the other hand, maintain that they cannot possibly accept the strict commitments of the snake mechanism without sufficient credit lines to offset the potentially very large "speculative" international capital flows. The debate goes on and probably will go on for some time. I sense a growing tendency to carry the problem outside the community, to larger international forums such as the Group of Ten and the IMF, ostensibly because the amounts involved are often so large as to require participation by the other major economies of the world. Another reason that is not often mentioned openly is the growing feeling that the imposition and enforcement of strict economic policy conditions can be realized better on the IMF level than within the circle of immediate colleagues. If that is true, the wider implications for the working of the EEC are rather dismal.

The Adjustment of Central (Cross-) Rates. One of the agreed aims of international monetary reform was to ensure prompt and adequate adjustment of par values. In its report to the Board of Governors of the IMF, the Committee of Twenty stated that it might be necessary to put teeth into the agreement by means of "graduated pressures." Such pressures could be imposed by discretionary action on the part of the IMF, or they could be activated by objective indicators, operating either as presumptive or as automatic triggers.[10] The distinction among discretionary action on the part of an international decision-making body, presumptive indicators, and automatic indicators is, I believe, a

---

[10] International Monetary Fund, *International Monetary Reform: Documents of the Committee of Twenty* (Washington, D.C., 1974).

useful one that can be applied in the European context as well. One might, however, add a further possibility that the deputies of the Committee of Twenty, loyal civil servants that they were, hardly dared to mention, namely, fully automatic adjustment. Since the countries of the EEC are in principle willing to accept stronger commitments than the world community, one cannot exclude such automatic mechanisms a priori.

This is not the place to go into the economic merits and drawbacks of the different sets of methods to ensure prompt adjustment. I will limit myself to presenting a few comments on each of them from the policy maker's point of view, together with a subjective judgment on their chance of being accepted in the foreseeable future as part of a renovated European snake mechanism. Since it is good parliamentary practice to start with the most far-reaching proposal, I shall start with the automatic systems of adjustment.

Automatic Mechanisms. Automatic systems of adjustment imply the legal obligation, imposed on the monetary authorities of the participating countries, to adjust the central rates of their currencies periodically, as a predetermined function of the change in some objective parameter. Among the many indicators examined by the deputies of the Committee of Twenty, it seems to me that only two types are potentially suitable candidates for such automatic systems of adjustment: the crawling peg and indexation on the basis of some index of differential rates of inflation. All others are either clearly inadequate as sole parameter or subject to such margins of interpretation and manipulation that they could not possibly function as parameters in an automatic mechanism of adjustment.

The different versions of a crawling peg all share the drawback that one must either impose severe constraints on the country's intervention and money market policies or accept that the crawl can be manipulated by policy measures. The former is probably unworkable and in any case very unlikely to be accepted by national monetary authorities as long as they still have substantial national autonomy.[11] If the monetary authorities could, and therefore presumably would, manipulate the crawl, the scheme would lose much of its function as a device to enforce prompt adjustment of central rates. The crawling

---

[11] Intervention in the exchange markets for the purpose of manipulating the crawl could be prevented by disallowing intramarginal intervention or by allowing it only by common consent, as in the present snake arrangement. But that still leaves money market policies and possibly also exchange control measures (especially those that regulate capital flows, including the external position of the banking system).

peg would then become an annoying complication for the management of exchange and money markets rather than an automatic system of adjustment. I for one would certainly prefer managed floating to a system of managed crawling peg.

I am far more attracted, at least on the conceptual level, by a system of automatic indexation of central rates on the basis of some index of differential rates of inflation, as proposed in the Optica 1976 report.[12] The authors correctly point out that differential rates of inflation (competitive price and cost performance) are the major factors requiring adjustment of exchange-rate relationships. Studies of the IMF confirm this proposition: the changes that have taken place since the early 1970s have for the most part just offset the differential rates of inflation.[13] If it is true that "fixed but adjustable" par values tend to be too sticky when left to autonomous government decision, it would appear quite sensible to build an automatic correction for differential rates of inflation into the system. On top of the automatic correction, it would have to be possible to adjust central rates by discretionary action as well, in order to take account of factors other than differential rates of inflation. Such discretionary adjustments would have to be subject to community supervision so as to prevent the automatic mechanism from being frustrated by national action.

In commenting briefly on the Optica proposals, I shall ignore the many problems involved in making them fully operational: the choice of the appropriate price index, including the tricky question of whether and by what procedure to correct for "special factors";[14] the length of the reference period and the frequency and timing of adjustment, both as related to the question of market speculation; the problems of interdependence (should we opt for a system of unsynchronized separate adjustments or for periodic mini-Smithsonians?); and so forth. All these

---

[12] Study Group on Optimum Currency Areas (Optica Group), *Inflation and Exchange Rates: Evidence and Policy Guidelines for the European Community* (Brussels: Commission of the European Communities, 1977).

[13] International Monetary Fund, *Annual Report 1976*, pp. 31–32.

[14] In my own country, for example, what about a rise in the price of crude oil and natural gas? It would probably affect our wholesale price index more than that of most other countries since these products play a relatively large part in domestic production and in our international trade (especially if one includes the large transit trade of oil and oil-based products). It would at the same time improve our current-account position because of our large exports of natural gas. A correction of the automatic mechanism would certainly be in order; but what of the many other conceivable cases of perverse relationships and the many relevant factors other than prices, such as shifts in the capital account? Experience indicates that once one embarks on the road of correction and refinement, the end is not in sight. What would it mean for the "automatic" system if it is to be so amended by discretionary "corrections"?

issues can in principle be resolved. In terms of the practical politics of international negotiation, however, they do present serious obstacles to reaching agreement within a reasonable time. I consider this a fatal flaw of the proposal, but I realize that such cynicism is an insufficient basis for rejecting it out of hand.

What are the chances of the community's agreeing even on the general principle of the Optica proposals? I have very serious doubts on that score as well, not only because national policy makers are by nature reluctant to abandon what they rightly or wrongly consider an important policy instrument, but also because indexation in any form is generally regarded as one of the mechanisms of self-reinforcing inflation. This is not the place to go into the economic reasoning behind the vicious circle thesis. Rightly or wrongly it does play a role in the minds of policy makers. They will not want to give up the possibility of defending the effective exchange rate against depreciation, for example, as part of an anti-inflationary program. Defending the rate may require restrictive domestic monetary policies or the use of international reserves, but under certain circumstances countries may be quite willing to pay that price. And they may well be right at least in some cases: the automatic depreciation of the exchange rate on the basis of *past* inflation differentials may frustrate a correction of these differentials by *present* policies.

My principal objection to the scheme, however, is based on the simple observation that the countries of the EEC are manifestly not ready at this time or in the foreseeable future to accept an automatic mechanism for the adjustment of central rates. The present members of the minisnake are very unlikely to accept it; the present outsiders are very unlikely to be induced by such a mechanism to join a renovated all-community snake. If my judgment is correct, I am afraid that the community would waste its time if it were to embark on serious and undoubtedly very lengthy studies and discussions of these proposals. Far worse, it would be sidetracked from what I consider the most promising approach, that is, trying to make small, less ambitious, but meaningful steps in the right direction. The process of monetary integration is a long and arduous one: an attempt to make a great leap forward may well land us in a ditch and frustrate all further progress.

By all means, let us work on mechanisms that prod countries into action, that trigger consultation, and that at some stage may evolve toward gradually more binding policy commitments. In that scheme of things, relative price indexes might well play a role; but presenting them now as automatic determinants of central rate readjustments or even as forerunners of such a mechanism would, I believe, be highly counterproductive politically. The road would be blocked, and political road-blocks are often hard to remove. Let us therefore experiment with less ambitious schemes first and learn to walk together before we try to leap.

Discretionary Action by the Community. Proposals under this heading are necessarily procedural. They range between very strongly and very weakly supranational procedures. At one end of the scale, the EEC could be given the authority to impose a change of a country's central rate, after due process of consultation on the community level. At the other end of the scale, if a country does not adjust its central rate although the (great) majority of its partners deems this necessary, it might be forced to do so by a (strongly) qualified majority vote in the Council of Ministers, or it could be subjected to certain sanctions ("graduated pressures" in the terminology of the Committee of Twenty) imposed by the council. I do not put great faith in such proposals. Discretionary action by the Commission of the European Communities is clearly unacceptable for the time being. Procedures that require out-voting a country on such major policy decisions as the adjustment of central rates, even if accepted in principle (which I consider very unlikely), would probably not prove workable. The spirit of Luxembourg (no majority voting on "vital issues") is still very much alive in the community, even though Gallic nationalism has been replaced by the equally destructive "don't do unto others": the result is the same. Such procedures might conceivably work if based on a system of objective triggers for action to which countries had previously committed themselves. But that brings me to the last category of proposals.

Triggers for Action. The snake mechanism might indeed be improved by incorporating in it certain dynamic elements in the form of triggers for readjustment of central rates. The most sensible form of such a scheme would in my judgment be a system of presumptive triggers. Member countries would commit themselves to adjust their central rates when the trigger is activated, unless the presumption is overridden by an ad hoc decision. The community element in the decision to override the presumption could be gradually strengthened. At first countries might be allowed to take the decision unilaterally, but they would be obliged to consult with their partners and show cause why they should not adjust their central rates. When sufficient experience has been gained with the triggering mechanism, countries might be willing to accept further steps, such as giving the commission or the council the authority to block the national override, or even transferring the authority to override to the community.

The choice of the particular objective indicator that is to serve as presumptive trigger is both less sensitive and less difficult to agree on than in the case of automatic adjustment mechanisms. If countries can agree on a sensible index of relative prices, fine. If that turns out to be too difficult, a presumptive crawling peg might be acceptable for a first, experimental phase. As long as countries can override the presumption, they are less likely to manipulate the crawl. Possibly the system could be refined by additional triggering devices, such as cumulative net amounts of intervention or differential rates of interest prevailing over a certain period. These devices have the disadvantage that they cannot easily be used to indicate the size of the required adjustment, but one could—presumptively—set the required adjustment at half the total margin of fluctuation in the snake.

With a bit of imagination one can think of a great many variations on this theme. What is important in my judgment is that a start be made with a system that (1) is not too ambitious at first, so as to avoid the risk of its breaking down before it is fully developed; (2) is sufficiently flexible, and hence capable of being improved and strengthened, particularly in the direction of adding stronger community elements; and (3) induces a maximum of consultation on, and hopefully coordination of, policies that underlie exchange-rate developments both in the short run (intervention and money market policies, exchange controls, and the like) and in the long run (economic and monetary policies in the wider sense). This philosophy also underlies the Duisenberg proposals for exchange-rate management in the EEC during the period when not all countries are capable of joining or willing to join the present or a modified snake arrangement. I shall now turn to these questions of more immediate concern.

The Target Zone Proposals

General Spirit of the Proposals. In July 1976 Willem H. Duisenberg sent a letter to his fellow ministers of finance of the European Economic Community, in which he presented certain proposals concerning the coordination of economic policy and the management of exchange rates.[15] I shall limit my comments to the latter part of his proposals. It

---

[15] Letter of Willem H. Duisenberg, chairman pro tempore of the Council of Ministers of Economics and Finance, July 6, 1976. At its July meeting the council acknowledged the letter and requested the Monetary Committee, the Committee of Central Bank Governors, and the Economic Policy Committee to study it. Four months later the council had a first substantive discussion of the target zone proposals and asked the first two committees to examine how and when they could be applied in practice. The committees submitted their reports, and the council's first round of discussion on them was held in March and April 1977.

is important to keep in mind, however, that the so-called target zone plan is but one element of a more comprehensive package, which includes suggestions to improve the coordination of economic policies as a first priority. As a matter of fact, the target zones for floating exchange rates, which form the operational core of the proposals on exchange-rate management, are primarily intended to serve as a trigger for consultation and, it is hoped, for coordination of economic policy in general. They may also act as guideposts for the management of exchange rates, but that is not their main purpose. I want to stress this point at the outset, because the apparent similarity between target zones and the margins of fluctuation in a par-value system often leads to the entirely incorrect idea that the target zone plan implies the commitment of member countries to contain their exchange rates within these zones, if necessary by intervention in the exchange markets. That is emphatically not the case.

In order to dispel such misunderstandings at the outset, let me begin by giving a brief description of the target zone proposals, referring for a more detailed account to my earlier papers on the subject.[16] Duisenberg proposed that the countries of the EEC that now have floating exchange rates (individual countries as well as groups of countries such as the snake) establish a target zone for their exchange rate. Ideally, the target zone should reflect the country's assessment of future exchange-rate developments as determined, among other factors, by the policies the country intends to pursue. Since movements of exchange rates are relevant insofar as they imply changes in relative competitive positions, the target zone should be defined in terms, not of the exchange rate vis-à-vis one particular foreign currency, but of a trade-weighted average of exchange rates, that is, the *effective* rate. Target zones would be declared and adjusted by agreed procedures that would be developed over time, starting with no other constraint on national autonomy than the obligation to consult with partner countries and adding stronger community elements at later stages.[17]

The target zones are primarily intended to provide a framework

---

[16] The ideas were first presented in two speeches I gave on the subject as trial balloons before the plan was officially launched, one at the University of Edinburgh in May 1976 (published in *Common Market Law Review*, August 1976, pp. 301–14) and another at the Royal Institute of International Affairs in London in June 1976 (published in Chatham House, *The World Today*, August 1976, pp. 287–94).

[17] Williamson has made an interesting suggestion to put teeth into the obligation of countries to declare a target zone: without it, they would not be allowed to intervene in the foreign exchange market at all. John Williamson, "The Future Exchange Rate Regime," *Banca Nazionale del Lavoro Quarterly Review*, Rome, June 1975, pp. 127–43.

for meaningful discussion in the community on countries' economic policies in general and the management of exchange rates in particular.[18] They serve as a concrete trigger for and a focus of consultation: when a country's effective exchange rate moves outside the target zone, it has to enter into consultation with its partners as well as the Commission of the EC. At first this may be the only commitment, but it is one that is not entirely meaningless. The obligation to explain why earlier intentions were not realized or why the target zone must be adjusted, and the moral suasion that may be exerted by recommendations emerging from the review, do tend to have a certain influence on the national decision-making process. They may, for example, strengthen the hand of the minister of finance in taking unpopular measures to combat inflation.[19]

Present conditions in the community, in particular the strongly divergent rates of inflation, probably do not permit us to go very far in the direction of accepting concrete policy commitments in connection with the target zones for the time being. When international monetary developments have quieted down sufficiently and some experience has been gained with the system of target zones and the accompanying consultation procedures, countries should be willing gradually to accept stronger policy commitments. We might begin, for example, by introducing certain limited, essentially negative obligations in policy areas directly related to the management of exchange rates (in particular money market and intervention policies). These obligations could be similar to the guidelines for floating recommended in 1975 by the Board of Governors of the IMF: countries should not take measures that tend to push the effective exchange rate outside or further away from the target zone.[20] As the basic economic developments in the different countries of the community begin to converge, governments might in

---

[18] When referring to the management of exchange rates, I am thinking of money market policies, intervention in the exchange market, measures to influence the external position of the banking system, official or officially backed international borrowing, financial incentives and penalties or direct controls to influence capital movements, and other forms of exchange control.

[19] The term "target zones" is really not very appropriate for the initial phase in which the system does not impose any policy obligations that tend to bring actual exchange rates in line with the target zone. The resistance to the proposals on the part of the Bundesbank is probably in large measure because of the association of the concept of a target with the intervention obligations of a par-value or a snake system. I have considered changing the wording to "reference zone," but an already established terminology is hard to drop, and "reference zone" would completely omit all allusion to the policy obligations, however limited, that, it is hoped, the system will be made to carry at a later stage.

[20] International Monetary Fund, "Selected Decisions of the International Monetary Fund," no. 8 (Washington, D.C., May 10, 1976), p. 21 ff.

addition accept certain positive policy commitments, in particular with regard to monetary policy and possibly also in the area of economic policy in general. Essential to the target zone proposal, however, is that countries not be in any way obliged to maintain their effective exchange rate within the target zone by intervention in the exchange markets. That is the basic difference from the snake system. If and when countries with an individually floating currency *are* ready to assume such strict obligations, they should join the snake.

It is also important that the policy obligations, if any, should be deliberately asymmetrical to compensate for the inflationary bias in the world of today. The general spirit of the policy commitments should be to prevent further inflationary developments that would cause a significant movement of the effective exchange rate *below* the target zone. There should be no corresponding obligations in the case of an appreciation above the target zone, except in those cases where a review clearly indicates that the country concerned carries out policies that seriously depress its domestic economy and that cause significant damage to its partners. In no case should a country be asked, induced, or forced to adopt policies that add to domestic inflation.

So much for the general spirit of the target zone proposal. The many loose ends will be picked up in the next sections. Before turning to these essentially technical issues, I would like to comment briefly on the political and economic motives behind the Duisenberg plan. A quotation from his original letter may serve to give the flavor of these motives:

> We are worried about the exchange rate developments in the Community. There is at present no effective Community framework for the coordination of policies in this area among all members, while recent developments have surely indicated the urgent need for common action. The large movements of exchange rates have affected our relative competitive positions, in some cases rather strongly, and have created pressures for protection. Moreover, there is a danger of a growing divergence between the countries that participate in the European snake arrangement and the other countries.
>
> A weakening of the snake arrangement, which would allow these other countries to join, does not seem to us the best way to bridge the gap. Rather, we would suggest creating a general Community framework for consultation and surveillance of exchange rate policies, based on the "guidelines for floating" which we have agreed to recommend for adoption in the context of the International Monetary Fund.
>
> As you know, these guidelines centre around the concept

of agreed "target zones" for exchange rates. I would emphasize that the guidelines do not impose any obligation on a country to keep its exchange rate within the target zone, but they do create the presumption that countries will not engage in policy measures that are designed to push the rate away from the target zone. Periodic review of the target zones, and Community surveillance of national policies on the basis of such guidelines, could provide the start of an effective framework for Community action in this area.

The economic motive is clear: the wide swings in cross-rates the community has experienced in recent years threaten its economic cohesion; they are destructive for common policies (especially the common agricultural policy); and they may rightly or wrongly be regarded by some countries or by certain sectors in these countries as a distortion of competition, which creates the danger of protectionist tendencies. In order to combat these dangers we need a two-pronged approach: to remove as much as possible the basic causes of divergent economic developments by effective coordination of economic policies and to prevent swings in exchange rates that do not reflect underlying economic developments. The target zones are instrumental in both areas. They may be an almost empty box at first, but they have a dynamic potential in the direction of policy coordination and policy commitments.

The main political motive is equally clear: to prevent a growing divergence between snake and non-snake countries, in which the snake countries become more and more snake-centered and inclined to consider the snake mechanism the sole road to virtue in the community[21] and the "individual floaters" are excluded more and more from the only policy discussions in the community that have any real content. The latter may be overpessimistic, in view of the lack of real policy discussions in the snake, but the danger of divisive tendencies is certainly there.

Definition, Initial Declaration, and Adjustment of Target Zones. The Duisenberg plan proposes to define the target zones in terms of effective exchange rates, with weights derived from the specific composition of each country's foreign trade.[22] This has two advantages over exchange rates defined in terms of a specific currency. First, effective rates reflect

[21] See, for example, the report by Belgian Prime Minister Tindemans, submitted to the heads of government of the European Communities on December 29, 1975.
[22] To ensure calculation of effective rates in a consistent manner, the weights to be used could, for example, be those employed in the Multilateral Exchange Rate Model of the IMF. Figure 2 shows the development of effective exchange rates.

FIGURE 2

EFFECTIVE EXCHANGE RATES: PERCENTAGE CHANGES FROM FIRST QUARTER 1970

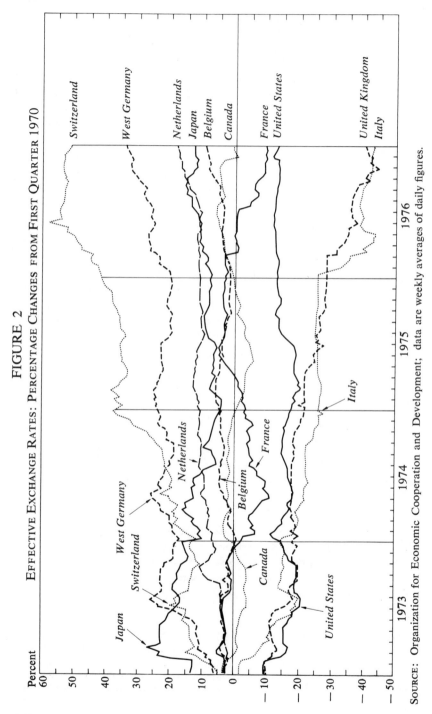

SOURCE: Organization for Economic Cooperation and Development; data are weekly averages of daily figures.

international competitive positions and are therefore more relevant for economic policy than the exchange rates measured in one currency or a standard (non-trade-weighted) basket of currencies. Second, they are less likely to create unrest in exchange markets. Such unrest could be created by the movement of an exchange rate outside its target zone, even though it would not be very likely in a system that does not oblige countries to take concrete action. The second point does seem to be important in practice, or at least exchange dealers think so. Although anyone can calculate the effective rate (indeed, in some countries, it is published regularly), the movement of the effective rate outside the target zone creates a less obvious target for speculation than a similar event in terms of market exchange rates, if only because the effective rate is an abstract concept, an index number; it is not a price at which market operators buy and sell foreign currency.

The width of the target zone should presumably be the same for all countries, although some systematic difference could be considered as a function of, for example, the percentage of the country's foreign trade that takes place within the community (the band being narrower, the larger that percentage). The margin should not be so narrow as to trigger consultation with every small and temporary movement of the effective exchange rate. On the other hand, it should not be so wide as to make the target zones operationally meaningless. In view of the fact that effective exchange rates tend to fluctuate less than exchange rates in terms of individual currencies, a margin of 3 percent above and below the initial value would seem a reasonable starting point. The figure could and should be revised in the light of experience gained in running the system, and it should be narrowed as the economic development in the different countries converges.

The initial target zone will be declared by the country concerned, presumably in the form of the agreed percentage margin around the effective rate prevailing at the start of the system. In other words, if the effective rate at the start of the system is set at 100, the initial target zone would be a band for the effective rate between 97 and 103. A country might wish to set the initial zone slightly higher or lower so as to take account either of special factors influencing the initial position or of expected changes in the effective rate.[23]

---

[23] Since an asymmetrical target zone would seem to imply that the authorities have certain expectations concerning the future course of the effective rate, it is rather unlikely that a country would declare an asymmetrical target zone. It is even more unlikely that any country would be inclined to declare an initial zone that does not include the initial value of the effective rate (for example, a zone of 92–98).

Since the country concerned has some degrees of freedom in setting the initial target zone—it can influence the initial value of the effective rate by policy measures, and it can declare an asymmetrical band around that value—the initial target zone should be set in consultation with the other community countries and the Commission of the EC. The partners and the commission could be given the right to object to a proposed initial target zone if it is considered manifestly out of line with underlying economic factors. The final decision would, however, rest with the country concerned.

The target zone could be a stationary band, with adjustment only as a result of a new policy decision, or it could be a moving band. For reasons I have set out, it seems to me rather unlikely that countries would accept any kind of automatic adjustment mechanism. During the initial stages at least, adjustment of the target zone would be a decision of the country concerned, to be taken at any moment but only after prior consultation within the community. When experience has been gained with the system, the community element in the adjustment of target zones should be gradually strengthened. My own preference would be to introduce such elements according to an agreed, pre-determined time schedule, a procedure not unknown in the history of the community. I have indicated some of the many conceivable methods of strengthening the community element. Whereas I expressed doubts on the political acceptability, at least in the foreseeable future, of meaningful discretionary action by the community with regard to central rates, I am somewhat less pessimistic when we are dealing with the less sensitive, because less coercive, system of target zones. If the granting of such discretionary powers to the community proves to be not yet acceptable, the adjustment of target zones could be aided by introducing certain presumptive triggers as discussed above.

A final word on procedure. Exchange rates are highly sensitive issues. Procedures will have to be devised to ensure strict confidentiality of any discussions on the adjustment of target zones, while still allowing a fully effective consultation and coordination on the community level. This will not be easy, but a way must be found. Fortunately politicians, public opinion, and the world press have become used to exchange-rate changes and no longer get excited by any hint of a discussion on such matters. But exchange market operators are still nervous characters who will often speculate or run for cover at the slightest rumor, however unfounded or irrelevant. Special care will have to be taken to ensure that the consultations in the framework of the target zone system do not have this effect.

The Snake in a System of Target Zones. Why maintain the snake within the broader system of target zones? There are essentially two sets of reasons: the interests of the snake countries themselves and the wish to maintain alive and operational a system of exchange-rate management that may one day serve the community as a whole. As I have indicated, the smaller countries of the minisnake find it to their advantage to anchor their exchange rates to the currency of their major trading partner. Given that West Germany has been able to keep its rate of inflation at substantially lower levels than its snake partners and given that it has consistantly run a current surplus, the smaller countries find that the snake obligations impose constraints on them that act as a stimulus to economic and monetary discipline. Moreover, the snake mechanism has various advantages compared with an informal pegging (as practiced by Austria and to some extent by Switzerland): it provides for a multilateral intervention system, it implies consultation on intervention in dollars, it provides a framework for multilateral decisions on the adjustment of central rates, and it contains effective credit and settlement arrangements. The fact that the countries of the minisnake are determined not to abandon the arrangement or weaken it in any way is sufficient reason to shape the system of target zones so that it is compatible with the snake.

The next question is, then, whether the minisnake countries should participate in the target zone system at all. It could be argued that these countries have far stricter mutual obligations than the weak commitments under the target zone system and therefore need not participate in the looser system. In other words, would it not be logical to give a country of the community a choice, either to declare a central rate in the snake or to declare a target zone for its effective exchange rate? The answer should clearly be negative, if only because the nonparticipation of the deutsche mark bloc would render the target zone system entirely meaningless. For political as well as economic reasons, it is clear that the snake countries, either individually or as a group, should participate in the system of target zones. It is politically inconceivable that the community would accept a system of target zones, which aims explicitly at bringing the snake countries and the individually floating countries together, and yet exclude the snake from such a system. The economic rationale of the snake countries' participating is obvious as well: the development of the effective exchange rates of the snake countries is as relevant to intracommunity relationships as that of the non-snake countries.

Should the snake countries participate individually or as a group? It is far more logical, as well as desirable, to have the snake as a whole participate rather than declare individual target zones for snake members. It is more logical because the exchange rates of the snake members are tied together by the strict rules of the snake arrangement: what really counts in a system of target zones is the position of the snake as a whole. It is more desirable because target zones for individual countries defined in effective exchange rates might occasionally be inconsistent with the margins defined by the snake arrangement.[24]

A target zone for the snake as a whole could be defined in terms of some weighted average of the effective exchange rates of the individual snake countries, possibly excluding their trade with one another. When the EEC is ready to accept certain policy obligations in the framework of a target zone system, a procedure would have to be devised to translate such obligations in the case of the minisnake into policy obligations of individual snake countries. In principle this would be a matter of adequate policy coordination within the minisnake, rather than a concern of the community as a whole. So as not to impair the community character of the system, however, these consultations should not be limited to snake countries but should be held at the level of the community as a whole.

Consultation and Policy Commitments. I shall not attempt to spell out the many possible options with regard to consultation procedures and policy commitments. I have given some broad indications on these questions already. Let me add only that, as in the case of adjustment procedures, I would prefer to introduce additional commitments on the basis of an agreed, predetermined time schedule. But I concede that this is probably not realistic for the time being. Decisions to increase the policy content of the target zone system will probably have to be taken ad hoc, whenever the economic and the political climate is ripe for them.

Consultation will take place when an exchange rate moves significantly outside the target zone for some time.[25] The country concerned

---

[24] For example, a substantial appreciation of the dollar could affect the effective exchange rates of the individual snake countries differently, depending on the relative importance of their trade with the dollar area. However, a conflict between snake obligations and target zones is not very likely, nor does it matter very much so long as the target zones serve only as triggers to consultation. One might even argue that such a conflict, if it arises, might well serve as a useful trigger for discussions within the snake on the possible adjustment of central rates. The sensitivity of snake countries to anything that might interfere with the internal operations of the snake seems to be such as to exclude the option of separate target zones for the individual snake countries.

[25] The exact operational definition of the qualifications "significantly" and "for some time" will have to be worked out on the basis of practical considerations.

could then (1) indicate that it considers the rate movement to have been caused by temporary, erratic factors; (2) present projections, including policy intentions, that imply that the rate will return to the target zone within a reasonable time; or (3) announce its intention to adjust the target zone. Consultation would also take place when a country proposes an adjustment of its target zone without its exchange rate having moved outside the zone. At a later stage, the commission and the partner countries might be given the right to initiate a consultation procedure as well.[26]

In all cases consultation will involve a thorough review of the country's general economic development, including in particular the situation and prospects of its balance of payments and a discussion of the economic policies it intends to pursue. The review should also pay attention to the policy areas that have an immediate impact on the balance of payments and the exchange rate, in particular money market policies. The consultation would normally end either with tacit approval of the country's views and policies, possibly as modified in the process, or in a confidential recommendation. In certain cases a conflict of views might be carried to the political level in the community. As I have mentioned before, effective safeguards would have to be devised to ensure strict confidentiality of the consultations and any conclusions drawn from them.

On the subject of policy commitments, I want to emphasize the importance of monetary policy, particularly in the early stages of the target zone system. Monetary policy is probably more amenable to effective policy coordination than are fiscal and incomes policies. For one thing, the interdependence between countries is more immediately obvious, and the effects of measures in this area on the domestic economy as a whole are less pronounced. Past experience confirms this proposition: central banks have been able to coordinate their policies more effectively than governments, not because governments are less willing or less able to do so, but because fiscal and incomes policies raise far more sensitive issues than does monetary policy. For example, it would be easier to accept and to carry out the obligation not to offset the restrictive effect of balance-of-payment deficits on the domestic money supply than to accept community directives (even if they were arrived at by a strongly qualified majority) to decrease the budget deficit in case of a depreciation of the effective exchange rate below the target zone.

---

[26] It would obviously be desirable to establish some link between these consultations and the similarly oriented consultations in the framework of the IMF, but so far practical as well as political difficulties appear to have inhibited fruitful cooperation in this area. The question should be given serious consideration.

Monetary policy is also more important than intervention in exchange markets. In my opinion, the latter has received far too much attention, presumably because it is the most dramatic expression of the obligations under a par-value or snake-type system. Past experience, for example, the recent mini–exchange crisis in the minisnake, has shown that intervention is in fact less important than money market management, even in a system of fixed margins. *Without* supporting monetary policy, intervention may be worse than useless: it often leads to very large movements in official reserves that are not sustainable and that tend to trigger destabilizing speculation. *With* adequate monetary policies, intervention can usually be limited to supporting operations and smoothing out minor fluctuations in the market.

Even though I consider intervention basically of secondary importance, the need for coordination is obvious. National policies in this area can easily be conflicting instead of mutually supporting. Certain rules of the game for intervention in the exchange markets can therefore serve a useful function. Such rules might be concerned with the direction of intervention and with the currency or currencies in which intervention takes place. With regard to the direction of intervention, the community could take its cue from the IMF's guidelines for floating, which encourage smoothing-out operations, to be carried out asymmetrically when the effective rate has moved outside the target zone, and which prohibit aggressive intervention unless it serves to bring the effective rate within or closer to the target zone.[27]

Hard and fast rules with regard to the currency of intervention are difficult to devise. So far the non-snake countries of the community have intervened almost exclusively in dollars, while snake countries have increasingly done so as well, even though the snake agreement provides for a multilateral intervention system. Occasionally the actions of snake and non-snake countries have been conflicting, in the sense that one country pushed up the value of the dollar by buying while another depressed it by selling. It would be rational to include in the target zone system an agreement to set up adequate procedures that aim at avoiding such conflicts and at promoting techniques of intervention that are mutually supporting whenever possible. Such procedures would almost inevitably have to depend on ad hoc consultation; the experience of the snake countries proves that such ad hoc consultations can yield entirely satisfactory results.

---

[27] The IMF guidelines are not limited to intervention but apply to all policy actions that influence the exchange rate. They are phrased in terms of market exchange rates rather than effective rates.

The Duisenberg Proposals and European-American Monetary Relations.
To the extent that the target zone system operates only as a device to
strengthen consultation on and coordination of economic policies in the
EEC, its effect on U.S.-European monetary relations would obviously be
limited. However, any discussion on the course of effective exchange
rates will inevitably involve a discussion of the movements of exchange
rates vis-à-vis the rest of the world, in particular the dollar. This need
not at all imply the development of a common "dollar policy," in the
sense of agreements to hold the dollar rate at a certain level or within
a certain range. But it does imply a discussion of and possibly active
measures to influence the development of the dollar rate. In fact, this
already takes place in the community, both at the regular meetings of
the Committee of Governors of the Central Banks and ad hoc whenever
a member of the snake intends to intervene in dollars (which is in
principle permitted only by common consent of the snake partners,
a procedure that in practice includes all community countries). These
consultations are in effect a common dollar policy, albeit an incomplete
and not always explicit or fully thought out one. The system of target
zones as well as the snake mechanism does put the question of a
common dollar policy on the agenda of the community as a whole, and
it does create the instruments for an active common dollar policy.

Obviously a common dollar policy in the case of so large a
monetary unit as the community cannot be carried out successfully
without the cooperation of the United States. Regular consultations on
intervention policy are already taking place. When Europe organizes its
external monetary policy in the framework of the target zone system, it
would seem advisable—and indeed necessary, considering the weight
of the dollar in the effective exchange rates—that consultation with the
United States and other major economies be strengthened, intensified,
and broadened to include other areas of policy relevant to the
management of our exchange rates. Exchange-rate management is by its
nature a multilateral affair. We should organize European-American
monetary relations to take account of that fact in order to avoid conflicting policies and to exploit our common interests to the full.

I shall end on a question mark concerning the most appropriate
institutional setup for such discussions. As long as Europe is still a
collection of more or less autonomous units, it is difficult to achieve an
effective dialogue with the United States and other major economies.
It is to be hoped that the Duisenberg proposals will contribute to creating sufficient "solidarity of fact" with regard to monetary matters that
the community will in future be able to speak really *una voce* rather
than continue to present the familiar façade of unity that falls apart on
the first challenge.

PART
FIVE

PROBLEMS OF GLOBAL
MONETARY INTEGRATION

INTERNATIONAL COORDINATION OF NATIONAL ECONOMIC POLICIES: COMMENTARIES

Assar Lindbeck

Three Reasons for Policy Coordination. When discussing international coordination of national stabilization policies, it may be useful to make a distinction between three different, though related, purposes of such coordination: to influence the business cycle, to influence the long-term price trend, and to avoid inconsistencies among national policy targets.

To influence the business cycle. The first purpose of coordination is to influence the pattern of macroeconomic instability—domestically and globally. In a deep, synchronized international recession, such as in 1974–1976, the purpose of coordinated domestic expansionary actions is, of course, to prevent governments in individual countries either from waiting for export-led expansions generated by domestic demand management in other countries or from trying to engineer export-led expansion all by themselves—a beggar-thy-neighbor policy. The argument for coordinated actions is partly symmetrical in the case of synchronized inflationary booms, as in 1972–1973. Since prices of tradable goods are to a large extent formed on international rather than national markets, in particular for European countries, a main purpose of coordinated actions is to prevent governments from trying to take "free rides" on anti-inflationary policies in other countries, in particular on actions taken by the large countries.

Thus in both recessions and booms a main argument for concerted action is that some of the benefits of policy actions tend to wind up in other countries. In recessions, there is the additional argument that all countries may gain by agreeing to abstain from using policy instruments that shift unemployment to other countries.

In the case of more "normal" business cycle situations, such as during the main part of the period from the early 1950s to the mid-1960s, the argument for coordination of national stabilization policies is quite different. The purpose would then be to bring about a *desynchronization*, rather than a synchronization, of macroeconomic

223

fluctuations, in order to avoid global recessions or booms. For it is quite clear that the most severe macroeconomic developments during the post–World War II period in individual countries have taken place exactly when the business cycle has been strongly synchronized among nations—both in the relatively deep recessions of 1958 and 1974–1976 and in the inflationary booms of 1950–1951 and 1972–1973.

It is far from clear how such a coordination for desynchronization could be brought about. Perhaps it is tempting to argue that a completely uncoordinated policy, by a pure random process, is more likely than a coordinated policy to result in a desynchronization. This is a rather fragile hope, however, since the world economy is strongly dominated by a handful of major countries that can pull the whole world economy one way or the other. The world economy and the group of developed market economies are simply too "asymmetrical" to allow us to rely on "the law of larger numbers" of national policy actions to achieve a desynchronization of the business cycle.

A realistic approach to the task of policy coordination should, I think, start from the assumption that each government is concerned mainly, or perhaps only, with the welfare and approval of its own constituency and that these considerations tend to have systematic consequences for the pattern of macroeconomic instability during the course of the election period. More specifically, it would seem that governments usually take expansionary actions during the year immediately before an election and restrictive actions after the election—except if inflation is so high immediately before the election, relative to unemployment, that politicians believe that more votes can be gained by restrictive than by expansionary actions. A policy conclusion from these observations is that a desynchronization of the business cycle could perhaps be achieved by changing the constitutions of the major countries so that their general elections would not coincide. It is, of course, an open question—perhaps even a naive one—whether changes in the political constitutions in major countries really could be engineered in this way to avoid clustering of elections.

To influence the long-term price trend. Since any trend is a cumulation over time of short-term developments, the long-term price trend for the world economy is largely determined by the time-path of short-term macroeconomic policies pursued in various countries. However, one of the determinants of these policies is the path of the supply of international liquidity and international reserves—somewhat as the time-path of gold production was an important factor behind the price trend for the world economy during periods of the gold standard.

During the early post–World War II period it was perhaps reasonable to make a sharp distinction between private liquidity and official reserves, as well as between national and international credit markets, but these distinctions have recently become increasingly difficult to maintain because of the integration of national credit markets and the integration of private and public credit markets. With national governments borrowing heavily on "private" international credit markets in competition with private agents and being exposed to about the same kind of scrutiny as they, the distinction between public reserves and national and international private liquidity is becoming vague.

In fact, it is not unreasonable to argue that the international credit market has become similar to the banking system in the United States before the creation of the Federal Reserve System. The function of lender of last resort and of regulator of the degree of tightness or ease in international credit markets is mainly performed by the aggregate, usually rather uncoordinated, actions of a great number of national central banks and national governments, in a complicated interplay with the actions of private agents. Thus there seems to be a strong case for coordination of national monetary policies to get some control over international liquidity, the supply of which at present seems quite elastic. Of course such a control is no guarantee that the price trend for the world economy will become the "desired" one; there are simply too many slips between international private liquidity and international reserves on the one hand and domestic economic policy and prices on the other.

To avoid inconsistencies among national policy targets. In case of strong differences in the "revealed preferences" among nations concerning the price trend, the obvious answer is, of course, not policy coordination but highly flexible, or even floating, exchange rates. To some extent highly flexible exchange rates may also help to reconcile different national targets for capacity utilization and unemployment. However, there is hardly any theoretical reason, or any empirical evidence, to indicate that even highly flexible exchange rates are *very* efficient in shielding domestic economies from international macroeconomic fluctuations, or for that matter in bottling up domestic macroeconomic fluctuations. As is by now rather well understood, exchange rates in floating rate systems are determined so as to achieve equilibrium between stock-demand and stock-supply of financial assets in various currency denominations—which certainly does not necessarily mean that exchange-rate variations also keep national export and import volumes unaffected by macroeconomic fluctuations in other countries. Moreover, the short-term elasticities in demand for exports and imports are simply not high enough for even "well-behaved" changes in ex-

225

change rates to counteract completely the effects on the domestic economy of shifts in income and economic activity in other countries. In other words, highly integrated commodity and credit markets make nations "open" economies regardless of the exchange-rate system. Thus floating exchange rates cannot be expected to eliminate the disadvantages of conflicting targets among nations for capacity utilization and unemployment.

The argument for target coordination to avoid inconsistencies presumably becomes even stronger when we look at the third major target of stabilization policy (in addition to unemployment and inflation)—the balance of payments or, in floating systems, the exchange rate. This issue is, of course, closely related to the old issue of the sharing of the burden of adjustment between surplus countries and deficit countries, a problem that has obviously been accentuated by the contemporary problem of the sharing of the oil deficit.

The shift to more flexible exchange rates has most likely helped solve this problem. However, floating rates certainly do not *remove* the argument for some policy coordination for balance-of-payments adjustment. There are several reasons for this: (1) countries are not indifferent whether adjustments take place on the current account or the capital account; (2) there is a common interest among nations that the size and distribution of debt among countries not lead to an erosion of the creditworthiness of some countries and therewith connected speculation in bankruptcies; (3) all countries tend to gain if deficit countries and countries that experience a contraction of their currency area (such as the United Kingdom) do not use adjustment methods that harm the world community as a whole—low capacity utilization, direct controls on trade or capital movements, or mercantilist subsidies of exports and the production of tradables; moreover, it is important that (4) "cobweb" types of fluctuations in exchange rates or interest rates are not created by aggressive or inconsistent interventions by governments in the markets for foreign exchange or domestic financial assets.

For instance, attempts by individual nations to pull in or push out financial capital by interest-rate changes may, also in highly flexible exchange-rate regimes, result in a general *level* of interest rates regarded by most governments as undesirable from the point of view of aggregate demand management or growth. Moreover, since exchange rates have a profound influence on prices, profitability, and investment incentives in the tradable sector of various countries, individual nations have a strong interest in the operations by other countries in both exchange markets and domestic financial markets.

In fact, it may be argued that changes in exchange rates have stronger effects on some basic target variables in the national economies than do changes in reserves (brought about by the same underlying changes in circumstances). From that point of view, it is not unreasonable to argue that the need for coordination of national monetary policies is quite as strong under floating as under fixed exchange rates— or perhaps even stronger.

Thus even though in floating-exchange-rate regimes the balance of payments is not a restriction, the price trend can be chosen rather independently of the outside world, and domestic control of interest rates and monetary aggregates is considerably easier than in fixed-rate regimes, the case for monetary policy coordination certainly does not become invalid.

Countries may, of course, increase their policy autonomy somewhat by using other instruments than exchange and interest rates to influence trade, the balance of payments, profits, and investment— instruments such as taxes and subsidies on trade, on the production of tradables, on investment in the tradable sector, or on capital flows. However, this means mainly that the arguments for policy coordination are expanded to these instruments, with strong cross-country effects as well.

Moreover, since shifts in the supply and demand of financial assets brought about by monetary or exchange market policy strongly influence not only interest rates and exchange rates but also prices for real assets, such as land and primary products, such policies may have a rather strong *direct* effect on prices, besides the effects through changes in capacity utilization. This suggests that some prices—for instance, for land and primary products—are more affected if a given change in capacity utilization is brought about through monetary than through fiscal policy. I think we may therefore say that monetary policy has a comparative advantage in influencing *prices*, whereas fiscal policy has a comparative advantage in influencing output and employment. These considerations become an international concern because the markets for some real assets, such as primary products, are truly international markets. For instance, it is tempting to argue that the dramatic price boom for primary products in 1972–1973 was fed by a remarkable expansion of international and national liquidity through a very expansionary monetary policy in a number of nations, including the largest reserve currency country, the United States.

Drastic swings in the supply of international reserves are less likely to occur if reserve currency countries have highly flexible exchange rates than if they have fixed rates. Thus it would seem that the case for coordinated actions to prevent a sudden overexpansion of inter-

227

national reserves is somewhat weaker now than before. Nevertheless, the case for some coordination of national monetary policies remains valid, for reasons discussed above.

Alternative Strategies. I want to end by emphasizing that there are many alternative strategies to deal with the problems of having an international economic system interacting with a great number of national political systems.

One strategy would be to try to reconcile the international character of the economic system with the national character of the political system. This might be achieved by relying as much as possible on automatic adjustment mechanisms between countries, such as floating exchange rates and better functioning international markets for factors and financial capital—including markets between governments. Such a reconciliation might also be brought about by using domestic policy tools with a minimum of cross-country effects, such as income-compensating schemes and mobility-increasing policies within countries.

A second strategy to deal with the apparent inconsistencies between the economic and political systems would be to adjust the economic system to the national character of the political system by way of a return to protectionism and autarky.

However, the topic discussed here has been whether it is possible and useful to adjust the political system to the highly international character of the economic system by increasing coordination of national policies of governments. Nevertheless, the strength of the case for coordination of national policies depends to a considerable extent on what is done along the lines of the first two strategies, that is, to what extent the tensions between the economic and the political systems are either reconciled (by automatic adjustment mechanisms or by developing domestic policy tools with limited cross-country effects) or reduced by a retreat in the international character of the economic system.

Even if some such reconciliation or some retreat in the economic internationalization process is brought about, it is highly unlikely that the usefulness of policy coordination would disappear. This leaves us, of course, with the fundamental question: Who should do the coordinating? It may then be useful to make a distinction between coordination of rules and guidelines and coordination of actual policies.

Coordination by Whom? For coordinating general rules and guidelines, in particular for the use of policy instruments with strong cross-country effects, international organizations, such as the IMF and the General Agreement on Tariffs and Trade (GATT), as well as regional organizations, such as EEC, are obvious candidates—in the future as in the past. Obvious responsibilities of the IMF are (1) the establishment and surveillance of rules about exchange rates to prevent what has recently been called "aggressive" interventions that considerably disturb other countries, as well as (in cooperation with GATT) of other policy instruments with similar cross-country effects, such as aggressive interventions by taxes or subsidies in trade, production of tradables, or foreign exchange transactions; (2) advice to countries about economic policy; (3) actions to reduce problems of solvency and liquidity for individual countries, and (4) the pooling and transmission of information among agents in international monetary and financial fields to reduce uncertainty. The fund also has a responsibility for (5) the supply of international liquidity and reserves, although it would seem that this is more under the influence of national central banks and governments.

A cosmopolitan view of the world would suggest that as many countries as possible should participate in the coordination of actual stabilization policies, undertaken within the framework of established rules and guidelines: the United Nations, the OECD, or organizations such as the Group of Ten or the Group of Twenty. In view of the difficulties of achieving agreements among—and within—nations, however, a more pragmatic and, I think, more realistic view would be to involve as few countries as possible in such coordination attempts, which means that coordination would be pursued mainly by the major economic powers of the Western world. This approach is bound to result both in some criticism from the smaller countries for being sidestepped and in some attempts from them to take "free rides" on coordinated actions undertaken by the large countries. However, there may be no other effective approach, since decisions about coordination of short-term stabilization policy, unlike decisions about rules and guidelines, have to be taken rapidly to be of much use.

A third way of assigning responsibility for policy coordination is to rely on the same mechanisms that have traditionally been used to coordinate decentralized decision making by private agents: the market system. In fact, as pointed out earlier, the internationalization of credit markets and the integration of governments in those markets as regular lenders and borrowers, as well as the increased importance of market forces for exchange-rate determination, mean that the coordination of government actions is increasingly brought about by "the invisible hand of markets" rather than by the more visible hand of government authorities. Flexible exchange rates and the recycling of the so-called oil deficit on private markets are obvious examples. Thus, when discussing the possibility of coordinating decentralized decision making in inter-

229

dependent systems, we should perhaps not altogether forget that the coordination of government decisions can to some extent rely on the same mechanism that is used for the coordination of decentralized decision making in the private sector.

Stephen N. Marris

It used to be taken for granted that international coordination of national policies was required. It is very salutary, particularly for an international civil servant such as myself, that this proposition is frequently challenged today. I am not talking about international cooperation that involves only the exchange of information or the policing of certain basic rules, such as not having trade restrictions. I am talking about the circumstances in which countries are required, and must in some way be persuaded, to take action that is not in their immediate short-term interests but in the interests of the system as a whole.

I think that I, at any rate, realize more clearly now that the existence of such circumstances depends very crucially on the way in which exchange markets work. The model often put forward is that of a world in which each country is doing its own thing—each is printing a different amount of money and has a different rate of inflation and a different interest rate—and exchange rates smoothly and beautifully move apart in a way that seems to keep the whole thing in equilibrium. I believe that model of how the world really works is as unrealistic as the neoclassical models of income determination, which ensured full employment through the flexibility of real interest rates and real wages— and for exactly the same reasons, the existence of stickinesses and lags in the system.

The unique feature of the exchange market is that it not only influences very large flows of income and expenditure but also is overhung by enormous stocks of financial and real assets. The reaction times in the different markets are very different; it may take hours or days for financial markets to react, months for cost and prices, and years for real trade flows, particularly when such questions as product design, sales networks, and investment are involved. And it is essentially because of these differences in reaction times that we need coordination of national economic policies.

At present, as Shonfield has said (see Part II), West German monetary policy is determining the level of unemployment in the United Kingdom. I do not expect that everybody would fully agree with that, but most of us might think there was some relationship between the two. Why is that? It certainly is totally inconsistent with the theoretical model. If the United Kingdom does not like its level of unemployment, theoretically it need only expand and allow the exchange rate to go down. This should soon produce the extra exports needed to restore balance in the exchange market. The fact is, however, that because the effects on domestic costs and prices come through much more quickly than the effects on the volume of trade, expansionary action is more likely to lead to higher inflation than to less unemployment, and the United Kingdom feels highly constrained.

As Lindbeck mentioned (in the preceding commentary), this predicament is not entirely symmetrical. In a world inflationary situation, the Dornbusch effect works the other way around. A country that wishes to opt out of an excessively inflationary world environment can, in fact, gain on the swings and the roundabouts; currency appreciation resulting from a restrictive policy will dampen domestic inflation with a relatively small negative effect on export demand. But as Lindbeck also said, such a country will probably nevertheless find that it has a considerable interest in the policies being followed by other countries because those policies will have an important effect on the terms of trade between primary commodities and manufactures in the world as a whole. Since the country is probably either a net importer or a net exporter of raw materials, it will find that its economic situation is indeed affected by the degree of inflation in the rest of the world.

Thus a country's ability to achieve its aims with respect to inflation and employment depends significantly on what is going on in the rest of the world. Under floating exchange rates, this proposition is much less theoretically obvious than is often realized. Hence the case for international coordination of national policies depends crucially on the way in which exchange rates are thought to influence the real and nominal variables in the economy.

There are four points I wish to make. First, I hope that we have now buried the naive model of the vicious circle. Willett's paper shows clearly, and I think rightly, that a movement in the exchange rate that is in line with the differential inflationary movement cannot be regarded as a source of inflation. Indeed, if such a movement does not take place, there is a kind of borrowing of price stability from other countries.

Second, "overshooting" is a possibility not only in theory but also in actuality. The events of 1976 were, I think, fairly conclusive in that respect.

Third, we have discovered after a brief period of euphoria that external discipline under the present exchange-rate system is tougher than it was under the previous exchange-rate system. Any indulgence in vice is consumed at home; both the static processes and the more dynamic processes of changes in expectations set off within the vicious circle have such great power that those countries that have come anywhere near them have a very strong desire to avoid them in the future.

Fourth, and perhaps the most worrying, is that the disequilibrium between our countries has gone on for so long that it has become embedded in the structures of our countries, in the structure of our industry, and in attitudes and behavior. I am still quite unclear how this has happened. Is it because of bad policies or different initial positions or, more fundamentally, are there different species in the world—a Homobritannicus, a Homogermanicus, a Homojapanicus, and so on? Are they fundamentally different, and do they produce different economies?

If countries wish to experiment with somewhat different economic arrangements, let them do so and discover that those arrangements do not work either. But that is a fairly high-risk policy to adopt in such a very interconnected system.

William Fellner

Types of Coordination. I will distinguish two meanings of the ambiguous term "international coordination," and I will suggest an unconditionally favorable appraisal of the concept in one of its two meanings. As concerns the concept's other meaning—in my presentation, its second meaning—I will express a favorable appraisal when the concept is applied to some specific problems but an unfavorable one when it is applied to problems of a different kind to which it has nevertheless been applied in recent policy debates.

The first meaning—the meaning of which I have an unconditionally favorable appraisal—is that of adjusting one's own policies to the policies that other countries are about to put into effect, and to do so on the basis of dependable current information supplied by the others. That is clearly desirable simply because of the superiority of informed over uninformed decision making. In practice the desirable procedure is apt to involve a process of successive approximations, because the impending policy measures of a country will influence the desired policies of other countries and vice versa, and methodologically it would be utopian to assume the existence of dependable models that provide simultaneous algebraic solutions for all countries given a whole range of potential values of policy variables. What matters, however, is that international coordination in my first sense is clearly desirable.

The second, more ambitious interpretation of the concept of international coordination would require countries partially to subordinate their own interests to those of others. This way of describing the willingness to be influenced by the interests of others becomes somewhat ambiguous in cases in which the other countries could retaliate, and, even aside from conscious retaliation, there is some ambiguity in all cases in which damage done to the others is apt to have an adverse feedback on the country itself. Leaving aside the question what elements of long-run self-interest could conceivably be said to enter into what is normally considered a regard for the interests of others, we may safely conclude that there does exist a case for trying to get countries to subordinate their immediate interests to those of others in various specific respects. Trying to enforce abstention from so-called beggar-my-neighbor policies is an obvious illustration. Another relates to situations in which countries performing well give assistance to countries endangered by poor economic performance and in which such assistance—ranging from otherwise unattainable loans and loan guarantees to outright grants—needs to be made dependent on a significant improvement of the recipient country's performance. Whenever such assistance is considered desirable, a coordination of policies is needed, and the avoidance of "free riding" does call for making concessions at the expense of the immediate interests of individual countries.

Exerting Pressure on Others to Expand Demand and the Problem of the Oil Deficit. Having so far accentuated the positive, I now turn to the negative part of my remarks. It is much more true of some countries than of others that internal political circumstances force them to look at their own interests from a short-run point of view. The attempt to reduce unemployment by inflationary policies reflects this kind of short-run orientation. No reasonable case can be made for trying to force the countries capable of resisting this temptation into acting like those not at present capable of resisting it. To be specific: if the experts of a country that is capable of taking a longer view believe that stepping up their country's rate of expansion would destabilize their domestic economy, it is unreasonable to require that country nevertheless to become more expansionary to raise the exports of other countries. If such an effort were made and were successful, the risk would be high that the economies of the countries performing well would in fact become destabilized and that with a brief lag this would damage the other countries as well. Any willingness to assist other countries that are overcoming their difficulties should express itself in loans, guarantees, or even grants made conditional on improved performance; the idea that one can help others by destabilizing one's own economy is

233

thoroughly ill conceived. In a general way this may by now be rather widely realized, but the idea seems to be still alive in a different and less transparent garb.

Judging largely by the current political controversies, in which, however, professional experts have also played a role, it seems that the idea of helping others through engineering more than the domestically desired expansion has recently acquired a somewhat less crude form, but this semisophisticated version is equally misleading. It came to life in an international environment largely influenced by the oil deficits of the countries dependent on imports of energy materials. This version recognizes that the experts of the countries performing well are those likely to have the most competent judgment of the desirable degree of expansion of demand in their own countries. It recognizes also that a country would do no service to other countries by overexpanding. However, in its new, semisophisticated form, the view maintains that an oil-consuming country that is not bearing its share of the oil deficit but is instead running a current-account surplus should shift resources from its export industries to the industries producing for its domestic markets, thereby enabling the countries running high current-account deficits to increase *their* exports. At the same time, a more expansionary domestic demand policy is alleged to be a corollary of the effort to shift resources out of the export industries into those oriented to domestic markets.

Behind this thesis is first the question whether an oil-consuming country running a current-account surplus is in any sense violating the rules of good behavior, that is, whether such a country takes insufficient account of the interests of others. Only if it can be argued with reason that the surplus of the country is developing because of the promotion of the country's exports beyond the level determined by competition or because of obstacles placed in the way of its imports, can a case be made that there is such a violation. It should be added that if assistance is being given to countries that can straighten out their problems only gradually and that meanwhile find it difficult to import the capital corresponding to their deficits without losing their soundness as borrowers, differences of opinion may well develop concerning not only the size and conditions of such assistance but also the appropriate share in the assistance of the well-performing countries, including those running a current-account surplus. Yet these differences of opinion should concern the terms on which countries make funds available in specific cases, not any obligation to reduce or eliminate the country's surplus. To repeat, the claim that such an obligation exists is reasonable only to the extent that the surplus may reasonably be said to result from artificial interference with the workings of market forces.

But assume now for the sake of argument that a case *can* be made for a country's obligation to shift part of its resources from its export industries to those producing for the domestic market; and assume also that the country can achieve that objective by changing specified policies regarded as objectionable. Even in this event there is no reason to believe that the country should create either more or less effective demand in terms of its domestic currency than it would otherwise create. To be sure, no proposition as comprehensive as that I am formulating here is ever valid *entirely* without qualifications, but I shall argue that the qualifications to which my proposition is subject relate to second-order effects and that these may influence the conclusion in either direction.

The proposition that shifting from exports to domestically absorbed products requires no stepping up of demand creation in terms of domestic currency is supported by the following argument. Regardless of whether a specific part of a country's output will or will not represent "net exports" (positive or negative), the country needs to create in terms of its domestic currency an amount of effective demand corresponding to its domestic output at the projected price level. Any country in the process of winding down inflation (or having already established practical price-level constancy) will aim for demand creation at a rate enabling the markets to bring forth the output compatible with an acceptable behavior of the price level, and a consistent policy of this sort will gradually achieve its price-behavior objectives. Output targets incompatible with such price-behavior objectives cannot be achieved over a reasonable time. Given a reasonable time horizon, this sets limits to achievable output objectives, and at least in a good first approximation those limits should be regarded as independent of the algebraic sign of any current-account imbalance.

An export surplus implies that the domestic purchasing-power equivalent of the exported output is acquired by foreign buyers whose money holdings in their currency are acquired by residents of the exporting country; and an import surplus implies that foreigners are acquiring the currency of the importing country in order to finance (directly or indirectly) investments in goods that remain located in the importing country. These are merely *swaps* of money holdings, and they do not change the outcome, which needs to be the creation of effective demand corresponding to the planned domestic output. It is bad practice to adjust the desired demand creation upward to accommodate the rise in prices of traded goods that may occur under flexible rates when the current account moves toward a deficit, because that policy merely covers up for a while an inevitable real burden and thus has all the longer run disadvantages of policies based on short-run Phillips trade-offs.

As I see it, this last proposition possesses general validity, but in a more ambitious analysis some of the propositions here developed would, of course, have to be refined. For example, I have used the concept of the effective demand corresponding to a given domestic output but have not discussed the bearing of the difference between output and final sales or the bearing of varying volumes of intermediate transactions on this concept as it is usually defined. What is more important, I have not gone into the complications that arise because all methods of aiming for a specific amount of effective demand are indirect and because a policy should presumably be regarded as having become more expansionary or less so if, in order to create the same effective demand, it must create a larger or a smaller addition to the money supply. Swaps between domestic residents and foreigners—the swaps considered above —may exert an influence on the liquidity ratio describing the habits of the average moneyholder, and hence such swaps need not always be of negligible importance for demand-management policy. Changes in gold holdings may call for a similar qualification, which, however, would have to be expressed in a somewhat different terminology because gold is no part of the money supply.

But usually all these are second-order considerations, and it would be difficult in some instances to generalize about the algebraic sign of the allowances they might call for.

Conclusions. Putting pressure on a country that is performing well to serve the interests of others by engaging in more rapid expansion than it considers desirable is an ill-conceived policy. The claim that a country, to share in the aggregate deficit of the oil-consuming countries, should eliminate its current-account surplus (or increase its current-account deficit if that deficit is relatively small) is *not* a generally valid claim. That claim is defensible only if the current-account position of such a country can be viewed as resulting from interference with the forces of competition. In that event a case does develop for requiring that the country give up those practices, but even then there is not normally a case for trying to influence the country to adopt more expansionary policies. Overexpansion is not an effective method of giving assistance to other countries.

Jacques J. Polak

I should like to deal with this subject in a somewhat methodological framework. To do this, I would rephrase the title of the subject, perhaps somewhat provocatively, as a question: "Coordination or Adjustment?"

It is perhaps not obvious at first sight that the coordination of national policies and adjustment are two essentially different, indeed alternative, approaches to the management of the international economy.[1] The coordination approach starts from the assumption that if, in a given situation, countries pursue their preferred policies in an uncoordinated way, the result for themselves or for the world economy will be unsatisfactory, or at least suboptimal. The adjustment approach is more atomistic. It sees each country as facing the world, that is, many other countries, and asks that each country adopt measures designed to bring about the necessary correction in its position.

Which of the two approaches, coordination or adjustment, is to be preferred? Can one specify certain circumstances in which one or the other is more suitable? Can these questions be answered by objective criteria, or is the choice merely a reflection of one's attitudes toward social and economic arrangements in general, those having a socialist or *dirigiste* bent tending to favor coordination of national policies and those with greater confidence in the free market system tending toward the adjustment approach?

I would venture the view that there is more to this choice than the reflection of general attitudes and that a review of the extensive experience embodied in international negotiation and in the work of international organizations would bring out certain objective rules. I will limit myself here, however, to a discussion of three cases and hope that this discussion may give some inkling of the possible content of such rules.

Before coming to those cases, let me moderate somewhat the contrast between the two approaches, which—for purposes of shock effect—I have so far presented starkly in black and white. The adjustment approach is not, or need not be, a purely nationalistic, each-country-on-its-own approach. Adjustment can be subject to international rules on the avoidance of particular types of adjustment measures that, if generally applied, could easily have destructive international effects. Thus competitive depreciation is banned as a means of adjustment by the Articles of Agreement of the IMF, and trade restrictions are normally prohibited by the GATT rules.

[1] This approach is broadly in line with that in my paper on the subject of policy coordination presented to the Netherlands Economic Society in December 1961 and published as "International Coordination of Economic Policy," *IMF Staff Papers*, vol. 2, no. 2 (July 1962), pp. 149–81.

In addition to these negative rules, adjustment, to be effective, may require the framework of positive international provisions, in the absence of which it could again become destructive. The clearest example of this was the establishment of the special drawing rights (SDR) facility in the IMF. This was a response to the proposition that countries required a secular increase in their reserves, while the supply of traditional reserves was, for various reasons, believed to be limited. Thus there appeared to be a risk of competition for a limited supply of reserves, which could lead to internationally undesirable consequences. The solution to this problem was not to attempt to persuade countries to coordinate their reserve policies so as to make do with what was available, but to create globally adequate reserves and let each country adjust its reserves to its needs within this framework. The oil facility in the IMF can be seen as a somewhat similar policy response of creating a framework to discourage undesirable national action. To make it possible for countries to adjust not too abruptly to the increased cost of oil exports, the oil facility provided them with the possibility of financing the impact of the new shock on attractive terms.

Now I turn to my three cases, starting with an easy one: the reduction in the world supply of coffee that has been brought about recently by a number of exogenous factors. As everyone knows from experience, this shortage of coffee imposes a severe hardship on adults over a large part of the world, and one could imagine coordinated governmental action of the importing countries to allocate the hardship in some fair way and perhaps in the process to reduce it somewhat—for example, by some rules on limiting coffee stocks. But no move in this direction has been noted, and both internationally and nationally demand is being adjusted to supply through the price mechanism. But I think it is necessary to realize that this is the preferred international approach to this particular shortage because it is of coffee. If a similar shortage of wheat or petroleum occurred, the coordination approach would almost certainly commend itself for the international allocation of available supplies.

The second case relates to the conduct of monetary policy in the United States and West Germany. In both countries this policy has been overwhelmingly conducted to meet domestic objectives, with the result that differences between the two countries in cyclical phasing or in the outlook for inflation control frequently led to large swings in their relative interest rates. Since the floating of the deutsche mark–dollar rate, the resulting balance-of-payments pressures were absorbed—"adjusted"—by swings in that exchange rate. It would clearly not be an easy matter to prevent the need for such adjustment by the coordination of monetary policy between the two countries. In its 1975 *Annual Report*, the IMF concluded that effective multinational coordination of monetary policy for balance-of-payments purposes could not be an immediate goal.[2] Yet it is hard to believe that, for *two* countries, *no* coordination of monetary policies and full reliance on adjustment through the exchange rate constitute an optimum solution. This would be the case only if it were overwhelmingly important for the success of domestic policy that the stance of monetary policy be exactly right at any moment of time and if zero importance were to be attached to cyclical fluctuations in the exchange rate. I am aware of the saying that there is no such thing as a "right" rate of exchange, but I would take that simply as a pithy way of debunking any excessive belief in fixed rates and their defense. We have, indeed, much cause to be modest about our knowledge of the right exchange rate, but we do know that excessive exchange-rate variability has negative effects. There is surely also a case for some modesty as to what is the "right" monetary policy. It follows from this alone that there would be benefits from policy coordination in the monetary field. Among further ramifications of this approach, I will mention only the importance of reduced reliance on monetary policy and greater reliance on fiscal policy as a further means of avoiding unnecessary fluctuations in exchange rates.

My third case is more difficult and more complicated, and it will take up the rest of the time I have available. It deals with the effects on the world economy of the increase in the price of oil or, more precisely, with one of its inevitable consequences, the persistent current-account surplus (around $40 billion a year) of a few Middle Eastern oil-exporting countries. This surplus has to have its counterpart in current-account deficits elsewhere in the world. But where? Should these deficits be allocated or distributed by some mechanism of policy coordination? Or should one rely on adjustment, that is, on action by individual countries in a suitable world setting to produce a satisfactory structure of surpluses and deficits on current account? Until recently much of the international discussion on the subject seems to have proceeded from the assumption that this was a problem for multinational coordination, of a type never previously exercised. Any approach under which a given deficit has to be shared almost inevitably leads to the rather simplistic conclusion that every non-oil country has to accept its fair share of the total. We have indeed seen the emergence of a new morality in international economics: that every industrial country should have a current-account deficit (the old morality, which reigned

---

[2] International Monetary Fund, *Annual Report 1975*, p. 20.

in certain OECD committees five to ten years ago, was that *no* industrial country should have a current-account deficit). One has also heard frequent observations that, because of insufficient coordination of policy action by the industrial countries, too large a share of the oil deficit had to be absorbed by the developing countries.

The attempt to solve this problem predominantly by coordination strikes me as essentially wrong in its direction, apart from being devoid of practical means of implementation. It overlooks certain salient facts of the present situation. As Table 1 shows, the $40-odd billion current-account surplus of the oil exporters is of the same order of magnitude

TABLE 1

SHIFTS IN GLOBAL STRUCTURE OF CURRENT-ACCOUNT BALANCES
(billions of dollars)

	1967–1972 Average			*Difference between Projected 1977 Balance and Rescaled 1967–1972 Average*
	Actual current account balance[a]	Rescaled to 1977 prices and levels of real output[b]	*1977 Projections*	
Major oil-exporting countries	0.7	3	42	39
Industrial countries	10.2	30	2	−28
Other non-oil countries:				
More developed	−1.7	−6	−10	−4
Less developed	−8.1	−27	−29	−2
Total[c]	1.1	—[d]	5	—[d]

[a] On goods, services, and private transfers.
[b] Scale factors for prices are based on a general index of world trade prices; scale factors for growth are based on average rates of increase in real GNP (or GDP) in each group of countries.
[c] Reflects errors, omissions, and asymmetries in reported balance-of-payments statistics, plus balance of listed groups with other countries (mainly the Soviet Union, other nonmember countries of Eastern Europe, and the People's Republic of China).
[d] In rescaled version of 1967–1972 average, this residual figure is primarily a reflection of asymmetries in the treatment of listed groups and thus does not lend itself to meaningful interpretation.
SOURCE: Research Department, International Monetary Fund.

(in real terms and adjusted for economic growth) as the traditional pre-1973 current-account surplus of the industrial countries. On the same basis, the current-account deficit of the LDCs, at some $30 billion, is no larger than it was before 1973. Far from decrying this amount, one should wish that it were substantially larger, under the right financing conditions, which would mean that the promise of an increased flow of real resources to these countries would have materialized. While one should, of course, be careful not to overlook the wide differences among the positions of individual countries, it is nonetheless fair to conclude from the table that it contradicts the notion that the non-oil developing countries bear a highly disproportionate share of the collective current-account deficit of oil-importing countries.

The oil price increase has not altered the basic structure of the external accounts of the primary producing countries. Collectively they are still large net importers of capital and aid and of the goods and services thus financed. It is true that the oil price increase has added a relatively intractable lump sum to their import bills, but they do not, in general, import oil on a scale comparable to that of the industrial countries. The main counterpart of the foregoing broad shifts in current-account balances is that national savings of the oil-exporting countries have displaced national savings of the industrial countries as the ultimate net source of funds flowing in various forms to the non-oil primary producing countries. A relatively small part of the oil countries' funds goes directly to the final recipients, while the bulk moves through financial intermediaries in the industrial countries.

Can the problems inherent in the present international payments structure be resolved by the adjustment approach? This depends on the answer to two other questions, the first related to the level of aggregate demand in the world and the second to the flow of finance from countries with current-account surpluses to those with corresponding deficits.

The first question—prompted by the sluggishness of real activity since 1974—is whether the world economy can be expected to attain a reasonably high level of employment in view of an autonomous source of saving (in a limited number of oil-exporting countries) that still amounts to more than $40 billion a year. However, the combined current-account surplus of the industrial countries having virtually disappeared, such an amount is not unduly high when properly compared with the pre-1974 experience. The figures in the table therefore do not support a basic pessimism about the "oversaving" or "underconsumption" in the world economy. The subnormal performance of the world economy over the past few years is rather to be attributed to the restraint that national authorities have maintained over monetary and fiscal policies because of the severity of the inflation problem and because of concern in some countries over the balance of payments as the need for individual adjustment made itself felt. It may also be noted that the widespread suggestion that West Germany and Japan should expand somewhat faster to enhance the speed of worldwide recovery does involve a form of policy coordination. These countries are being asked to use their available policy instruments in a somewhat different way, and with different intensity, than they would have preferred from a purely national point of view.

The second question—concerning the flow of finance from surplus to deficit countries—is equally important, because successful functioning of the international adjustment process presupposes a satisfactory solution to the problem of financing the capital needs in developing countries and elsewhere. On the whole, the recycling process has worked reasonably effectively over the last few years. The extent to which this process relies on short- or medium-term credit through the commercial banks has, however, raised certain problems that suggest the need for some international action to improve the framework in which adjustment is to take place. The need for policy action can be seen in several fields, including improvement in the flow of aid from developed countries, promotion of long-term capital flows from the oil exporters and other surplus countries, and larger intermediation by international financial institutions.

It would appear that with such action to provide a stronger framework—which is within the realm of feasibility—the adjustment approach to this major problem can reasonably be expected to work. I should add that I would be more than dubious, on the basis of past attempts in this field, about the likelihood of success of an approach that would coordinate current-account positions of industrial countries to make them add to a given total.

I would conclude, therefore, that to resolve this most difficult problem of international disequilibrium we will have to rely chiefly on adjustment—within an appropriate framework and subject to appropriate adjustment rules—rather than on coordination.

Charles Frank

I should like to comment first on some of the issues raised by Fellner and Marris concerning relative rates of expansion and the sharing of the deficits. Not all the differences between the United States, West Germany, and Japan on these issues stem from differences in values. To some extent they derive from differences in perceptions of the effects of policies. There are those in the U.S. government, for example, who feel that an expansionary policy would not be very inflationary because of the great excess capacity and high rates of unemployment we now suffer. Others, however, are more concerned that increased government expenditures will increase inflation. There are differences on these issues between officials of the United States and officials in West Germany. The difference between these two countries may not be so much in honest policy differences as it is in expectations about the results of particular policies in terms of inflation.

Special circumstances in Japan operate to constrain the degree to which the Japanese government can move toward more economic stimulation. Premier Fukuda has a very thin margin in the Diet. Acceptance of his budget by the Diet is very important to him politically and to his ability to maintain control in the Diet. He cannot modify the budget easily in these circumstances. There are ways of speeding up expenditures, which the Japanese recently said they would do and which can accomplish the same expansionary effect without necessarily increasing the budget.

I am not quite so gloomy as Marris about the policy differences between the United States, West Germany, and Japan. I am not sure that the benefits from greater expansion in the surplus countries are necessarily that important. Perhaps the most serious problem that we face right now is that of financial intermediation of the large surpluses caused by the very high price of oil. If the United States, West Germany, and Japan increased their combined deficits by $5 billion, that would still leave a very large amount of financial intermediation to take place. Most experts agree that, although the commercial banking sector has played an important role in performing that intermediation, its role must be supplemented by more official international finance.

Another important issue, perhaps even more critical than that of coordinating monetary and fiscal policies, relates to international trade. The United States is faced with a number of important decisions. The International Trade Commission has made findings of injury and recommended import restraints in a number of cases, the most important of which is shoes, for which a presidential determination has to be made by April 9. There are also cases pending for sugar and television sets, for which presidential determinations have to be made about a month later.

The U.S. decisions on these particular items are enormously important for our domestic economy but probably more important for the impact they might have on the international economy and for the degree to which there might be retaliation if the United States were to raise its import barriers. This problem is a very serious one, which could, if it got out of hand, overwhelm some of the other economic problems that we face. We must find ways, particularly in the United States, to meet the problem of increased import penetration in a manner that is consistent with our international obligations.

Another issue that concerns me is the energy policy. We face the possibility in July of another 5 percent increase in the price of oil. Such a price increase could have a serious deflationary impact on the world economy, and at the same time it could also add to world inflationary trends.

It is important that the major industrial countries have a common view as to the effects of that oil price increase. Our various representations to the major oil-exporting countries will be more effective if we agree that a price increase is going to have a serious macroeconomic impact on the world economy. A common understanding of these macroeconomic effects is also important so that industrial countries can factor the oil-price problem into their own economic planning in a consistent manner.

Another policy issue that has important implications for the functioning of the global economy is that of international commodities. In the 1972–1974 period, a run-up of commodity prices significantly added to world inflationary trends. At present a number of mineral prices are quite depressed, while other mineral prices are high and are expected to go up. Some agricultural commodities are in very short supply and others, like sugar, are in oversupply. Now is the time to give some thought to ways that we might coordinate international and national buffer stocks to mitigate the effects of rising commodity prices, at least to avoid some of the more inflationary effects of the 1972–1974 period. There is a particular need to discuss how we might coordinate national stockpiling policies for grains.

Let me say in conclusion that policy areas other than domestic demand management affect the macroeconomic performance of the world economy, and they are, in many ways, just as important to world recovery and world economic stability as the questions we have discussed so fully—the sharing of the oil deficits and appropriate fiscal policies in the industrial countries.

THE EVOLVING
EXCHANGE-RATE MECHANISM
AND ITS CONTROL

Thomas D. Willett

The Bretton Woods system was based on the premise that exchange rates were a matter of international as well as national concern.[1] The international economic disasters of the interwar period had clearly demonstrated the dangers of treating trade and balance-of-payments measures as purely unilateral national concerns. On the other hand, the major countries were anxious also to preserve freedom to pursue their newly found interest in active domestic macroeconomic policies. They were mindful of the costly economic consequences of Churchill's decision to subject the domestic British economy to the dictates of a particular exchange-rate goal.[2] Thus they were unsympathetic to the idea of giving international authorities exclusive control over the de-

---

Note: This paper represents the author's personal views and not necessarily those of the U.S. Treasury.

[1] For example, in his testimony before the House of Lords on May 23, 1944, John Maynard Keynes described the Bretton Woods proposals as setting up "an international institution with substantial rights and duties to preserve orderly arrangements in matters such as exchange rates which are two-ended and affect both parties alike, which can also serve as a place of regular discussion between responsible authorities to find ways to escape those many unforeseeable dangers which the future holds."

Of course, in academic writings the concept that exchange rates are a matter of international concern goes back much further. An interesting example is found in Palgrave's *Dictionary of Political Economy*: "It will thus be seen that every country, by altering its mint regulations, has power to alter the metallic standard of value *pro tanto* in every other country using a metallic standard; and from this point of view the contention of those who desire to make currency arrangements a matter of international agreement may be accepted."

I am indebted to Edward M. Bernstein for calling both these quotations to my attention.

[2] Keynes, of course, was a leading advocate of this view. See his book *The Economic Consequences of Mr. Churchill* (London: L. and V. Woolf, 1925). The essay, "The Economic Consequences of Mr. Churchill," was published in his *Essays in Persuasion* (London: Macmillan, 1931), pp. 244–70. For a recent review and references to the literature on the interwar periods, see Gottfried Haberler, *The World Economy, Money, and the Great Depression, 1919–1939* (Washington, D.C.: American Enterprise Institute, 1976).

termination of exchange rates.[3] What was sought was a compromise between national and international interests and control such that countries would have freedom as they saw fit, subject to limitations on blatant beggar-thy-neighbor trade and exchange-rate policies.

Our international exchange-rate system has, of course, been changed substantially during the 1970s, the par-value or adjustable peg system adopted at Bretton Woods giving way to a system of managed floating. The same basic issues of international surveillance remain, however, albeit in some instances with changed manifestations and degrees of seriousness. Contrary to the initial fears of many, the adoption of widespread floating of exchange rates has not led to a breakdown in international financial cooperation even under the extremely trying circumstances caused by the huge increase in the price of oil. And while the operation of our new floating-exchange-rate system has certainly not been free of criticism, there is a fairly strong consensus that, in Edward M. Bernstein's words, "as a practical matter the system of fluctuating exchange rates has worked reasonably well, much better than would have been possible if attempts had been made to perpetuate the Bretton Woods system of fixed parities by patchwork here and there."[4] Thus it seems safe to assume that for the indefinite future our new system of flexible exchange rates is here to stay.

Within the framework of a system of managed floating, there has been a good deal of discussion about the need for international stabilization loans to allow countries to break the alleged vicious circle between exchange-rate depreciation and inflation. I have been asked to discuss this issue briefly before turning to the question of international surveillance of exchange-rate policies.

It is difficult to present a comprehensive analysis of the vicious circle hypothesis, as so many different versions of it abound. In the next section, I shall attempt to analyze several major variants, recognizing full well that I cannot do justice to all the more sophisticated versions

---

[3] For a discussion of Harry Dexter White's early ideas along this line, see David Rees, *Harry Dexter White* (New York: Coward, McCann and Geoghegan, 1973).

[4] Edward M. Bernstein, "The Monetary Authorities and the Free Exchange Market," speech before the Foreign Exchange Conference of the American Bankers Association, New York City, November 4, 1976. For an evaluation of the experience with floating rates to date and extensive references to the available literature, see Thomas D. Willett, *Floating Exchange Rates and International Monetary Reform* (Washington, D.C.: American Enterprise Institute, 1977), chap. 2. For a wide spectrum of views on the experience with floating, see Jacob S. Dreyer, Gottfried Haberler, and Thomas D. Willett (eds.), *Exchange Rate Flexibility*, proceedings of AEI-U.S. Treasury Conference on Flexible Exchange Rates, April 1976 (Washington, D.C.: American Enterprise Institute, 1978).

of the hypothesis that may be held by some of the participants in this conference. As this section displays a considerable lack of enthusiasm and some might even say hostility toward vicious circle adjustments, I should make clear at the beginning that it is directed primarily toward the more naive versions of the hypothesis, for example, those that assume that any exchange-rate depreciation is necessarily the cause of additional inflationary pressures rather than perhaps the reflection of underlying inflationary forces.

It is possible to construct particular scenarios in which exchange-rate depreciation can be an additional cause of inflationary pressure. For example, if destabilizing speculation drove the exchange value of a currency below its equilibrium level, this would worsen the short-run inflation-output trade-off facing financial authorities and could induce additional monetary and fiscal expansion. In such an instance, over-depreciation of the exchange rate, operating on a government reaction function, could create higher rates of inflation, which might legitimately be termed a vicious circle.

In my judgment, however, actual examples of this process operating to a significant degree have not often occurred. Some, however, see vicious circles as a frequent phenomenon. For example, the impression is sometimes given that if one adopts a monetary or asset market approach to exchange-rate determination and assumes that asset markets adjust faster than goods markets, one is likely to have overshooting of exchange rates and the preconditions for a vicious circle as a frequent occurrence. Recent research, however, has raised serious questions about the prevalence of overshooting of exchange rates, whether because of badly behaved speculation in the foreign exchange markets or because of faster adjustment of asset markets than goods markets.[5] It furthermore does not seem always to be realized that if the world does operate according to the monetarist overshooting models any vicious circle could quickly be broken. A tightening of monetary policy would cause a short-term overappreciation of the currency, breaking the exchange-rate-related part of the vicious circle.

In empirical investigation of overshooting questions, we must recognize that the current state of the art does not allow us to calculate unambiguously "correct" exchange-rate levels or zones with any high degree of accuracy. It is well known that equilibrium exchange rates can differ considerably from purchasing power parity (PPP) calculations and that PPP calculations can themselves vary widely depending

---

[5] For extensive references to this literature, see Willett, *Floating Exchange Rates*, chap. 2.

247

on the particular price indexes used.[6] Thus the use of different models or judgments and different sets of expectations about the future can give a wide range of exchange rates, which cannot be definitely labeled as too high or too low. We can also investigate patterns of exchange-rate dynamics that would be implied by various models of destabilizing or insufficiently stabilizing speculation or by monetarist overshooting.

The various empirical studies done by a number of my former colleagues in the Office of International Monetary Research at the U.S. Treasury (Sven Arndt, Dennis Logue, Charles Pigott, and Richard Sweeney) and me do not strongly support the prevalence of such patterns, especially after the first year or so of generalized floating. While this sheds some doubt on the prevalence of overdepreciated exchange rates, the necessary precondition for valid vicious circle arguments, it does not show that exchange rates were generally at the "correct" levels within a fairly narrow range. The advocates of the prevalence of the more sophisticated versions of the vicious circle generally have a good deal more confidence in their ability to judge what are right and wrong exchange rates than I believe is justified by our current state of scientific knowledge, but by the same token, they cannot clearly be shown to be wrong.

I would certainly not be one to argue that the market is always right, but I do have a fairly strong bias against attempting to alter market outcomes unless I am fairly confident that they are wrong and that I know in what way they are wrong. Thus I tend to see many fewer episodes that I would judge to meet the preconditions for a vicious circle than do others who have greater confidence in their own ability to decide what are incorrect exchange rates.

We can all agree to the advantages of eliminating temporary overshooting of exchange rates. The problem is to know beforehand which exchange-rate movements are likely to be temporary. Where such incipient fluctuations would clearly be temporary, the private market will generally have profit incentives to smooth them out without the need for official intervention. Thus the question becomes, in what instances can official intervention be expected to perform more successfully than private speculation? While I hope that we are making considerable progress in securing agreement among international monetary experts on the appropriate type of analytical framework

---

[6] For a recent excellent review article on the difficulties of using PPP calculations as guides of correct exchange rates, see Lawrence H. Officeu, "The Purchasing-Power-Parity Theory of Exchange Rates: A Review Article," *IMF Staff Papers* (March 1976), pp. 1–60.

from which to analyze the vicious circle hypothesis, I do not anticipate the rapid emergence of a consensus on empirical judgments.

I should also state my belief that it would have been much more productive if recent debate about appropriate intervention and stabilization policy under floating exchange rates had not so frequently been labeled debate about vicious circles. The more sophisticated versions being discussed at a conference like this are really quite different from the naive versions frequently discussed in other circles, and support for sophisticated versions of the vicious circle hypothesis can frequently be mistaken as support for more naive versions. The use of this simple label for a quite complicated set of issues has also all too often tended to generate theological debate instead of serious analysis and discussion. Thus while I do believe that many of the issues raised in the vicious circle debate are important and that we have reached a better understanding of current international monetary problems by discussing them, I do wish that the label could be made to disappear.

In the final section, alternative approaches to international surveillance under floating exchange rates are analyzed. It is concluded that the world of international finance has sufficient complexity and uncertainty that no simple set of statistical indexes or forecasts can form a sufficient basis for effective international surveillance to prevent countries from "manipulating exchange rates or the international monetary system in order to prevent effective balance of payments adjustment or to gain an unfair competitive advantage" (new IMF Article IV, Section iii). Nor, given the zealousness with which governments attempt to maintain the appearance of national sovereignty, are detailed formal public procedures for exchange-rate policies likely to be nearly as effective in practice in inducing countries to modify antisocial policies as are quiet discussions and informal pressures. This argues that formal public agreements on international surveillance should be at the level of basic principles whose meaning will gain greater precision through time as case histories accumulate, rather than attempts to establish initially a long list of detailed guidelines and regulations.

Vicious Circle Arguments for the Control of Exchange Rates

According to the vicious circle hypothesis, as frequently expounded in its more "modern" versions, it is more difficult for countries to bring inflation under control under flexible exchange rates because inflation causes exchange-rate depreciation, which immediately boosts import costs. This in turn causes the aggregate price indexes to rise further, which causes further depreciation of the exchange rate, and the circle starts all over again.

249

While it is frequently not mentioned in standard expositions, almost all modern advocates of this vicious circle argument would grant that such a cumulative circle would not go on and on unless validated by expansionary financial policies. Their charge is rather that floating rates make the process of reducing inflation more difficult and tend to widen the differences in inflation rates between high- and low-inflation countries. In other words, the charge is that floating rates cause additional inflation. Even in this revised form, however, typical modern vicious circle arguments are subject to confusion between statistical and behavioral relationships and generally fail to distinguish between the systems of adjustable pegs and floating exchange rates.

Calculations of the inflationary impact of exchange-rate depreciations are generally based on the mechanical relationship between import prices and aggregate price indexes. For example, if import prices carry a weight of 10 percent in a particular country's wholesale price index, a 20 percent depreciation in the exchange rate, if fully reflected in higher import prices, would increase the domestic price index by 2 percent. More sophisticated calculations may also take into account impacts on the domestic prices of exported products and import substitutes and induced reactions of wages as estimated from some macroeconomic model. Despite this increased sophistication, such calculations share the basic limitations of the back-of-the-envelope calculations. They do not speak to the issue of causation. Without establishing causation, such calculations can give no insight into the validity of the vicious circle hypothesis, any more than can the well-established empirical correlation between high rates of inflation and depreciating exchange rates. The calculations of the mechanics of inflationary impacts tell us nothing about whether the price increases were caused basically by underlying inflationary pressures in the country or by some capricious and unjustified movement in the exchange rate.[7]

---

[7] For further discussion on this point see Charles Pigott, John Rutledge, and Thomas D. Willett, "Some Difficulties in Estimating the Inflationary Effects of Exchange-Rate Changes," a paper presented at the Western Economic Association meetings, June 1978, and available as a Claremont Economics Discussion Paper (Claremont Graduate School, Claremont, California 91711).

Strictly speaking it is not correct to speak of causation running from inflation to exchange rates or vice versa. Both exchange rates and prices are endogenous variables, determined by underlying factors such as monetary and fiscal policies and productivity growth. When one speaks of causation running primarily from prices to exchange rates, what is really being said is that the underlying macro variables that determine prices are also the main determinants of the exchange rate. Likewise, the statement that causation runs from exchange rates to inflation implies the belief that the exchange-rate change is exogenous to the domestic inflationary process. (Of course, even in this case, the import price effects of the exchange-rate change would have to be validated by domestic macroeconomic

Suppose, for example, that a country begins to inflate more rapidly than its neighbors. Other things being equal, the resulting demand and supply shifts will cause the equilibrium exchange rate to depreciate and observed import and export prices to rise. This decrease in the exchange rate, however, is clearly the result of changes in underlying inflationary pressures, rather than being the independent cause of inflation.

Consider the following simple example. In a simple quantity theory world with full employment and efficient speculation, expansion of the money supply by 10 percent will, in a closed economy, eventually lead to a 10 percent increase in prices. In an open economy with floating rates, the same theory will apply: while domestic prices are rising by 10 percent, import prices will also rise by 10 percent. If other countries are also inflating at 10 percent, the increase in the home country's import prices will come directly from the increase in foreign exporters' prices with no change in the exchange rate. If, on the other hand, there is no inflation in the home country's trading partners, its import prices will still rise by 10 percent, and its exchange rate will depreciate by 10 percent. While in a mechanical sense one could say that the exchange-rate depreciation was what caused the import price increases to keep up with the general level of inflation, it would clearly be wrong to use this mechanical relationship to blame the import price increases on the exchange-rate depreciation. Nor would these import price increases be the cause of further exchange-rate depreciation, as is frequently assumed in presentations of the vicious circle hypothesis. The initial depreciation and import price increases would be the reflection of the already existing expansion in aggregate demand, not the cause of further inflation.

Of course, by running down its reserves and borrowing abroad, a country could for a time keep the full effects of expansions in aggregate demand from showing up in domestic prices. In the example above, by keeping its exchange rate from depreciating, a country could for a time keep its aggregate price index from rising by the full 10 percent. But such subsidizing of domestic absorption cannot be continued indefinitely. When it comes to an end, the exchange rate has to depreciate.

Some proponents of the vicious circle hypothesis would presumably grant that to the extent that exchange-rate depreciations were the direct

policies to have a significant effect on the overall price level.) All empirical studies that I have seen on the effects of exchange-rate changes on inflation assume that exchange-rate changes are exogenous. That assumption makes the statistical results of limited value in analyzing the interrelations between exchange rates and inflation under floating exchange rates.

result of domestic inflation, they could not legitimately be labeled a cause of additional inflationary pressures. But such proponents would go on to argue that exchange-rate depreciations frequently tend to be exaggerated because of destabilizing speculation or other shifts in capital flows and that it is these exaggerated depreciations that are the cause of additional inflationary pressures.

This more limited version of the vicious circle hypothesis is on a sounder analytic foundation. Various types of disturbances can certainly cause exchange-rate movements under floating rates to alter short-run inflation-unemployment trade-offs from what they would be in a closed economy or in an open economy under fixed exchange rates. Proponents of vicious circle arguments have a tendency, however, to focus primarily on examples of disturbances that worsen the inflation-unemployment trade-off in high-inflation countries. And in making judgments about actual developments, they frequently assume that any large and rapid depreciation and any depreciation greater than inflation differentials are evidence of exaggerated or excessive exchange-rate movements that do cause a worsening of inflation-unemployment trade-offs.

Such criteria are seriously deficient, however. It is well established in modern economic analysis that, once the important role of expectations in economic behavior is recognized, it becomes difficult to infer causation from the leading or lagging relationship of one statistical series or another. Indeed, this point was applied specifically to the vicious circle question by Gottfried Haberler more than forty years ago (in his classic book *The Theory of International Trade*)[8] to explain why one would frequently expect the building up of domestic inflationary pressures to lead to a depreciation of the exchange rate more rapid than the initial inflation in domestic prices. The lag in domestic prices behind the exchange-rate depreciation, however, did not imply that causation ran from depreciation to domestic price increases.

There has been much discussion through the years of the role of the discipline of fixed exchange rates in discouraging inflationary policies. What was frequently not made clear in such discussions was that the truth of this argument with respect to genuinely and permanently fixed exchange rates does not carry over to the case of adjustably pegged exchange rates. There is the possibility of endless debate over whether exchange-rate depreciation with freely floating, or balance-of-payments deficits with genuinely fixed, exchange rates would be likely to provide a stronger source of discipline against inflationary policies. But I believe that there can be little doubt that adjustably

---

[8] Gottfried Haberler, *The Theory of International Trade* (London: William Hodge and Co., 1936), chaps. 6 and 8.

pegged or heavily managed exchange-rate systems would score the lowest marks. An attempt to establish genuinely fixed exchange rates would hardly be realistic (even if desirable). This leaves floating rates as the best practical system for reducing governments' propensities to engage in inflationary policies.[9]

Compared with adjustably pegged or heavily managed exchange rates, floating also gives low-inflation countries greater ability to shield themselves against the inflationary policies of others and reduces the inflationary pressures generated by the massive movements of capital internationally in response to anticipations of exchange-rate realignments. There can be no question that at times under floating rates private speculation will cause rates to depreciate "too far" as determined ex post, just as at other times it will not move rates far enough. But it is extremely difficult to imagine that under floating rates the inflationary consequences of such lack of perfect foresight in the private market could come anywhere near equaling the inflationary pressures generated by the operation of adjustably pegged and heavily managed flexible rates.

Nor is this conclusion altered by the so-called ratchet effect associated with asymmetrical upward and downward flexibility of wages and prices: when an exchange rate falls, prices and wages rise, but when an exchange rate rises, wages and prices do not fall or do not fall as much. Thus exchange-rate movements are said to ratchet up wages and prices. Despite the frequency with which such ratchet effects are discussed, it is extremely doubtful that in reality they have accounted for even a tiny fraction of world inflation. In the first place, such asymmetries are relevant only in instances in which exchange-rate movements are not the result of relative underlying inflationary pressures—that is, only in the minority of instances in which exchange-rate movements are primarily a cause rather than a consequence of past or anticipated price changes.

Second, it must be recognized that even in the instances in which such asymmetries would be relevant, their magnitude can easily be exaggerated. While it is certainly true that there is very little downward flexibility of wages, there is a good deal of downward flexibility of prices, especially of the prices of internationally traded goods. Thus in

---

[9] According to two papers on this topic, when the full range or even several of the major ways in which exchange-rate systems can influence inflation are taken into account, it is not possible to conclude that either genuinely fixed or floating rates are inherently more inflationary (see Emil-Maria Classen, "World Inflation under Flexible Exchange Rates," and W. Max Corden, "Inflation and the Exchange-Rate Regime," *Scandinavian Journal of Economics*, vol. 78, no. 2 [1976], pp. 346–65 and 370–83, respectively). See also Andrew Crockett and Morris Goldstein, "Inflation under Fixed and Flexible Exchange Rates," unpublished paper, International Monetary Fund, 1976.

practice it is doubtful that significant asymmetries would be likely to operate unless the exchange-rate changes were maintained sufficiently long to be incorporated into wages. And exchange-rate changes that are maintained long enough to be incorporated into wage bargains are unlikely to have been caused simply by exaggerated speculative movements not reflecting the true underlying degree of inflationary pressures.

One must also consider the inflationary impact of the monetary asymmetries that operated because of speculative capital flows under the par-value system. As Otmar Emminger and Leland Yeager argue, under the adjustable peg, capital inflows into surplus countries generated additional inflationary pressures for those countries, while there was very little tendency for the corresponding deficit countries to allow the capital outflows to tighten their domestic monetary conditions.[10] Thus speculative capital flows under the old par-value system tended to ratchet up the overall rate of monetary expansion. Given the huge magnitude of such capital flows during the last several years of the adjustable peg system, there can be little question of the quantitative significance of this type of asymmetry.[11]

Another type of argument that floating rates make it more difficult to implement anti-inflation policies successfully runs along the following lines: when a country has been suffering from serious inflationary pressures, the market reacts not just to past inflation but also to expected future inflation rates. But there are lags in the effects of macroeconomic policies on the economy. Thus even when a sound stabilizing policy is implemented, it will take a good while for its real effects to show up. In the meanwhile speculation will have caused an exaggerated depreciation of the exchange rate, forcing up import prices and causing further inflation and undermining the initial stabilization policy. In other

---

[10] Otmar Emminger, *Inflation and the International Monetary System* (Washington, D.C.: Per Jacobsson Foundation, International Monetary Fund, 1973), chap. 6; and Leland B. Yeager, *International Monetary Relations*, 2d ed. (New York: Harper and Row, 1976).

[11] There is considerable empirical evidence that in actual practice there was a good deal more sterilization of capital inflows under the adjustable peg than is assumed in many analyses. For example, Herring and Marston found almost full sterilization of payments imbalances for West Germany during the 1960s. There can be little question, however, that although the huge payments imbalances of the early 1970s caused much less than a one-for-one increase in monetary expansion in the surplus countries, there still was a significant net expansionary impact on world monetary aggregates. On these questions, see Richard J. Herring and Richard C. Marston, *National Monetary Policies and International Financial Markets* (Amsterdam: North-Holland, 1977), pt. 2; and Thomas D. Willett, "The Eurocurrency Market, Exchange Rate Systems, and National Financial Policies," in Carl M. Stem, John H. Makins, and Dennis Logue, eds., *Eurocurrencies and the International Monetary System* (Washington, D.C.: American Enterprise Institute, 1976), pp. 193–221 and the references cited there.

words, in such a situation the stabilization policy is not given time to take hold. The frequently advocated "cure" for this brand of vicious circle is a large international stabilization loan that will allow the country to prop up its currency in the foreign exchange market while its domestic policies are taking hold.

In its extreme form, however, this argument rests on a very peculiar view of how the market works, which is difficult to reconcile with actual international monetary experience. According to this view, the problem is that the private market is farsighted, but apparently only in one direction. That is, the market will incorporate expectations of future high inflation rates into the current level of the exchange rate, but for some reason, when a strong domestic stabilization policy is implemented, there is no corresponding immediate strengthening of the spot exchange rate because of anticipations of lower future inflation rates.

It is, of course, easy to construct a theoretical model of the economy that would behave in this way. All that would be needed, for instance, is to assume that expectations of future inflation rates are based on a mechanical extrapolation of past inflation rates. But such an assumption would hardly conform to reality. There is, of course, no doubt that the past behavior of both government policies and inflation rates heavily conditions expectations about the future, but this does not occur in general in a simple mechanical way.[12] Even a cursory following of foreign exchange market developments shows how often exchange-rate expectations are based directly on expectations about such key factors as the macroeconomic policies governments will adopt and the likelihood that those policies will be maintained.

Many episodes of a strengthening or a weakening of a currency are explained by exchange market participants as primarily reflecting changed expectations about the course of national budget or monetary policies. There can be little question that government policies can influence expectations immediately. If a *credible* stabilization program is implemented, the effects on confidence and exchange rates need not operate only with long lags.

It is quite true that government announcements of stabilization objectives frequently fail to influence private expectations. But this is hardly surprising given the frequency with which such announced targets fail to be met. In short, the composite of private expectations is neither infinitely malleable in response to announced government targets nor unalterably based on the mechanical extrapolation of past statistics. The

---

[12] On the effects of government policies on conditioning expectations, see particularly William Fellner, *Towards a Reconstruction of Macroeconomics* (Washington, D.C.: American Enterprise Institute, 1976).

track record of government anti-inflationary pronouncements has in many instances strained the credibility of such pronouncements. Given this inheritance, current governments must work harder to reestablish confidence in the credibility of stabilization programs. That means that they must not merely announce stabilization policies but take credible steps toward implementing and maintaining them before their full extent is reflected in private expectations and in the exchange markets.

During this process there may sometimes be a useful role for exchange market intervention, but the case for such intervention can easily be exaggerated. The main point is that if really adequate domestic stabilization policies are adopted in such a way that their continuation is ensured, little intervention is likely to be needed; if such domestic policies are not adopted, even a huge international stabilization loan would be inadequate. There is little basis for the notion that the operation of a vicious circle under floating rates would undermine the operation of domestic stabilization policies that would otherwise have been adequate.

There are, however, times when international loans can make an important positive contribution to domestic anti-inflationary policies. Private market participants will quite rationally want to wait for more proof of the likely success of new stabilization efforts when a government has inherited a long string of past failures of such efforts than when it has a good record with respect to stabilization policies.

In such instances, as part of an overall stabilization program, it may be a wise investment for a government to devote some of its resources to temporary support of the exchange value of the currency. And if the stabilization program looks sufficient to international officials, it may be wise for, say, the IMF to lend funds to the country for this purpose. Indeed, given the international reputation of the IMF for financial responsibility, such loans can play an important direct role in bolstering private confidence in the likelihood of the success of national stabilization efforts.

It is very important, however, that the positive potential for such loans not be squandered. The market will follow the track record of IMF loans just as much as national stabilization efforts, and any persistent failure to use such loans productively will serve to undermine confidence in the IMF, as well as in the national authorities. One of the quickest ways to undermine the potential productivity of such international stabilization loans would be to use them to attempt to maintain some specific exchange-rate target.

Of course, some hold the view that the exchange market behaves in an essentially irrational manner; in particular, that any depreciation of the exchange rate will set off a chain reaction of further depreciation as traders mindlessly extrapolate from the change in the rate today to the change they expect tomorrow. In this view official efforts to prevent the exchange rate from depreciating would stabilize expectations, even if the national authorities were piling up huge international debts in the process.

If indeed expectations in the exchange market were predominantly formed so myopically, the arguments for using international stabilization loans to maintain some target level of the exchange rate might make some sense. But it is hard to believe that anyone with any knowledge of how foreign exchange markets work would give credence to such a hypothesis. The behavior of private participants in the foreign exchange markets has not been dominated by destabilizing bandwagon effects.[13] Nor has official intervention to maintain particular exchange-rate targets had a predominantly stabilizing influence. On the contrary, the market has learned from experience to be quite suspicious of government efforts to maintain pegged exchange rates. If the market comes to believe that funds from stabilization loans are being spent in an effort to pursue a specific exchange rate that the market considers untenable, such funds could be dissipated in very short order and to very little effect in aiding domestic stabilization.

The potential magnitudes of private capital that can flow internationally when an officially pegged exchange rate comes under suspicion are much greater than the limited resources available for official international lending for stabilization purposes. Over the medium term, official efforts to maintain a particular narrow range of exchange rates would seem much more likely to endanger than to enhance the chances of success of domestic stabilization efforts. Both the credibility and the lending power of the IMF and other official international lending sources are much too important and scarce to be squandered on ill-conceived efforts by inflationary countries to maintain particular exchange-rate targets.

In summary, there are some substantially modified versions of the vicious circle hypothesis that are legitimate theoretical possibilities. One can imagine particular types of episodes in which greater inflationary pressures would be generated under freely floating rates than under realistic alternative exchange-rate regimes. In actual practice, however, episodes of any great significance are rare. On balance, when

---

[13] See, for instance, Willett, *Floating Exchange Rates*, and Dennis Logue, Richard J. Sweeney, and Thomas D. Willett, "The Speculative Behavior of Foreign Exchange Rates during the Current Float," *Journal of Business Research*, no. 2 (1978), pp. 159–74.

our experience under relatively freely floating rates is compared with our experience under adjustably pegged and heavily managed flexible exchange rates, there can be little doubt that the latter facilitate the generation and international transmission of inflationary pressures. This, of course, is not to argue the other extreme—that floating rates are a panacea for the world's inflationary problems. As was clearly recognized in the Rambouillet and Jamaica agreements, no international monetary system can be a substitute for sound domestic economic and financial policies. But the various vicious circle hypotheses do not present a convincing case that a greater degree of exchange-rate pegging would contribute to the efficiency of our evolving exchange-rate system.

Alternative Approaches to International Surveillance under Floating Exchange Rates

A Brief Review of Surveillance Issues. The Bretton Woods arrangements were remarkably successful in preventing a return to the autarkic days days of the 1930s. As the postwar period evolved, the major difficulty in the operation of the international exchange-rate system became not that countries were too anxious to alter their exchange rates to obtain competitive advantages but that they were too hesitant to make the changes in exchange rates called for by changes in underlying economic and financial conditions.

It became increasingly clear that revisions were needed in what had become the operational surveillance principle of the par-value system, that it was only changes in exchange rates that were a matter of substantive international concern. It became apparent that the failure to change an exchange rate in the face of an underlying balance-of-payments disequilibrium could not be excluded from substantive international surveillance. (Of course, the founders of the Bretton Woods system were not oblivious of this problem, as is witnessed by the scarce currency clause, but in practice the par-value system was much more effective in discouraging disequilibrating changes in parities than it was in encouraging equilibrating changes.)

In contrast to the 1930s, the basic fabric of international financial cooperation has been strengthened to the point where I would judge that, under managed floating, the greater ease of allowing rates to adjust to prevent or remove disequilibrium substantially outweighs the greater ease of implementing beggar-thy-neighbor manipulative policies. In other words, as contrasted with the par-value system, managed floating probably does increase the scope for following beggar-thy-neighbor policies, but it also reduces the cost of following cooperative policies.[14]

My reading of our experience under managed floating to date suggests that the latter effect has been of much greater importance than the former, and I am fairly optimistic that this is not likely to be reversed over the coming years. Thus I view the basic framework of our new exchange-rate system as favoring the promotion of international co-operation on exchange-rate issues.

This, of course, does not mean that the adoption of widespread floating obviates the need for international surveillance of the exchange-rate system. Surveillance might become redundant if all countries adopted completely freely floating exchange rates, but our emerging system of managed floating is a long way from that extreme ideal or horror, depending on the commentator.

Even apart from continuing pegged rate arrangements such as the snake, official management of floating rates by many countries is still quite heavy. Indeed, in a number of instances official management under floating has been more reminiscent of the operation of the adjustable peg than of the leaning-against-the-wind intervention that has traditionally been practiced by Canada, much less of freely floating rates. Under the managed float to date, there may very well have been more disequilibrium generated by attempts at excessive pegging of rates within a narrow range in the face of changing equilibrium rates than by disequilibrating depreciations of exchange rates caused by official manipulation or destabilizing private speculation.

Attempting to draw such a balance would be primarily of academic concern, of course, for the task of international surveillance is to reduce as much as possible such disequilibrating and disruptive tendencies. A finding that there were more attempts to maintain overvalued currencies than undervalued ones is not an argument against attempting to discourage attempts at undervaluation.

Some commentators have expressed disappointment that the Rambouillet and Jamaica agreements did not provide for more formal and detailed procedures and guidelines for monitoring the operation of the international adjustment process. Fears have often been expressed that the greater freedom of exchange-rate movements under floating would be used in a beggar-thy-neighbor manner. With the huge increases in oil prices in 1973 and 1974, concerns about these problems were

---

[14] It should be remembered, however, that the beggar-thy-neighbor policies of the 1930s were carried out primarily through changes in adjustably pegged rather than in floating exchange rates.

greatly multiplied.[15] It was soon recognized that an aggregate payments problem would not result for oil-importing countries since oil exporters collectively had no choice but to put the money they earned back into the oil-importing countries in the form of purchases of goods and services and short- and long-term investments.

But many fears were expressed that, despite the absence of an overall aggregate payments problem, serious difficulties would arise from the distribution of payments positions among oil-importing countries. For example, if the aggregate current-account deficits of the oil-importing countries fell primarily on a few major countries, those countries might find such large current-account deficits unacceptable, and a scramble of beggar-thy-neighbor policies of the 1930s type would be initiated, as the major industrial countries attempted to pass the aggregate current-account deficits with oil exporters around from one to another. Indeed discussions of the distribution of the burden of the oil price increases among oil-importing countries focused as frequently on who would "bear" the current account deficits as on how the real economic costs were distributed. Numerous proposals were put forward suggesting specific formulas for "allocating" the aggregate current-account deficits.[16]

Fortunately such fears have proved greatly exaggerated. In fact, the primary problem in the adjustment process since the oil shock is not that countries have tried to adjust too quickly and too much, but rather that many countries have postponed sufficient adjustment measures for too long. Initially, the major concern was how countries could be induced to borrow sufficiently to avoid disruptive and self-defeating attempts to adjust individually more than was collectively feasible. But it has turned out that the aggregate willingness of countries to borrow internationally was much greater than had been anticipated. As a result, in the first several years after the oil shocks, only a small part of the aggregate current-account deficit of the oil-importing countries "fell" on the countries in the strongest international financial positions, such as West Germany and the United States. This was not, however, primarily

---

[15] This and many of the other oil-related international monetary issues are discussed in Thomas D. Willett, *The Oil Transfer Problem and International Economic Stability*, Princeton Essays in International Finance, no. 113 (December 1975), and references cited there.

[16] For discussions and analysis of such proposals, see Andrew D. Crockett and Duncan Ripley, "Sharing the Oil Deficit," *IMF Staff Papers*, vol. 12, no. 2 (July 1975), pp. 284–312; Robert Solomon, "The Allocation of 'Oil Deficits'," *Brookings Papers on Economic Activity*, no. 1 (1975), pp. 61–87; John Williamson, "The International Financial System," in Edward R. Fried and Charles L. Schultze (eds.), *Higher Oil Prices and the World Economy* (Washington: Brookings Institution, 1975), pp. 197–225; and Willett, *The Oil Transfer Problem*.

the result of efforts by such countries to take explicit adjustment actions to achieve trade surpluses, as many had feared by analogy with the 1930s. Rather it largely represented the effect of many countries' hesitating to begin adjustments.

Our success in avoiding the worst of the conceivable outcomes of the oil shocks should not, however, be allowed to lull us into a false sense of security. We have been fortunate that adjustment initially took the form of countries' being too willing to run payments deficits rather than too eager to compete for surpluses. But the absence of an aggregate international financial problem associated with the oil-related current-account imbalances does not mean that the accumulation by individual countries of economic indebtedness has no consequences for international financial stability. We have reached the point where, to secure a sounder world payments structure, more emphasis must be placed on making greater adjustments by a number of countries that have much larger payments deficits than can be accounted for by increased oil payments.

The need for a more balanced world payments structure was one of the major items on the agenda at the IMF annual meetings in Manila in September 1976. Achieving better balance will require both more adjustments by countries with excessive deficits and the willingness of financially strong countries to abstain from policies that would frustrate these attempts. The achievement of better balance can be greatly facilitated by the informed analysis and discussions that are a part of multilateral surveillance of the adjustment process. The process of multilateral surveillance will take place in a wide variety of forums— bilateral discussions, regional groupings, small groups of heads of state or top financial officials, and the meetings of such organizations as the OECD. The IMF retains the prime responsibility for "umpiring" or overseeing the adjustment process.

In such discussions it is important to distinguish between the ex post pattern of current-account deficits that occurs and the way it comes about. For example, it is frequently argued that the current-account surpluses of West Germany and Japan intensify balance-of-payments pressures on other countries. That is clearly true if their current-account surpluses are the result of *active* policies to acquire or maintain strong current-account positions. In such instances the strong countries are impeding the efforts of financially weaker countries to adjust, and it is certainly appropriate to exert pressure on such countries to keep them from undercutting the operation of the international adjustment mechanism.

However, suppose a country permits its current account to be determined by market forces and other countries' adjustment policies. If it still runs a current-account surplus, it does not seem at all clear that this should be judged as significantly intensifying the pressures on other countries.

Since the current system is one of less than completely freely floating rates, there are still some elements present of the old "who should adjust" problem that existed under Bretton Woods. Thus some encouragement for positive government actions in the strong countries may be a desirable complement to encouragement of countries with excessive deficits to adjust, but this should be clearly distinguished from the much stronger presumption against active policies to thwart other countries' adjustment efforts.

The Rambouillet and Jamaica agreements were based on the recognition that there are no easy statistical shortcuts to monitoring the operation of the international adjustment process. This does not mean that extensive use should not be made of statistical indicators or that measures of reserve movements and their substitutes should not be used as important factors in determining disequilibrium and manipulation. But even with respect to reserve indicators, it would probably be unwise to attempt to secure international agreement on definite quantitative limits. Such a view is not in basic conflict with the reserve indicator approach proposed by the United States during the C-20 negotiations.[17] Rather it is based on recognition of the difficulties of designing any one statistical series that will capture tolerably well the effects of direct government influences on the foreign exchange market.

This difficulty is compounded by the tendency of countries zealous over their formal sovereignty to cooperate in practice far more fully than is implied by the formal international commitments they are willing to undertake. Thus, even if the overwhelming technical problems could be overcome so that a good set of reserve indicators could be constructed, it is doubtful that explicit quantitative limits could be negotiated that would be sufficiently "tight" to be very useful. Indeed, such an agreement could even be counterproductive, since countries would have a stronger defense for manipulative actions if they were still within such internationally agreed limits. Thus greater cooperation can perhaps be secured by informal than by formal methods.

An example of this point is that, despite the widespread unwillingness to accept the U.S. reserve indicator proposals to limit fluctuations in countries' gross reserve levels, there has in general been much less fluctuation in recent reserve positions of the industrial countries than

---

[17] For a review of the discussions of reserve indicator proposals, see Thomas D. Willett, *Floating Exchange Rates*.

would have been allowed under even the most stringent versions of the U.S. proposals.

Difficulties of the Target Zone Approach. The difficulties of attempting to negotiate a detailed formal set of reserve indicators hold even more strongly for approaches that attempt to set international allocations for current-account positions or target zones for exchange rates.[18] It is true that, if international experts could forecast perfectly and national governments succeeded in shedding all concerns for national sovereignty, these approaches would present a feasible and perhaps even desirable way of ensuring the most efficient possible operation of the adjustment process. But in the world as it is, neither national nor international officials have any hope of being able to calculate "correct" patterns of exchange rates with a high degree of accuracy, much less secure the willingness of national officials to have their exchange rates set by international authorities.

Proposals for allocating current-account deficits have tended to focus primarily on what the pattern should be and have given less attention to how it would be achieved. As I have argued elsewhere,[19] desires for current-account surpluses are largely a political phenomenon. There is no single economic calculation that can be used even conceptually to determine an optimal allocation of current-account positions. The economic criteria that might be relevant are too numerous and complex to allow a "scientific" formula for allocation, even if attention were limited to purely economic factors.

Perhaps even more important, proposals for allocating current accounts have seldom considered how an agreed pattern of current accounts would be achieved. The world is just not sufficiently predictable to put much faith in balance-of-payments forecasts of the degree of precision necessary for such approaches to be workable. With

---

[18] The target zone approach calls for countries to announce what they believe is an appropriate range for their exchange rates to lie within and to intervene to move exchange rates toward or at least keep them from moving away from this zone. As frequently expounded, the target zone approach differs from the old par-value system with a wide exchange-rate band in that the zone is usually thought of in terms of a trade-weighted or effective rate measure and the zone approach is somewhat looser, both in the frequency of revision and the degree of willingness to defend the outer limits of the zone. Still, references to the target zone approach as a back-door attempt to reestablish a par-value system are not entirely inappropriate. The IMF guidelines for floating encourage but do not require countries to establish target zones in consultation with the IMF.

There is also a looser type of target zone proposal, which has been advanced in Europe by C. J. Oort and others, that treats the limits of the zone as consultation points rather than necessarily as intervention points.

[19] Willett, *The Oil Transfer Problem.*

TABLE 1

OECD CURRENT-ACCOUNT FORECAST ERRORS FOR 1974 AND 1975
(billions of dollars)

Country	1974	1975
United States	5.6	19.2
United Kingdom	5.8	2.7
France	5.2	6.5
West Germany	8.6	2.2
Italy	6.4	5.2
Japan	4.2	0.7
Total	35.8	36.5
Average	6.0	6.1

SOURCES: Thomas D. Willett, *Floating Exchange Rates*, appendix A; and *World Financial Markets*, various issues.

perfect foresight and knowledge of economic parameters, the technical problems of implementing such an approval would be trivial. Once the current-account targets had been determined and underlying economic and financial policies projected, the pattern of exchange rates that would bring about the desired pattern would be calculated.

Econometric models and estimates exist that in principle could allow such an exercise to be undertaken. But in practice the accuracy of such models and estimates is far less than sufficient to make such an approach viable, as is clearly illustrated by the huge forecast errors frequently made by even the best balance-of-payments models and judgmental forecasts. For example, while discussions of the "appropriate" allocation of current-account balances are frequently conducted in terms of an accuracy of at least to the nearest one or two billion dollars, the average annual error of the projections of the OECD secretariat for the six major industrial countries was approximately two billion dollars for the 1969–1975 period.[20] And this was for forecasting only one year in advance. Many discussions of target zones have envisaged selecting a zone that is expected to hold over several years.

Furthermore, with all the underlying instabilities in the world economy in recent years, forecast errors have risen dramatically. For

[20] See Willett, *Floating Exchange Rates*, appendix A. It should be noted in defense of the technical experts at the OECD that their freedom in forecasting is circumscribed by the policy assumptions they must use. Thus they are presenting projections rather than true forecasts. Nevertheless, their accuracy has not been notably less than forecasters free of this constraint.

1974 and 1975, the average error of the annual current-account projections by the OECD was approximately $6 billion for the six major countries (see Table 1). And the error for the U.S. current account in 1975 was an incredible $19 billion, the actual result being a surplus of $11.7 billion and the projected *deficit* $7.5 billion. These errors do not occur because the OECD is a particularly bad forecaster. Errors of similar direction and magnitude were made both in internal U.S. Treasury forecasts and in the published forecasts of Morgan Guaranty. Indeed, as shown in Table 2, the average error for Morgan Guaranty forecasts as published in *World Financial Markets* was almost identical with that of the OECD for 1975, although Morgan did hold an edge for 1974.

Such figures certainly raise questions about the ability of international authorities to determine a viable pattern of exchange rates for any significant length of time. As soon as any of the forecasts on which the exchange rates were based began to go wrong, which would be frequently, a renegotiation of the target exchange-rate pattern would have to be undertaken. Of course, some degree of uncertainty could be handled by the adoption of fairly broad target zones for exchange rates, but if the target zones were allowed to be broad enough to take ad-

TABLE 2

Morgan Guaranty Forecast Errors for Current-Account Balances
(billions of dollars)

Country	1974			1975		
	Forecast	Actual	Absolute difference	Forecast	Actual	Absolute difference
United States	−2.00	−2.25	.25	−6.50	11.70	18.20
United Kingdom	−6.00	−8.75	2.75	−8.50	−3.80	4.70
France	−4.50	−5.50	1.00	−3.50	.30	3.80
West Germany	−3.50	9.25	12.75	10.00	3.80	6.20
Italy	−5.50	−9.50	4.00	−4.50	−.50	4.00
Japan	−7.00	−4.50	2.50	−.50	−.70	.20
Total			23.25			37.10
Average			3.90			6.20

SOURCES: Thomas D. Willett, *Floating Exchange Rates*, appendix A; and *World Financial Markets*, various issues.

equately into account the difficulties of estimating "correct" exchange rates, especially for the time horizon of several years frequently specified in such proposals, they would become much too loose to yield a strong linkage to current account positions.

Reference Rate Proposals. To a lesser degree, these difficulties apply to the reference rate proposals for international surveillance of floating rates. As propounded by Ethier and Bloomfield and by Williamson,[21] the reference rate proposal would retain the Bretton Woods idea of parities but reverse their relation to official intervention. The Bretton Woods regime focused on when intervention was required. The reference rate proposal focuses on when intervention is prohibited. Under the Bretton Woods regime, countries were required to intervene to keep exchange rates from moving away from parity by more than a specified amount. The reference rate proposal, on the other hand, prohibits official intervention to sell foreign exchange when exchange rates are below the reference parity or zone and prohibits the purchase of foreign exchange when the exchange rates are above the parity zone.

Intervention to move exchange rates toward the reference parity or zone would be allowed but not required. On the assumption that it could be effectively enforced, the advocates of the reference rate proposal make a convincing case for its superiority over the old par-value system. It is also much less likely to lead to undesirable intervention and contribute to international financial instability than the target zone approach encouraged in the 1974 IMF guidelines for floating,[22] which has been recommended by several economists and officials in recent years. The more ambitious target zone approach would in addition require, or at least strongly encourage, that countries intervene to dampen exchange-rate movements away from and reinforce movements toward the target zone.

But the reference rate proposal is not completely free of dangers as the basis for international surveillance of the adjustment process.

---

[21] Wilfred Ethier and Arthur I. Bloomfield, *Managing the Managed Float*, Princeton Essays in International Finance, no. 112 (October 1975); and John H. Williamson, "The Future Exchange-Rate Regime," *Banca Nazionale del Lavoro Quarterly Review*, Rome, no. 113 (June 1975), pp. 117–44.

While some have likened the looser Oort target zone approach to the reference proposal because of the lack of required intervention, the focus of the two types of proposals is really quite different. The Oort type still focuses, though in a weaker form, on when an exchange-rate zone should be defended, and the reference rate proposals focus on when intervention should be prohibited.

[22] For a critical review of the IMF guidelines, see Raymond Mikesell and Henry N. Goldstein, *Rules for a Floating Regime*, Princeton Essays in International Finance, no. 109 (April 1975).

For example, Williamson sees the reference rates as providing a focal point for stabilizing speculation. Thus he would see the scheme as not only safeguarding against antisocial exchange-rate manipulation but also leading to greater stability in the foreign exchange markets. Such an outcome, however, is crucially dependent both on the assumed nature of the behavior of the private exchange market and on the ability of governments to speculate better.

It is clearly difficult to judge conclusively whether official or private speculation has performed better (or less poorly) on balance under the current float or what is the best role of official intervention in supplementing the private market. But in my judgment the available technical studies do not generally support the view that private speculation has tended to behave in a systematically perverse manner. And it does seem fairly clear that the countries whose official intervention has been most effective (or least ineffective) in promoting stability have been those that did not become strongly committed to defending particular rate levels for any significant period of time.

The reference rate proposal runs the serious danger that it would generate pressures on financial authorities to defend reference parities or zones. In other words, it just may not be possible to generate an officially sanctioned set of reference rates without setting up pressures that would in practice convert the reference rate scheme into the target zone approach.

Even apart from this major problem, some technical questions must be raised about the advantages claimed for the reference rate approach over other proposals for guidelines for floating. For example, Ethier and Bloomfield argue that the reference rate proposal is easier to implement than a reserve indicator approach because it avoids the problem of defining reserves.[23] But this gives a misleading impression of the comparative difficulties of the two approaches because Ethier and Bloomfield do not deal sufficiently with the question of how to define intervention. This question, if addressed realistically, is open to almost as many ambiguities as is the meaning of reserves.

Ethier and Bloomfield also argue the superiority of the reference rate over reserve-based proposals on the grounds that

> at a more basic level, the fundamental goal of any proposal is presumably to maintain an approximation to an equilibrium structure of exchange rates. There is, in truth, no such thing as as equilibrium structure of reserve levels. When reserve levels are used to define permissible intervention, they are really

---

[23] Ethier and Bloomfield, *Managing the Managed Float*, p. 19.

serving as proxies for exchange rates, and they need not be very exact proxies.[24]

This again is a misleading formulation. Ethier and Bloomfield appear to assume implicitly that they can know within a fairly close range what equilibrium rates are. But this assumes away the real problem, that it is difficult to "know" what the equilibrium rate is.

There is usually no dearth of commentators willing to offer their opinion on the subject, but seldom is there a wide consensus among experts that the market rate is very far from this equilibrium rate.[25] In practice, one would expect the relative accuracy of the pure reserve indicator and reference rate approaches to vary at times both from country to country and from episode to episode. It is clearly understandable that at times national officials in some countries will want to "take a view" on their exchange rate and that, in confidential discussions of balance-of-payments financing and surveillance of the adjustment process, international officials may sometimes have a particular range of exchange rates in mind as "appropriate" for a particular country at a particular time. But it is quite a different matter to make use of the reference rate approach in such an informal context than to attempt to determine and keep up to date a full set of internationally sanctioned reference rates.

In other words, the reserve approach assumes that market forces are generally a fairly reliable determiner of equilibrium exchange rates, and the best evidence of substantial disequilibrium is usually the existence of sizable government influences on the exchange market through official intervention or various types of substitute policies. The reference rate proposal, on the other hand, assumes that, because of poorly behaved speculation, market exchange rates will frequently diverge substantially from equilibrium rates. In pure form the reference rate proposals implicitly assume that officials can fairly consistently forecast better than the market behaves. One need not be a naive believer that the market is always right to have serious qualms about

---

[24] Ibid.

[25] In general, if there is a broad consensus among both private and official experts, it will be reflected in the market rate. Conceptually it is possible where the supply of speculative funds is highly limited—that is, where there is little elasticity in the speculative schedule—that the market rate could differ substantially from the view of a vast majority of experts. Indeed, there is some evidence that this occurred at times in the early days of floating as the market was becoming accustomed to the new arrangements. There is little evidence that this is a common phenomenon today, however. In general, experts' opinions that an exchange rate is substantially above or below "equilibrium" are balanced by the opposing opinions of others.

the general accuracy of this assumption, especially given the difficulties of initially negotiating official exchange-rate norms and then keeping them updated. A much more flexible and productive way to make use of the reference rate idea is to discuss staff estimates where appropriate in private, rather than attempt to establish a full set of publicly announced reference rates.

Disorderly Exchange Markets and Obligations for Official Intervention.
On one major point the reserve indicator and reference rate approaches are in basic agreement. That is that the primary emphasis of surveillance should be on avoiding manipulative acts that influence the exchange rate. Under neither approach in pure form would countries be required to undertake active intervention to influence the exchange rate.

This focus coincides with the emphasis in the new IMF articles on avoiding manipulation. But, as Bernstein has pointed out, "What remains uncertain in the new article is whether a member has any responsibility for exchange rates that fluctuate excessively because of market forces when its own exchange rate policy is completely passive."[26]

The Rambouillet agreement among the major industrial countries did carry the obligation to seek to avoid disorderly exchange market conditions. But it did not imply a necessary obligation to intervene to avoid fluctuations in exchange rates. In devising principles for the international surveillance of exchange-rate policies, one should be wary of using variations in exchange rates as evidence per se of disequilibrium and disorderly market conditions. The 1974 IMF guidelines for floating implicitly endorsed this view, by indicating that official intervention should be used to oppose large, rapid movements in exchange rates. While the view that any rapid change in an exchange rate must be strong presumptive evidence of destabilizing speculation is still held in some quarters, investigations of the behavior of the foreign exchange market raise serious doubts about such a presumption. Concern with avoiding disorderly markets should not be formulated in terms of monitoring the variance of countries' exchange rates. This, of course, does not mean that sudden large movements in rates should not be one of the many factors that would serve as warning signals of the need for a full analysis by those concerned with international surveillance. But it should not be taken as necessarily creating a strong presumption that such movements should be countered by official intervention.

The avoidance of disorderly market conditions does involve both positive and negative obligations, however. The most commonly dis-

---

[26] Bernstein, "The Monetary Authorities and the Free Exchange Market."

cussed obligation under this heading is a positive obligation for foreign exchange market intervention to make a market where for some reason the functioning of the private market has become disorderly and normal transactions cannot be carried out or can be accomplished only with extraordinary difficulty. The emergence of such disorderly market conditions requires a judgmental determination and cannot be reasonably indicated by the use of objective statistical indicators alone. It is also generally a fairly short-lived phenomenon. Thus, in practice, except perhaps for the possibility of after-the-fact reviews of previous episodes, international surveillance of countries' obligations on this score must rest on the network of frequent communication and consultation among the finance ministers and central banks of the major countries.

A second aspect of the obligation to avoid disorderly exchange markets, perhaps even more judgmental than the first, is the avoidance of official actions likely to generate disorderly conditions in the private market. The most clear-cut examples of such actions is official intervention to maintain an unrealistic market rate. Many examples can be cited where such actions have generated disorderly market conditions. Thus the obligation to seek to avoid disorderly market conditions may sometimes call for less rather than more official intervention. Only in this kind of case, however, could we expect surveillance through the IMF to play a major role.

On the IMF's role in fostering official intervention to counter erratic exchange market conditions, I would have to agree with Bernstein that "no doubt the Fund could make representations that the fluctuations in exchange rates are excessive and that they have an adverse impact on other countries. . . . It would be unreasonable, however, for the Fund to go beyond that and require a member to intervene in the exchange market."[27]

The Need to Adopt a Case History Approach. The fears that the Jamaica agreements are seriously deficient because they do not provide detailed rules for exchange-rate behavior are understandable but not well founded. The IMF has been charged in the Jamaica agreements with developing specific principles for the international surveillance of the adjustment process. They should be fairly general principles. More specific interpretations may be codified over time from the case histories of judgments on particular circumstances, that is, through development of precedents.

There are some imaginable actions that would clearly be deemed manipulative or beggar-thy-neighbor, and there are others that clearly

---

[27] Ibid.

would not be. But there is a wide gray area of actions that cannot easily be labeled one or the other a priori. These will have to be settled case by case by multilateral judgments. In the process, greater clarification will gradually be achieved as the gray area is narrowed.

There are just too many conceivable gray area cases to make it wise to attempt to secure precise international agreement ahead of time on all possible types of cases. These considerations are reinforced when it is recognized that the seriousness of the consequences of a particular policy action, even whether it is on balance desirable or undesirable, may be crucially dependent on the surrounding circumstances.

Furthermore, it must not be forgotten that the ability of the international community to influence and penalize nations' behavior is not unlimited. Attempts to enforce prohibitions on too many minor abuses might well undercut the ability of the international community effectively to discourage major abuses. The development of too detailed a list of dos and don'ts would court the danger of undermining the effectiveness of international surveillance.

At this stage in the evolution of international financial cooperation, it appears that countries are more likely to modify somewhat inconsistent targets for the structures of their balance of payments (for example, individual targets for trade or current-account surpluses that are not collectively feasible) on the basis of quiet discussion among national and international financial officials than they would be to accept and follow a highly detailed set of guidelines promulgated by an international body. On such issues, national officials seem much more likely to modify positions if it does not appear publicly that they have been pressured into it. There is to some degree an analogy here to the proven need to make international agreements sound sufficiently ambiguous that all major parties can claim some measure of victory.

There may likewise be little point in attempting to construct a more graduated set of formal IMF sanctions, such as were discussed in the C-20 negotiations. Moral suasion against countries with undervalued currencies and the withholding of credit from countries with overvalued currencies are probably in practice the IMF's most potent potential weapons, limited though they are.

The absence of a long list of specific international guidelines or regulations should not be taken as failure to recognize the importance of fostering cooperation and discouraging manipulative exchange-rate and balance-of-payment policies. Nor should the fact that there are many cases that cannot be evaluated unambiguously keep us from focusing on less ambiguous cases.

In almost all countries there are pressures for protectionist trade and exchange-rate policies that must continually be fought. Both the formal mechanisms for international surveillance through the IMF and other international organizations and frequent informal contact among top officials of national governments are important weapons in that fight.

COMMENTARIES

John Williamson

Before turning to the subjects on which I disagree with Willett, I would like to stress the areas in which I endorse the views he expresses in his paper:

- His proposition that managed floating has performed markedly better than the adjustable peg could have been expected to
- His advocacy of a positive but cautious role for the IMF in underwriting stabilization programs
- His recognition that "there are no easy statistical shortcuts to monitoring the operation of the international adjustment process" (It is not clear who has ever claimed there are, apart possibly from those who saw reserve indicators serving in what I have elsewhere termed a "diagnostic" role.[1])
- His assertion that rapid exchange-rate changes are not per se evidence of disequilibrium or disorderly markets.[2]

There are other points where I am open to persuasion that Willett is correct, although I would have found some empirical documentation more convincing than his unsubstantiated opinions. I refer in particular to his dismissal of the vicious circle hypothesis, where the essential question seems to be the empirical one of how frequently an exogenous decline in the exchange rate provokes additional cost-push inflation that is subsequently validated by monetary policy, and his judgment that excessive intervention tending to prevent desirable rate changes may

---

[1] John Williamson, *The Failure of World Monetary Reform, 1971–74* (New York: New York University Press, 1977), chap. 5.

[2] I would, however, challenge his assertion that the IMF guidelines treated them as such. Guideline 2 permitted but did not encourage "leaning against the wind." Marcus Fleming, the principal architect of the guidelines, held views about the desirability of prompt adjustment when the occasion demanded very similar to those expressed by Willett.

have been a more important cause of instability than either deliberate disequilibrating depreciation or destabilizing private speculation (or inadequate intervention?).

There remain, however, a number of issues on which I am far from convinced by Willett's argument. I do not, to begin with, share his satisfaction with the operation of the adjustment process under managed floating or his belief that such failures as have occurred stem principally from the unwillingness of deficit countries to adjust. Willett argues that the fears expressed in 1974 about maldistribution of the oil deficit and consequential competitive payments policies have proved greatly exaggerated. Presumably no one would contest the view that the oil deficit has in fact been grossly maldistributed, and recent forecasts of the future trade positions of West Germany and Japan scarcely suggest that this maldistribution is about to be corrected. Overtly competitive payments policies have indeed been largely avoided, although one might interpret this as a welcome success for the efforts of the international community (expressed in the Rome communiqué) to outlaw such practices, rather than as an indication that the fears were misplaced. But the avoidance of overtly competitive policies is a minimal criterion of success. Excessively deflationary policies may have been adopted out of a desire for financial stabilization, but they need be no less detrimental for that.

The central fact that Willett overlooks, which seems to me for reasons developed below to be highly relevant to the surveillance of exchange-rate policies, is that the world has recently been suffering its most serious postwar recession. This recession was primarily caused by the priority given to financial stabilization, at the cost of a sacrifice in real output, in the countries whose position is now generally envied as "strong." Views can legitimately differ as to whether this priority was excessive, given the extent to which inflation had got out of hand in 1973–1974. But those who wish to argue that the currently "strong" countries were right to deflate as much as they did and that the real problem was the failure of the currently "weak" countries to follow their example must recognize that, had this advice been heeded, the "strong" countries would have achieved less financial stabilization at the cost of a greater sacrifice in real output than actually occurred.[3] Those who believe that the depth of the global recession was not inappropriate, in view of the need to reverse the rising inflation, may still believe

---

[3] If exchange rates adjust to neutralize partially (but only partially) a shock to the flow of current-account payments, it follows that a deflationary policy in one country will improve its current balance, reduce its output by less than world output, and reduce its inflation. A partner country will suffer a deterioration in the current balance, an output loss, and (at least in the short run) additional inflation. Proof of these propositions will be provided in a forthcoming paper.

that the maldistribution of the oil deficit and the polarization into "strong" and "weak" countries were aggravated by the uneven adoption of deflationary policies. Those who believe the depth to which the recession was allowed to develop was a mistake have even more reason to be critical. But it is hard to see what basis there is for satisfaction in the operation of the surveillance process.

In our present world there exists a collective oil deficit, acceptance of too large a part of which undermines a country's creditworthiness, and this burden—for it is a burden—can be reduced by deflation. This world is also one of floating rates, which generally adjust only a part of the way needed to offset the impact of shocks to the current account, and this implies that deflation can allow a country to reduce its inflation at the expense of its partners while exporting some of the cost in unemployment to its partners. Contrary to the theory of floating exchange rates as developed in the textbooks, floating does not eliminate the international spillover effects of a country's policies. Multilateral surveillance remains as necessary as it has ever been if a collectively appropriate conjunctural policy is to be developed.

What mechanisms can be devised to promote the development of such a policy? Will "quiet discussions and informal pressures" suffice? Or can a more explicit definition of countries' obligations play a constructive role? If so, what form should this definition take?

If the problem were confined to that of restraining overtly competitive policies, I could see that Willett's prescription of quiet discussions and informal pressures, building up case studies, and so on, might suffice. But if it is the more general problem that I have argued it is, of ensuring consistency in macroeconomic policies in a world where international spillover effects remain important despite the adoption of floating rates, I find it hard to believe that his approach will get anywhere beyond adding to airline revenues. Something more explicit is required to define what a country's responsibilities are.

For as long as the problem of the oil deficit persists—that is, as long as the aggregate borrowing desired by willing, creditworthy borrowers on resource-allocation grounds falls short of the current surplus of OPEC when the world economy is operating at a satisfactory level of demand—the natural place to start is with current-account targets. Reasonable rules based on economic logic that can be applied with broad-brush justice to all countries have been suggested.[4] There need be no suggestion of penalizing countries for ex post deviations from these targets: we all know that economic forecasting is inaccurate. The rule

---

[4] Naturally I think the best logic is that embodied in my own paper cited in Willett's number 16.

would be used to test whether countries' policies are designed to guide adjustment in the appropriate direction.

If such a test is to be applied, it is necessary to have a forum in which adjustment policies are discussed and certain policy instruments that the international community is recognized to have a right to approve. Demand management policies are of course highly relevant, but it scarcely seems conceivable that countries would agree to any formal international limits on their freedom of action in this connection, except when they are reduced to last-resort borrowing. Hence the natural candidates for this role are the two that Willett considers: reserves and exchange rates—the two policy instruments with the most direct international repercussions.

A rule that effectively prohibits reserve use—Willett's "reserve approach"—makes sense if and only if one believes that the market will normally do a better job of settling on the optimal (not equilibrium) exchange rate. Although I would concede that free floating (which this rule would come close to enforcing) might in practice perform better than the management we are likely to see, the problem with this rule is that it provides no fulcrum for exerting indirect leverage on those other aspects of economic policy that the international community may wish to influence (despite the fact that it is in no position to enforce its wishes). One of the attractions of the reference rate proposal[5] is that it would go some way toward providing such leverage. In negotiating its reference rate, a country would have to show that its proposed rate was consistent with an expectation of adjustment toward its current-account target, given its demand management policy. If that policy were regarded by the rest of the world as unduly inflationary or deflationary, a reference rate could be approved only if set at a level sufficiently depreciated (and depreciating) or appreciated (and appreciating) to neutralize partner countries from the currently most urgent effects of the internationally inappropriate internal policies. Protection would not be complete; first, because the exchange-rate change that helps other countries in respect to payments and output worsens their position in respect to inflation; second, because the country could decline to agree to a reference rate and abstain from intervention. Incomplete protection is, however, preferable to none.

---

[5] Willett treats target zones as reference rates plus encouragement, or even an obligation, to intervene when the market rates deviate too far. I know of no proponent of the target zone approach who has proposed the imposition of such an obligation, which would amount to forcing a reversion to the par-value system. The essential difference between the two proposals lies in the fact that the reference rate proposal would prohibit all intervention unless a reference rate had been internationally agreed on.

In concluding, I return to another advantage that I have asserted for the reference rate proposal, which Willett challenges. That is the hope that such rates might provide a focal point for stabilizing speculation. Willett writes that "such an outcome . . . is crucially dependent both on the assumed nature of the behavior of the private exchange market and on the ability of governments to speculate better." I am not sure how to interpret the first condition, but I am unconvinced by the second. First, governments *ought* to be able to speculate better than the private exchange market, inasmuch as they ought to be in a better position to forecast their own policies (especially monetary policy), which have a far greater impact on future rates than the actions of any single speculator. Second, one of the major objects of the proposal is to force governments to declare their economic strategies more fully, thus making it less possible for them to pursue internally inconsistent sets of policies and increasing the information available to operators in the private market. The idea of using the proposal to improve the information base of the private sector would be defeated by Willett's misguided desire to keep secret any estimates of reference rates that might exist.

Henry C. Wallich

It is very difficult, at this stage, to say anything new. The best one can do is register one's preferences. It seems to me that any disagreement that may remain may have to do with the fact that everybody is trying to establish generalities, whereas actually we are dealing, of course, with the experiences of particular countries.

The United States, to begin with my own country, has been very comfortable under floating, for very particular, not generalizable reasons. There are two. One is that the albatross of convertibility has been lifted from us, so that the under secretary for monetary affairs no longer needs to travel around the world begging countries not to take gold, and we are helped to window-dress our balance of payments to make the deficit appear different from what it was, or from what some definition said it was.

The other benefit that the United States has enjoyed under the floating system is freedom from foreign determination of its exchange rate. Milton Gilbert to the contrary notwithstanding, I think that before 1971 the United States had very little ability, even by moving the price of gold, to change its exchange rate. I think what would have happened is a general move in gold prices and no move in exchange rates.

277

Under the floating system, the United States still has no control over its exchange rate, because trying to influence the dollar by intervention is a hopeless undertaking except in very small margins and perhaps in extreme cases. But nobody else has much control over the dollar rate either, so that the dollar cannot become as overvalued as it was in 1971, and that is benefit enough.

So long as things can stay that way, that is a comfortable position for the United States. West Germany and, I dare say, our Swiss friends, have also, I think, been comfortable, though for a different reason. Monetary policy has been freed from the need to buy up inflowing foreign exchange and from the need, therefore, to monetize the balance-of-payments surplus and to inflate the economy. That accounts for the satisfaction of another set of countries.

Other countries, I dare say, have been somewhat uncomfortable under floating. It is in these countries, of course, where floating has meant sinking.

I shall pay my respects very briefly to the circles in which we seem to be running around. The question of vicious circles, it seems to me, is all a question of, relative to what? What is the base on which to make a comparison?

Let me begin with a virtuous circle. I would think one might say that a fixed exchange rate is the base, because a country can, if it has a surplus, continue to have a fixed rate so long as it likes, since all that happens is to inflate the economy. For a country like West Germany or Switzerland that has a surplus pushing up the currency—higher exchange rate, lower import prices, less inflation, still higher exchange rate, still lower import prices, and so on—there is a virtuous circle. One could say that the process is one of equilibrium, but, relative to the base case of a fixed rate, it is a virtuous circle.

Let us take the opposite side, a deficit. If again we compare flexible to fixed rates, even the naive case is a vicious circle. If the exchange rate depreciates in line with purchasing power parity, the country is worse off as regards inflation than if it maintained a fixed rate. It must be granted, of course, that under a deficit a fixed exchange rate could not be maintained indefinitely. Hence one simply postpones to the future what would have to happen under floating right away.

Then there is the third case, overshooting. The exchange rate depreciates more than in line with purchasing power parity. I think it has been agreed that that is a vicious circle.

Let us then go to Willett's remedy, to bite the bullet, stiffen the upper lip, put in the right policies, show the market that the country is doing the right thing. The market will then prevent overshooting; in fact, the market will pull the exchange rate back up, and the country will be able to have stability. All this is perfectly true, but we have seen that it is not easy to do. Policies are not made in a vacuum. We have seen that countries caught in this situation have suffered. We have seen also that other countries that have been comfortable have been very aware of the emerging polarization. The weak got weaker; the strong got stronger. It does not help to say that polarization is the fault of the poor policies of the less strong countries. In fact, the stronger ones have felt constrained to make substantial financing available to overcome this polarization.

So it has been in the self-interest of the countries that have been comfortable with the floating system to avoid the extremes of polarization. Very dire things can happen, as Marris said earlier. One can imagine an end to the liberal trading system. Worse things, conceivably, could happen.

Vicious circle or not, something has to be done—and something, indeed, has been done—to provide very substantial financing of deficit countries. As Willett said about exchange-rate management, when we talk about intervention, we seem to think about the kind of thing that the Federal Reserve does, the Bank of Canada does, the Bundesbank does. A much more massive form of intervention, however, is the financing of a large payments deficit, regardless of whether that goes through the central bank or whether official agencies, or even private agencies encouraged by the government, do the borrowing abroad and feed the borrowed exchange into the market. This is a form of intervention. We do not call it that, necessarily. But I think we ought to be aware that, under our present system of floating, that kind of intervention, which really is BOP financing, has been massive.

From the experience of the countries that have been suffered under floating, I draw two conclusions. One is that the countries that seem to have benefited will want to help others through lending. The second is Lamfalussy's idea, which indeed seems plausible. If countries find that the benefits of floating are not what they thought, particularly if they find that their freedom of policy is stymied because they do not dare expand for fear of the BOP consequences, the attractiveness of adhering to an optimum currency area greatly increases.

This obviously may not be possible in the short run. Until policies are truly coordinated, there is no way for countries who have much above average rates of inflation to adhere to any optimum currency area. But a country might well change its mind about what is the more attractive position: to float, in effect to sink, and to have very little policy leeway; or alternatively, to adhere to a currency area and, while also having very little policy leeway, at least to have the benefits of partial stability in its external relations.

Willett makes surveillance a substantial part of his very interesting paper. It will have become clear, from what I said about the reaction of the United States to floating, that the United States has a strong interest in a clean float. Only then is the dollar exchange rate determined by the market, not by somebody else's intervention. Hence the United States would like to see a system in which floating is as clean as possible, and surveillance clearly can make a contribution to that.

There are subconcepts of surveillance: for instance, the question whether there should be target zones and target rates. The establishment of such zones and rates, if feasible, might have some advantages, but it would deprive a country like the United States of the benefits of floating. A foreign control over its exchange rate would be reestablished, and a convertibility obligation might reappear.

I am not arguing that the United States wants to escape convertibility obligations because it wants to conduct a wild career in monetary and fiscal policy. It is perfectly clear that no currency can remain a reserve currency unless it is solid and generally acceptable. We have just been through the sad experience of phasing out a reserve currency that had lasted for some 150 years. If I were to contemplate that happening to the dollar someday, I would see real injury both to the United States and to the world. There is every reason for the United States to be cautious and moderate in its policies. Nevertheless, freedom from convertibility is a significant policy advantage to all who have lived through the agonizing period of trying to maintain gold convertibility. Target zones and reference rates pose a new threat of that sort.

Surveillance also has to do, I suppose, with the allocation of current-account deficits. We have had a very interesting debate on that topic. It seems to me that, so long as the capacity to borrow is limited, countries cannot have the unlimited right to engage in policies that require other countries to borrow. In any event, some countries will find their surplus cut back or their deficit enlarged if borrowing capacity is limited. If deficit countries cannot or will not borrow, they will take actions that cut back others' surpluses or enlarge others' deficits. The question therefore is by what mechanism that adjustment should take place.

The solution that I see is neither exclusively domestic expansion nor exclusively an exchange-rate change. Under floating the exchange rate ceases to be a policy instrument. But I could visualize the stronger countries encouraging an adjustment process in the weaker countries that do much of the borrowing and thereby maintain their exchange rates. These weaker countries could allow their exchange rates to go down and reduce their borrowing. That means, of course, that the exchange rates of the stronger countries would tend to go up, thereby moving in the direction needed for adjustment. Since this would probably reduce the degree of expansion in the surplus countries—or low-deficit countries, since I include the United States in this category —some degree of fiscal or monetary stimulation might be appropriate. That would serve to restore the degree of expansion lost by the upward exchange-rate change.

Here we seem to be coming back to the old argument of the burden of adjustment. Is it the deficit countries that should adjust? Is it the surplus countries? Or is it both sides? We have heard this debate for the last fifteen or twenty years.

I support Willett's suggestion that the approach to surveillance should be evolutionary. I agree with him that countries will go much further in voluntary cooperation than they will in writing rules. Moving in an evolutionary way toward a development of the surveillance process therefore seems reasonable to me.

I would say, in closing, that such an evolution would guarantee us many more interesting conferences. All the arguments that can be conceived of in this area already exist and are unlikely to change; but, in the course of a series of conferences, the countries using the arguments would probably change.

Gottfried Haberler

Haberler found himself in substantial agreement with Willett and in some disagreement with Williamson.

He emphasized that any long-drawn-out inflation acquires vicious circle properties that are the consequence of inflationary policies and are independent of the exchange-rate regime. If there is overshooting of the exchange rate, the obvious remedy is intervention in the exchange market. But he was skeptical that such interventions would in fact be conducted efficiently. Thus Great Britain and Italy, the European countries most closely associated with the overshooting and VC argument, had for years intervened on a large scale in the exchange market and managed to finance a large import surplus. But their large borrowing abroad had not broken their vicious circle of inflation. Evidently the two countries had not used the breathing spell afforded by the intervention to institute effective anti-inflationary measures. Later they had had another chance under the guidance of the IMF to put their financial houses in order.

281

He next considered Williamson's view that the recession could be attributed to the priority given to price stability at the cost of real output. He felt that the choice was no longer so simple. He was impressed by the fact that in the post–World War II period there had been no case of inflation in the traditional sense of declining price levels or contraction of either the money supply (M) or money GNP (MV). In his view a clear-cut trade-off between employment and inflation no longer existed. And for economists and policy makers the choice between lower unemployment and lower rates of inflation was no longer available. In the era of stagflation, inflation and unemployment existed at the same time—in fact, inflation sooner or later produced or intensified unemployment. With the Phillips curve approximating the shape of a vertical straight line, we must expect inflation to accelerate quickly and output and employment to gain only little when expansionary monetary-fiscal measures are applied.

Haberler questioned whether the burden of the oil *deficit* (as distinguished from the higher oil price) had to be shared equitably so long as it could be financed by petrodollars. Similarly, if West Germany and Japan had an export surplus, it did not necessarily mean that they were exporting deflation and unemployment. If the surplus were financed by direct investments or portfolio investment abroad, they were exporting capital—in other words, "transferring real resources" to the deficit countries. Even if the surplus countries add to their international reserves, under floating the deficit countries were not compelled to deflate and accept more unemployment. No country in the modern (post-Keynesian) world has been willing to accept a real deflation.